MW00378811

ALIVE DAY

ALIVE DAY

FINDING HOPE AND PURPOSE AFTER LOSING EVERYTHING

CAPTAIN SAM BROWN

WITH AMY BROWN

HOUNDSTOOTH
PRESS

COPYRIGHT © 2024 SAM BROWN
All rights reserved.

ALIVE DAY
Finding Hope and Purpose after Losing Everything

FIRST EDITION

ISBN 978-1-5445-4602-5 *Hardcover*
978-1-5445-4601-8 *Paperback*
978-1-5445-4600-1 *Ebook*
978-1-5445-4623-0 *Audiobook*

To my Lord Jesus Christ—the Author and Perfecter of my faith

* * *

*Therefore, since we are surrounded by such a huge crowd of witnesses to the
life of faith, let us strip off every weight that slows us down, especially the sin
that so easily trips us up. And let us run with endurance the race God has set
before us. We do this by keeping our eyes on Jesus, the champion who initiates
and perfects our faith. Because of the joy awaiting him, he endured the cross,
disregarding its shame. Now he is seated in the place of honor beside God's throne.*

HEBREWS 12:1–2

* * *

To Amy, Roman, Esther, and Ezra

*May you find peace and hope through your faith—regardless of the
trials and suffering this life produces. Never forget that you have
a Father who loves and cares for you fully and perfectly.*

* * *

*Don't just pretend to love others. Really love them. Hate what is wrong. Hold
tightly to what is good. Love each other with genuine affection, and take delight
in honoring each other. Never be lazy, but work hard and serve the Lord
enthusiastically. Rejoice in our confident hope. Be patient in trouble, and keep
on praying. When God's people are in need, be ready to help them. Always be
eager to practice hospitality. Bless those who persecute you. Don't curse them;
pray that God will bless them. Be happy with those who are happy, and weep
with those who weep. Live in harmony with each other. Don't be too proud
to enjoy the company of ordinary people. And don't think you know it all!
Never pay back evil with more evil. Do things in such a way that everyone
can see you are honorable. Do all that you can to live in peace with everyone.*

ROMANS 12:9–18

CONTENTS

PROLOGUE

My younger brother Daniel and me in our new Christmas presents: US Army uniforms. Around 1988.

"You're invincible."

His voice came through clearly on my little cell phone, even though he was on the other side of the world. I slowly paced in the gravel circle of the motor pool, grateful that the sun was low enough in the sky that I could step away from the shade of our small combat outpost where the other guys were winding down. I grinned.

"I don't know about that, brother."

It was the first chance I'd had to touch base with Daniel in a few weeks. My younger brother and best friend, Daniel was following in my footsteps, completing his own military training at Fort Bragg. Only instead of pursuing a leadership role as an Infantry Officer, Daniel was training to be a Marine Corps Special Operations medic—formally known as a Special Amphibious Reconnaissance Corpsman (SARC). It was a perfect fit for him: from the time he was a kid, Daniel wanted to help people. He wasn't afraid of trauma, blood, or gore. He had a calm temperament in high stress—an invaluable quality in a medic who may be tasked with saving a life under fire. But as a Special Operations Medic, he also got to fight. In fact, he would be a warfighter first and medic when necessary.

Daniel always wanted me to divulge everything about my deployment, and I had to fight to keep the details confidential. It was a new form of the competition that had defined our youth together, each of us trying to win the tug of war.

"So, what have you been up to?" he asked at the start of the conversation.

"We're off the airfield now, interacting with some of the people in the local villages," I said, intentionally being vague.

"Any Taliban around?" he asked, deliberately probing for more specific details.

"There's been some 'bad guy' activity," I said, enjoying the contest and countering his probe with vagueness. "Nothing too close though." I grinned and turned the conversation. "Tell me more about what's going on in your medic training at Fort Bragg. I expect you're leading your class?"

As Daniel began updating me about his own experiences, I listened attentively to his descriptions of the leaders. One of the reasons that I made the leadership choices I did in my own platoon was because I wanted to support and love my guys in the way I hoped people would do for Daniel. I noted what he said about the leaders he liked and bristled when he described an officer or senior non-commissioned officer who led with insults and arrogance.

I didn't have long. "Daniel, I've got to get going," I said. "It's awesome to hear your voice and hear how things are going. Your team is going to be so blessed to have you after your training."

"Okay, wait—" he stopped me. "I've got one more thing to say to you. Nothing's going to kill you. You're invincible."

I tried to deflect the comment. Even so, he repeated himself: "I'm not worried. You're invincible."

I laughed. "Well, if you say so, it must be true. I better get going. Love you, bro. I'm so proud of you."

"Love you too. Proud of you too."

I hung up the phone and thought: *Invincible. Well—I'd better be. Can't let him down.*

My boots crunched on the gravel as I headed back toward the outpost. It was my favorite time of day in the Kandahar desert: sunset, before the chill of the night set in but after the blistering heat of the day had subsided. I took a deep breath, feeling the satisfaction and contentment I always felt after talking with Daniel.

It was the last conversation I had with him before the ambush, and the explosion, and the flames.

* * *

For most of our lives, Daniel had been the invincible one. Even though he was younger than me, he was tougher—though you could have never gotten me to admit it as a kid. We grew up in a rural area in Arkansas where our nearest neighbors were out of sight and earshot. Whenever we weren't in school, Daniel and I roamed around our property, playing soldier, hunting or fishing, and coming up with various ways to compete with each other.

One time when we were still young kids, we were playing on our trampoline under the shade of a big oak tree. The trampoline was half broken—missing a third of the springs, and even the ones that were left were badly rusted. We didn't care. It still worked well enough for us to play Crack the Egg and have bounce battles.

About forty feet away, one of our dogs started barking at the bush hog, the grass-cutting tool hooked up to our tractor. Another dog ran up and stiffened, then joined the barking. Daniel and I stopped bouncing. Tumbling over each other, we crawled to the edge of the trampoline. "What is it, boy?!" I yelled. "What's over there?!" Whatever it was, it couldn't be good. The dogs snarled like they were facing a threat.

I was the older brother—the biggest, fastest, and strongest. But I was afraid. "Go over there," I ordered Daniel. "Figure out what they're barking at."

Dutifully, Daniel hopped off the trampoline and ran over, right up to the dogs. "Oh no!" he yelled, then began running back to the trampoline. "It's a poisonous water moccasin! It was like two feet away from me in the shade of the bush hog!"

I *hated* snakes. I still do. One of my first memories from childhood was seeing a snake slither under the gap between the front door and the floor, sliding its way into the kitchen. Scarred me for life.

Daniel jumped back onto the safety of the trampoline. "We gotta get Father!" he said.

"Well, *I'm* not getting off!" I said. I wasn't about to risk getting bitten by a poisonous snake. "*You* go inside and get him."

Again, without questioning, Daniel jumped off the trampoline and ran inside. He came out quickly, tugging Father's hand toward the tractor. Father raised his .22, aimed, and shot.

That was the end of the threat from that snake. But it was only one of many times when Daniel showed himself to be braver than me.

Daniel was sent on his first deployment when I was still early in my journey of recovering at Brooke Army Medical Center. Like me, he was sent to Afghanistan—and, *because* of me, he went there on a blood mission, bent on revenge. Daniel looked for every opportunity to be in combat, making it his personal mission to cause as much destruction as possible to the people who had nearly succeeded in killing his brother.

He went back to Afghanistan on his second deployment. He went back again on his third. Each time, Daniel was looking for a fight. His weapon of choice was the M240B, one of the biggest machine guns an individual can carry and very unusual for a medic since they're also responsible for carrying all the medical equipment, in addition to the normal load and ammunition for their weapon. But, true to his nature, he was never afraid. He overcame every challenge to protect the men around him, always ready for a fight with the people who were responsible for nearly killing me and threatening his team.

During those three deployments, Daniel was exposed to countless blasts: grenades, mortars, recoilless rifles, and the constant concussions of the 7.62mm machine gun rounds he shot off. Those thousands and thousands of rounds had a cumulative concussive effect on his brain. The Taliban didn't get him in one fiery blast or an instantly fatal shot. But, his thirst for revenge and combat exposed him to events that wounded him in ways that could not be seen outwardly in passing.

By the time Daniel arrived home after his third deployment, he was a different person. He was deeply wounded and broken. His brain and personality were marred by what he privately confided in me was the only thing I ever knew him to fear: CTE, the neurodegenerative disease caused by repeated concussions. It caused his mind to break down, trapping him in a hellscape he couldn't wake up from. Over time, it got harder and harder for Daniel to distinguish between what his family would recognize as reality and the nightmare in his mind that he couldn't escape.

In that nightmare, Daniel was confronted with enemies. They told him he had a choice to make: either he kill himself, or—if he chose to live—his family would be murdered.

For more than a year, he lived under that threat. Over and over, he reached for rationality, telling himself that it wasn't real—that, even though he was receiving that input in his mind, it wasn't true. But it got harder and harder to separate truth from the nightmare as his brain continued to break down. In the end, he lost the ability to recognize that the threat to his family only existed in his living, delusional nightmares. He believed that everyone he loved was in imminent peril and only he could save us.

Daniel was always an active journaler. Toward the end, the entries got shorter and shorter. On July 27, 2022, in a messy scrawl, he wrote:

Said prayer to Jesus Christ to manifest to me and asked for forgiveness of my sins.

On August 1, five days later, Daniel took his life, believing it was the only way to save his family. He died as a hero to me, my family, and so many others because in the twisted reality of his deteriorating brain, he gave up his own life in exchange for ours.

* * *

For years, people have told me that my story gives them hope, that it reminds them of what the human spirit is capable of enduring. People have said they feel new strength to persevere after hearing what I've overcome.

And, for years, I let those comments pass by as simply a nice compliment or encouragement. In my mind, I deserve very little credit for enduring. I believe that the strength I've found has come entirely from God.

I've been told by some of those same people that I should write a book. I dismissed that idea for a long time too. Writing a book, to me, seemed like a vanity project. Particularly now that I've become a public figure—a politician, no less—a book seemed like a desperate attempt to show off, an obvious ploy for attention.

My brother, Daniel, during his first deployment

But the recent loss of my brother and best friend has shifted the equation for me. More than ever before, I see the importance of giving people hope who feel hopeless. More than ever before, I feel an urgency to inspire others to keep going—to persevere—to endure.

I've sought to relay my experiences as accurately as I can, although some points have been condensed for narrative clarity. Also, the accounts I share—especially around combat scenes—are told from my perspective, but I acknowledge that the fog of war is a real phenomenon and there may be other perspectives and memories that slightly differ from what I remember. I've conveyed my own memories of what transpired because ultimately it was that interpretation of my experiences that helped me form the meaning I've described in this book. Finally, I'll note that some names, titles, and details have been changed to protect privacy.

In some ways, we all have an "Alive Day"—a moment in life that signifies the crossing of a threshold, a day when we are forever altered from who we were before. For some, that may come in the form of loss: someone we love is ripped away from us. For some, it may come in the form of illness: an apparently healthy body is found to be corrupted with disease, vulnerable to death. For some, it's a loss of innocence: the day when a child's life is first marred by abuse, or when a marriage is found to be stained with adultery. In each case, a death occurs. The life that was, is no more.

But the reason I've titled my book *Alive Day* is because we have a choice in those moments. Will we choose to survive and find hope? Will we keep going, and let the painful journey usher us into a new identity that is defined not by what we've lost, but by what we've overcome?

My own hope in telling this story is to help you understand the depth of your own resilience. When we face the toughest of circumstances, there is a way through it. And in surviving the fire of an Alive Day, those moments can end up being the genesis of an extremely meaningful and powerful life. That meaning doesn't arrive overnight; it requires that we engage with the struggle for life. But by getting through those trials, we not only memorialize the death of who we were before, we also celebrate the birth of who we can become.

I've also written this book for my brother. I thought initially that I should make this book centered around advice: "Here's how to persevere. Here's how to claim hope." A memoir felt insubstantial by itself. But as I spoke with people who have navigated other challenges in life or mental illness, I was encouraged to let my story simply stand for itself. Perhaps people walking through the darkness don't need to know how to pull themselves up by their bootstraps. In my brother's case, that may have just added pressure to the weight he was already carrying. Perhaps they just need to know they're not alone.

Hear this: you are not alone. You can keep going. There is purpose and meaning behind the trial you're in. Your story may even deliver the hope that someone else needs to choose life when all seems lost.

I wish you were reading Daniel's story instead of my own. The stories he could tell about the people he interacted with, helped, and encouraged could fill volumes. I always felt like he lived ten lives, to my one. His potential to impact the world, I believe, was greater than my own.

I have wept and mourned my brother. I grieve the loss of his impact, which was stolen from him because of his wounds. I grieve the loss of my best friend, the person I looked up to most in the world. But I also rejoice, because I know this is simply an extended goodbye. We will have an eternal reunion one day in the presence of our Creator.

In writing this book, I seek to honor him. Based on my own experience, surviving physical pain is significantly easier than enduring internal anguish. The human body can withstand physical pain. It's when we lose hope that darkness can overtake us. The thing that defeats us isn't the pain itself; it's the hopelessness.

Yet even as Daniel was losing himself, he found ultimate peace through Jesus. And in my own story, the hope that kept me going wasn't strength that came from myself, or from any temporary goal. It was in believing that the life I fought for would have purpose and meaning which went beyond my last breath.

My Alive Day happened in the dark, in the desert. My mouth was full of dust and ash; my skin was roiled and melted. Yet in the moments after my soldiers had extinguished the flames, I realized that the death which had felt so certain was delayed.

I was alive. I would *live*. And that prompted a searing realization: *I was saved for a purpose. The life I live is not my own.*

The truth is: none of us are invincible. But we can trust that the pain we endure prepares us for a purpose that goes beyond our limited days—one that extends into eternity.

PART 1

DEATH AND DYING

CHAPTER 1

IN COMMAND
AND CONTROL

Mother, Father, me, and Daniel in Arkansas. Fall of 1988.

"It's so hot outside," I complained.

Mother's voice called up the stairs again. "If you and your brother can handle running around and playing in this heat, then you can handle mowing in this heat. Remember what your father said."

I remembered. If the property wasn't mowed by the time he got home from work, I wouldn't be allowed to ride my bike into town with my friends over the weekend.

"Can't I do it later?"

"Gonna storm this afternoon." One of my younger siblings started crying.

I sighed. Out of excuses, I trudged down the stairs and outside. The air was thick, wet, and still. Only the drone of the cicadas broke through the heavy blanket of humidity. By the time I got to the shed, I was already slimy with sweat. I pulled off my T-shirt and tossed it onto the workbench, then wrestled the push mower out from where I'd hastily stashed it last time, backing it outside and filling up the gas tank with fuel from the five-gallon red jug.

I yanked the pull cord. Could never get the motor started the first time. *Yank.*

Yank.

With a roar, the mower sprang to life. I steered it toward the house, where I'd kept the grass shorter and the mowing would be easier. I kept my eyes focused three feet in front of the mower, looking for holes or thicker patches of grass where snakes might be hiding.

It took an hour of pushing the mower back and forth in the yard right around the house until I reached the end of the grass I'd kept a handle on the previous weeks. Sometimes Mother and Father let me stop there, but I could see the grass around the ponds and in the fields was long enough that I'd get an earful if I didn't hit them too. Everything grew so fast in the summertime.

Gritting my teeth, I pushed the mower toward the first pond, knowing I'd better get them over with. The areas near the two ponds were the worst. Long, thick grass and that's where I was most likely to run into a snake. Slowly, I made my way around both. The mower quit on me twice, but luckily never made the dull *kerthunk* that indicated it had struck a reptile.

Relieved to have the area near the ponds done, I pushed over to the wooded areas. The roots were a pain, but the grass was shorter there and easier to cut. That part went fast.

By the time I finished around the trees, I could see the thunderheads building. I always loved the sight of the thunderheads: big towers of clouds—first white, and then growing into a threatening gray. Like an army gathering in the sky.

Better hurry up, I thought.

I pushed the mower over toward the pasture, which I knew would take the longest. The grass was long enough here that I had to lean against the mower at nearly a 45-degree angle to push it forward. In one thick patch, the eager, high-pitched roar of the mower changed to a lower, irritated grind. It slowed. Then it stopped.

"Come on," I muttered. My muscles were tired. It was harder to restart the mower every time. I pulled the machine back and kicked away the long grass from the blades. Wiped my hands on my cutoff denim shorts to dry the sweat.

Yank. Yank. Yank.

The mower rumbled to life again. I walked it farther back to give myself a running start, then rammed it forward. The mower seized on the longer grass, chewing it up, spitting it out. Pushing hard, I willed my eleven-year-old muscles to conquer the field. I began to see a longer stretch of mown grass spread out behind me. The sight was deeply satisfying.

Had to be past lunchtime, but now that I'd started, I didn't want to finish until I was done.

Nearly another hour subsided as I mindlessly strained against the mower, pushing it back and forth through the field of grass. My mind wandered, thinking about where we might ride on our bikes tomorrow. *The Cards and Comics shop. Get some new baseball trading cards. Buy a Sprite from the general store.*

I heard thunder rumble overhead as I drew near the dirt road. I rammed the mower through the last stretch of grass and shut it off at the mailbox. I looked back at the property. *Good.* I wouldn't have to deal with the pasture again for another two weeks. And now I could go into town with my friends.

Dust was settling over the road, a sign the mailman must have come in his truck while I had my head down with the mower. I wiped the sweat off my face and pulled down the front of our box. Several fat raindrops fell on my head and shoulders. It felt good.

There was the usual stack of envelopes and advertisements. Then, I pulled out something different. Someone had sent us a thick magazine. On the front, there were pictures of what looked like castles: high stone walls, arched windows, looming towers. I flipped the magazine open, ignoring another loud rumble overhead. On the inside were pictures of young people wearing uniforms. I stared at them, mesmerized. They seemed like they were from a different era.

"Samuel!" I could hear my Mother calling from the now-distant porch. "Better come inside!"

Thick drops splattered onto the magazine. I closed it quickly and tucked it under my arm, then thrust the rest of the mail back in the box. Grabbing the mower, I clumsily ran it back to the shed while holding the magazine tight against my side. As soon as I shoved the mower inside, I ran toward the house, my body bent over the magazine to protect it against the rain which was now falling hard and fast.

I ran up the stairs and leaped onto the porch. *Made it.* Mother had left me a sandwich and a glass of sweet tea on the table next to the rocking chair. I took a bite and a big drink, then sat down on the steps. I studied the pictures. Who were these people?

The rain poured down, louder than the cicadas. I didn't watch the lightning. I was too interested in the pictures. Daniel found me and wordlessly sat down, studying the images with similar attention.

When Father arrived home, I was still on the front porch with the magazine open. I heard the car door slam and looked up. With surprise, I realized the rain had stopped. The only drips now were the fat drops falling off the trees onto the lower steps and the roof of our well house. "What is this?" I called as he walked up. I held up the magazine.

Father studied the cover and smiled widely at me. "That's the West Point catalog. I reached out to them. Asked them to send us their materials."

He joined us on the porch and tapped the cover with his finger. "This is *West Point*," he repeated, making the words sound weighty and important. "It's a military academy. You could go there one day."

You could go there one day.

I tried to picture myself in one of those crisp, white and gray uniforms. Standing in front of a castle. Bearing arms. It felt like a far cry from where I sat: shirtless, in cut-off shorts, smelling of rain and sweat. "We could?" I asked.

"Sure. Why else would we have given you boys camo uniforms and dog tags? Why else would I have you doing drills all the time? All those push-ups and sit-ups and pull-ups and long runs—that's training." Father took the magazine and held the cover up to both of us. "You keep your grades up and do well in sports, this could be you."

He looked intently at both of us. "My expectation of you boys is that you'll grow up to serve your country. That's why I'm in the National Guard. And I would go on active duty if needed. I do that because I'm serving this country. I expect you boys to do the same."

We nodded, sobered by this sacred destiny.

"That's what our family is all about," Father emphasized. "We serve in the United States military armed forces." He paused, seeking a way to drive this point home.

"That's what Browns do."

* * *

Providing security for a convoy along a remote route in Afghanistan. August 2008.

"It's so hot outside," Philip Kopfensteiner complained from the back seat.

"Worse up here!" Kevin Jensen called from his gunner's turret. "What's the temp, Kopf?"

Our Humvee rumbled down the highway running through the Kandahar desert, second in my platoon's six-vehicle lineup. I stared out the window, watching the horizon ripple through the dry heat waves. Behind me, I could hear Philip, my Forward Observer, dig for the glass thermometer that hung on a keychain from his kit. "115," he called up to Kevin.

Kevin swore under his breath, a word that came through clearly into my headset from Kevin's mic. "It's probably over 120 up here then," he remarked, his Texas drawl thick. "Wish we were cruisin' in one of the MRAPs. What do you think the temp is in those?"

"A perfect seventy degrees," my driver, Mike Debolt, quipped.

"Hey, Lieutenant!" Kevin called.

"What's up, Jensen?" I said into my own mic.

"Any chance they're going to fix the A/C in our Humvees soon?"

Doubtful, I thought. But that wouldn't make Kevin feel better. "I can handle it, Jensen," I ribbed. "Can you?"

"It's hotter up here," he protested into the mic.

All of us in the Humvee were wearing the same thing: full sleeve uniforms, body armor, and gear on top of that. Each of us carried our own "kit," packed with the supplies we needed to carry out our individual roles. My kit included both my platoon network radio, strapped to my chest, and a larger radio strapped to my side which I used to stay in touch with Company Command, and—if we were close enough to be in range—Battalion. If we were farther out, I needed to use a third radio to reach Battalion: a large box radio, located next to me in the Humvee, shoved in between my seat and the driver's.

I shifted in my seat, trying to get comfortable. At six feet, four inches in height, there was never enough room for my legs in the passenger seat area.

Kevin started piping some of his good ol' Texas country music into my ear: "On the Road Again" by Willie Nelson. I grinned at the tune and, more so, at the sign of his changed morale. Kevin and I used our own private radio channel internal to the vehicle so that he could report anything noteworthy that he saw from his gunner's turret down to me, the platoon's leader. He had spruced up our setup by rubber banding one of the earbuds of his iPod to his little mic boom, which played the music through to me. My own personal DJ. I began tapping my finger where my arm rested next to the blast-proof glass window.

"Can't wait to get back to KAF and get out of this steel box," Philip remarked. After being out in the field for two weeks, we were packed up and set to return to Kandahar Airfield, a.k.a. "KAF," the closest thing to comfort we experienced during deployment. We'd head there as soon as we finished the afternoon's mission.

"Showers." Kevin sounded deeply satisfied. "And a real bed! Bet you're going to be glad to get off that stretcher, LT."

"Ha! True." A few weeks ago, right after arriving at our desert outpost Forward Operating Base, my platoon had discovered we were one cot short. For the last fourteen days, I'd been sleeping on a stretcher which I propped a few inches above the ground on MRE boxes—"Meals, Ready to Eat"—to avoid the camel spiders or other desert creatures that roam at night.

"A shower and a mattress sound pretty amazing," I agreed. "I'll shower last though. Cause the rest of you smell like shit." This comment had my intended effect: good-natured scoffs, mock offense, and a few choice remarks about my own subpar hygiene.

"If I smell bad, it's cause I was workin' up a sweat catching LT's touchdown pass last night," Kevin remarked.

"I didn't need to work up a sweat," Mike Debolt called back up to Kevin. "Sergeant Roszko's passes came right to me." He glanced over at me. "No offense, LT."

"No point trash talking now, Debolt," Philip said, leaning forward. "You guys *lost*."

Good, I thought, pleased at the signs of positive morale. I didn't want the guys thinking about the compromised security of our mission that afternoon, even though it was heavy on my mind. *Let's keep everyone focused on the good things waiting for us at the end of the day after we get the job done.*

My mind began to wander as I stared out at the vast desert landscape stretching in every direction. I liked being reminded of last night's football game. It had been one of my favorite evenings so far over here. After we'd finished chow and our other duties to prep for today's mission, I had grabbed the football I'd brought along to the Combat Outpost. "Sergeant Roszko," I'd called to Anthony. "You Captain one team. I've got the other."

Safe behind the blast-proof barriers, we'd stripped off our jackets and body armor. As we did so, we'd also taken off all the visible signs of rank. In our T-shirts, pants, and combat boots, running around in that gravel circle used as a Helicopter Landing Zone (HLZ), the weight of the deployment had momentarily lifted. It felt like we were back home, talking trash, eager to complete a pass, and looking to beat our opponent.

I'd laughed every time we dropped into formation, because Kevin—crouched next to me—was opposite Vincent Winston, who had some fresh new insult every time. It wasn't the ribbing itself that was funny—Winston was maybe the smallest guy in our platoon, but a great athlete, so he could have backed up his boasts. The funny part was hearing the trash talk come out of *Winston*. Vincent Winston had a heart of gold. He felt like everyone's kid brother and his ribbing was hilariously unexpected.

Equally funny had been Kevin's attempted responses—his thick drawl struggling to catch up with Winston's new choice remark. Every time, he'd only gotten out half a response before Anthony or I hiked the ball and we were all in play.

Staring out the window now, heat rising in ripples over the desert, I smiled at the memory. The sun had started to set as we chased each other around the gravel "field." Even when the light faded in the dusk, Sergeant Steven Smith had turned on a floodlight to keep the play going. Debolt had been right about Anthony's passes: they were strong and well-aimed. He hit his mark. My passes had been nearly as consistent though—one wobbly pass, notwithstanding. Anthony wasn't about to let me live that pass down. He gave me shit about it the rest of the night: "Didn't they teach you how to throw a spiral at your fancy military academy, LT?" Still—I'd thrown the pass that Kevin caught for the winning touchdown. That had felt good. My team cheered the victory while Anthony and his team demanded a rematch once we safely returned to KAF the next day.

I breathed a sigh of deep satisfaction. *Living the dream,* I thought to myself. This was what I'd worked my entire life to do—to serve in the US Army. I'd trained my mind and body to be an effective soldier. And, I led my troops by setting the standard of excellence, earning their respect, and providing the support they needed to accomplish the mission.

Now, it was happening. I had arrived. And the possibilities for my future in the military seemed as endless as the desert horizon.

Our Humvee hit a pothole in the pavement and my knees banged against the dash. That partially gravel-filled hole was only one of many pockmarks scarring the newly paved asphalt. The Taliban had a habit of planting Improvised Explosive Devices, or IEDs for short, in culverts running underneath the road, detonating them when they saw opportunities to harm their enemies. Dimly, I wondered if anyone had been hurt in the blast that left that particular pothole.

I studied the satellite navigation system in front of me. In military vehicles like the Humvee we were in, the driver always takes navigation from the passenger seat. It's not like you can glance down at a GPS map right by your steering wheel, the way most of us do when we're driving in the States. Out there in the desert, our rugged GPS navigation systems worked via a grid system where the numbers combined to define a specific point on a map. The grid was located in front of the passenger seat and—because of all the gear and machinery packed into the vehicle—the driver couldn't see it. He had to take directions from the passenger.

It wasn't easy to tell where we were by looking out the window. The desert in Kandahar is one vast, blank expanse, bordered by mountains in the distance and peppered with small villages made of dried mud that blend in with the earth. No signs. No city skylines. But according to the rugged digital mapping system, we were close to the mission staging area.

I held up the platoon radio and spoke into it. "3-4, this is 3-6. Our turn is approximately 200 meters in front of you."*

The radio buzzed back. "3-6, this is 3-4. Tracking." The music in my ear abruptly stopped. Now that we'd reached the mission area, Kevin's DJ time was over.

---

* A few notes on radio call signs: Comanche was my company's call sign. Ramrod was the Battalion call sign (higher up). "3" meant 3rd platoon; 1 through 4 designated a specific squad, and 6 meant leader of that unit. So, when people called through the radio to "3-6," they were addressing me.

Mike turned right off the paved highway onto a dirt road that stretched for several kilometers into the rugged mountains on the distant horizon. A cloud of dust arose from the lead vehicle. The "road" wasn't more than tire tracks in the desert, mostly made from our own activity in the area two weeks earlier, when the convoy had first passed through.

I didn't like seeing the evidence of our tracks.

When the convoy had headed into the mountains, they hadn't been subtle about it. The combined number of vehicles to carry new turbine equipment to a dam on the Helmand River in the neighboring province was rumored to be the largest military convoy since World War II. It was a massive international mission, all intended to bring electricity to parts of the country that didn't yet have it, in order to help the Afghan people and make the new Afghan government appear to be legitimately providing services for its citizens. The only problem was, these huge trailers and trucks got the attention of every single person in the area—including plenty of Taliban.

Now, the convoy was preparing to return along the same route it had come in on, through the area our Infantry Battalion had command and control over—and no friendly forces had been able to watch the road continuously between the convoy trips. Our region was large. For most of the previous two weeks, my platoon and others had been on assignment working in villages, trying to build goodwill and gathering intel about ways we could help provide resources to the local Afghan people. No other troops had been available to monitor the route on this particular stretch of desert.

The route, in fact, that we were driving on.

We had returned for the same reason we'd first come: two platoons were needed to provide security along the route while the convoy moved back through our Area of Operation (AO), shielding it from any attacks.

Providing security didn't bother me. What *did* bother me was that this massive convoy was coming back on the same route they'd used coming in, a violation of the principles of security I'd been taught in all of my military training. You *never* go in and out the same way.

That's inviting an ambush or hasty attack. On top of that, the convoy had been delayed in its return by over a week, providing plenty of time for any bad actor to bury landmines and IEDs beneath the tire tracks left in the dirt.

The radio chatter had quieted down now that we were in a high-risk area. I took a sip of water from one of the plastic bottles I'd grabbed out of the back of the Humvee. It was around the same temperature as the air outside: hot.

I scanned the long, flat expanse, my eyes always returning to the mountains in the distance. *That's where we'll see them. That's where the convoy will emerge.* Only a few more hours.

A massive *BOOM* suddenly ripped apart the horizon, causing it to disappear into a cloud of dust which swallowed up the vehicle in front of me. Pieces of the MRAP truck in front of us were blown off, somersaulting through the air. The realization hit me with the same force as the percussive blast. *They're hit. My guys are hit.*

"IED! IED!" I yelled into the radio. "React to IED battle drill! I'll take twelve o'clock! Let's *move!*" I yelled to Mike. "Drive around the right side, get up to the twelve o'clock position. Make sure we've got security at the front of our convoy!"

Our vehicle careened around the MRAP as I kept screaming into the radio. "3-2, go to three o'clock! 3-3, you're at nine. 3-1 and 3-7, you hold security in the rear!"

I quickly switched to our company radio channel. "Comanche 6, this is Comanche 3-6! 3-4 just hit an IED! We are currently executing the React to IED battle drill. More to follow, over!"

We abruptly came to a halt as the dust from the explosion began to settle. With the lurch of the brakes, I registered with shock what had just come out of me. I never yelled into the radio like that.

Taking a breath, I tried to settle. "3-4, this is 3-6, report your status. Are we dealing with fatalities?" There was a pause. My heart rate spiked again. "Come in, 3-4. Are we dealing with wounded or fatalities?" I peered through the settling dust at the exploded Mine Resistant Ambush Protected vehicle. Known as an MRAP, they were specifically built to withstand explosions, but we'd never taken a direct hit before. I didn't know how well they'd actually hold up. Had the IED penetrated the vehicle's armor?

The squad leader of the hit vehicle spoke through the radio. "3-6. This is 3-4." There was a long pause. One of the doors to the MRAP opened, and hung there outstretched, like a broken wing. No one got out.

"3-4, *what is your status?*" I demanded. "Do you have accountability of your guys?"

After another pause, his voice came back. "3-6, this is 3-4. Give me a moment." He sounded out of it. Was that just my imagination?

"Stand by," his voice came through again.

By now, the dust had settled enough that the MRAP's condition was more visible. Kevin's voice came through my headset. "LT, the rear axle and wheels have been blown off. Back of the vehicle looks pretty jacked up too."

"Gotta be deadlined after that blast," Philip mused quietly behind me.

We waited. I imagined the commander of that vehicle yelling into the back of the truck, getting a headcount, asking for a description of how everyone was doing. I closed my eyes and tried to breathe deep. *Why is it taking so long?*

Finally, I heard his voice again. "3-6, this is 3-4. We're all accounted for. Doesn't appear that we have any casualties or wounds. Just a little shook up and dazed by the blast."

I exhaled, feeling enormous relief. But as the fear of losing my guys dissipated, anger took its place. Who would *do* this?

I called through the radio to the rest of the platoon. "This is 3-6. Let's secure the site. We're going to be here for a while." The circle of vehicles which had gathered around the MRAP slowly made themselves permeable, soldiers and squad leaders hopping out, gathering around the smoking vehicle in the center. I jumped out of the Humvee, still inwardly fuming, only now my anger had turned toward my own higher ups. *I KNEW this was a risk. I told them this route was not secure.*

At the center of the action, the soldiers in the MRAP began climbing out. They were wobbly and seemed rattled, but I was relieved to see them moving under their own power. I put my hand on each of them as they walked over. "You okay? No blood? No broken bones?"

One of them gave me a shaky grin. "Don't worry, LT. I've been in bar fights worse than this."

I felt relieved at the joke. Their vehicle commander, one of my squad leaders, walked up to me and turned back to survey the vehicle. "That was a hell of a blast and the MRAP took it all. None of us anything more than concussed."

We walked toward the vehicle and bent down to examine the damage in the rear. Looking at the undercarriage, I had to appreciate the design of the MRAP. The underside of an MRAP is built of extremely heavy-duty steel armor, angled like a V away from the vehicle's center, deflecting the power of a blast outward and to the side, rather than absorbing the blast the way a flat-bottomed vehicle would. It was a shame we couldn't all travel in MRAPs, but they were so new to the war in Afghanistan, our platoon only had two. The rest of us were in much less armored and flat-bottomed Humvees.

The angled undercarriage of the MRAP was blackened from the blast, but still mostly intact. Then my eyes spotted the back axle. It was badly damaged. "Deadlined," I said quietly to myself. This vehicle wasn't going anywhere.

"Bet you regret turning down the MRAP now, LT." Staff Sergeant Anthony Roszko's voice pulled my attention out from under the vehicle. "You could have enjoyed a hell of a ride."

"No kidding," I mused.

I thought back to the conversation with my Company Commander several weeks earlier, when he had strongly recommended platoon leaders ride in the MRAPs. I didn't agree with his recommendation. In my mind, the two MRAPs in my platoon needed to be where the danger was greatest. Historically, the threat of IED blasts was highest in the first and last positions of our platoon's convoy lineup. Our practice had been for the platoon leader to be in a vehicle somewhere in the middle of the convoy—that way, the platoon leader could keep eyes on the front and give directions about what was coming up.

"Are you suggesting that platoon leaders ride in the first or last position?" I had asked my Company Commander.

"No," he said. "You keep your position in another spot in the lineup. But I suggest you should be in an MRAP. You platoon leaders need to be protected in the most heavily armored vehicles."

Immediately, I dismissed the recommendation. I wasn't going to have the last vehicle in my convoy be a Humvee, which was far more vulnerable to enemy attack. I also wasn't going to prioritize my safety over the safety of my guys. In my mind, their lives were more critical to the mission than mine. They were the ones actually *doing* the fighting and carrying out the work; I was simply the one doing mission planning and resourcing. And if anything happened to me, I had excellent Non-Commissioned Officers (NCOs) who could lead in my place. Either of my Staff Sergeant squad leaders, Anthony Roszko or Steven Smith, could easily take charge.

I didn't make a big deal about the vehicle order in the meeting in front of the other guys, but later, when it was just me and the commander, I explained I didn't intend to ride in the MRAP. "Sir, I just want to let you know that because of the risk to my guys in more highly vulnerable positions as we patrol in our vehicles, I intend to be in a Humvee. I'll use my MRAPs for my lead and my trailing vehicle."

After I finished explaining my rationale, the commander shrugged. "Lieutenant Brown, you can do what you think is best."

"Thank you, Sir."

"But as I mentioned before, I would prefer to have you in an MRAP."

I felt satisfied. We could agree to disagree. There wasn't necessarily a right or wrong answer except to us as individuals, and I was free to take the course I felt was best. When I gave the platoon sergeant instructions about which squad was going where, in what vehicle, I put the MRAPS in the first and last positions. I put myself in the number two spot—in a Humvee. But Anthony knew the CO had wanted me to be in the MRAP.

This conversation was fresh in my memory as I stared at the deadlined MRAP. Tearing my eyes away from the destroyed vehicle, I looked over at Anthony. "What the hell, right?" I said quietly.

Steven walked up to join us. "What the hell?" he repeated.

"This is exactly what we said was going to happen," Anthony fumed. I was gratified to hear the same anger in his voice that I felt. "We told them over and over that this route was compromised. How many more IEDs have been planted along this route? Battalion should have listened to you and taken this to the higher-ups who planned this mission. They should have had our back."

"Who are we?" Steven asked sarcastically. "Decisions about the convoy were made by leaders echelons above us. We're just the knuckle-draggers who have to execute when the higher-ups from this multi-national coalition blow off the fundamentals."

Inwardly, I seethed. *They make the decisions, but they don't suffer the consequences. They're not out here in harm's way. It's MY guys that have to execute their terrible plans. We don't have influence or power, but we have to deal with all the consequences.*

I knew I shouldn't say my thoughts out loud—I didn't want to add fuel to the fire when I could tell Steven and Anthony already agreed with me. I gave them a look that showed them I was just as pissed as they were. "Unfortunately, very predictable. And now we're down one of our MRAPs."

Steven shifted his demeanor. "Sir, there's a cluster of mud huts close by. Now that we've got the vehicle secure, we should probably do a quick sweep of the compound here to look for anything or anybody that could still pose a risk to us or those who will be following us later."

That made sense. I nodded. "Go ahead and take your squad to check it out. We'll keep security out here and you guys can run through it and report back. Let me know what you find." Moments like this always made me appreciate the fact that Steven and Anthony had prior deployments. Their experiences in combat gave them a streetwise savviness that benefited our platoon constantly—especially me as the leader, still cutting my teeth on my first deployment.

My company radio popped. "Comanche 3-6, this is 1-6." I heard the familiar voice of Austin Wallace, another platoon leader in Charlie Company and my former classmate at West Point. "Everybody okay?" I was grateful to hear the concern in his voice.

"1-6, 3-6," I returned. "Looks that way. Only casualty is the MRAP." I lifted my eyes to the horizon, back in the direction we'd come. I could see Austin's platoon idling on the highway: six unscathed vehicles, all in a row. The First Platoon had been charged with providing security for the southern part of the route—the area where we were currently stuck—and my platoon was supposed to head north. *Supposed to*. Once we cleaned up our mess.

"Roger that. We'll hold our position here while you guys cross-load. Let me know if you need support."

"Thanks, 1-6." I appreciated Austin. He was a good friend and a solid, steady leader.

I checked my watch. Thankfully, we still had several hours before the convoy was due to arrive. Nobody needed to rush north just yet.

My ride. That's Kevin Jensen in the gunner's turret and Mike Debolt at the front of the vehicle. The man sitting down is the Afghan interpreter who had been left back at the FOB on September 4, leaving me with an empty seat. This picture was taken earlier in the deployment, around August 2008.

Steven's voice came through my radio on our platoon's channel. "LT, we're inside the mud compound, and it's totally empty except for a sketchy-looking individual we found hanging out in here... We've got him secured. He's missing some fingers and a leg."

These details immediately aroused my suspicion. Missing limbs were often a telltale sign of a bombmaker. Steven's voice piped up again. "It'd probably be good for you to come in here and assess it for yourself."

"On my way."

I jogged toward the compound, thinking of my translator with regret. Due to the plans to return to Kandahar Airfield that evening, all the translators had been left behind at the forward operating base. I didn't know what kind of intel I'd be able to gather without him.

As soon as I entered the compound, it was obvious it had been abandoned for some time. The walls were bleached and cracked. There was no furniture, no fire pit with coals, no signs of activity or life—just a barren group of misshapen mud walls. On the northern outer wall, there was a smaller enclosed area. It looked like the kind of structure that, in an inhabited compound, would have been used as the latrine. Thin sticks lay on top of the walls to provide a bit of shade. That's where I saw my soldiers. They were standing around a lone Afghan man.

He wore traditional clothing—light-colored, baggy pants; a long sleeved tunic, and a dark colored vest. His turban was black: the sign of affiliation with the Taliban.

I walked up to him. He had deep-lined wrinkles and gray in his beard, his face weathered and beaten by the sun. He stared at me coldly.

"What are you doing here?" I asked, gesturing to the rest of the compound.

His face remained expressionless, the only visible emotion coming from his eyes which glowered like a thunderhead. He gave no indication that he understood anything I said.

I pointed in the direction of our smoldering MRAP, not quite visible over the outer wall. "Do you know anything about the bomb that just went off?"

The man spoke a few words in Pashtun, his tone even, his eyes boring into me.

I had no way to effectively question him. I was stranded without my interpreter—the only Pashtun phrases I knew were greetings or commands to stop. I stared at the man's hands. He was missing two of his middle fingers on his right hand and on his left, he was missing the pointer. Underneath one of his baggy pant legs, I saw what looked like a wooden stump. He had to be a bombmaker. Was this the man who had tried to kill my soldiers?

Frustrated, I spoke into the company radio. "Comanche 6, this is 3-6 with a status update. We've secured an individual in the mud compound near where the IED took out our MRAP. He's missing parts of his body that look like old injuries. There's no one else here... No signs of life or work equipment. Not sure why this guy would be here unless he was associated with the blast. Over."

"Comanche 3-6, this is Ramrod HQ." *Ramrod*—I was gratified to hear the call sign of the Battalion. That meant the higher-ups were tracking the situation and would provide support now. The voice on the other end continued. "Do you have any evidence that he set off the IED?"

I knew they were going to ask that. "Only circumstantial," I conceded. "He's missing limbs like a bombmaker. Black turban. He's got no apparent reason to be here, other than setting off bombs on us. Guessing he was alerted to the massive convoy approaching from the north and came here to set it off when they drove through. Or, who knows, maybe he just finished planting it and hadn't cleared out yet. But..." I paused. "But...no evidence to prove it."

"Does he have any weapons on him? Any bomb-making materials?"

"Negative. But we don't have our interpreters, so we can't properly question him. Do you want us to detain him and bring him back to the FOB for additional questioning?"

The radio remained silent. I spoke again. "Command, what do you want us to do?"

Another pause. "Comanche 3-6, this is Ramrod HQ. If there's no evidence to justify detaining him any further, let him go."

I caught Steven's gaze and could tell we were both thinking the same thing. There was no doubt in either of our minds that this guy was most likely responsible for the blast that nearly killed our soldiers. But we had no authority or legal power to do anything about it.

I jerked my head to my soldiers. "Let's go."

As we turned our backs on the Afghan man and started walking out of the compound, I suddenly recalled the warning we'd seen earlier that morning. Before we'd packed up for KAF and headed out to the convoy route, my platoon had gone out to the village to do a routine visit. But it hadn't been routine.

I could easily recall what Anthony had reported through the radio: "Lieutenant, we're seeing some fighting-age males moving quickly between buildings. Large groups of women and children appear to be exiting the area in a hurry. Heads up. Something might be about to go down."

Nothing had ended up happening in the village that morning, though we'd been on high alert. But walking out of the compound, I thought of his words again. They rose up in my mind like gathering storm clouds.

Heads up. Something might be about to go down.

I pushed the thought out of my mind.

Focus on the mission, I told myself. Clearly, our route had been compromised. What was my next move to mitigate the vulnerability of my guys? It was my job to lead and protect them. There were plenty of external factors outside of my control, but I intended to render control wherever I had the influence to do so.

I didn't need to worry. There was no point. Besides, wasn't this what I had prepared for? Wasn't this the culmination of the vast majority of my life? I'd played army in the woods around my house since childhood. I grew up watching Rambo in Vietnam. I spent my entire adolescence preparing for West Point, then I sought leadership positions throughout my West Point years. Then came Ranger School, then all the training prior to our deployment.

This is what I had been trained and equipped to do: Lead my troops. Complete the mission. Bring my soldiers home safely.

And if I was doing what I was supposed to do, and I'd prepared for what I was supposed to prepare for—what could stop me?

Not a bombmaker, or a deadlined MRAP. Not poor security planning, or all those "fighting-age males" that had run around the village earlier in the day. I'd spent my life preparing to take on all of them, and more.

I strode forward with the unshakeable confidence of a man who knows he is in command of capable warriors, and in control of his own destiny.

CHAPTER 2

PERFECTLY PREPARED

Crew at West Point. I'm in the first rowing position, in control as the Stroke. April 2005.

I gave an involuntary shudder after tossing my sweatshirt on a rock and wading into the water. As soon as we began rowing, I knew I'd warm up. But at 7:30 a.m. in March, even "balmy" South Carolina temps were just above freezing.

"So damn cold out here," I heard Erik's grim mutter behind me as we guided the shell deeper into the water. He sat in the number seven spot, just behind the stroke seat where I'd been assigned.

"Better than the Hudson," I rejoined, trying to convey humor I didn't feel. "We'd be dodging hunks of ice if we were still in New York."

Our coxswain, Nick, counted us down—*3, 2, 1*... On the final count, the eight of us transitioned smoothly into the shell and Nick settled into the coxswain seat right in front of me. As we began pulling the oars, I felt satisfaction, sensing the uniformity of our movement and timing. My favorite part of rowing on the crew team was the sensation of moving as a single organism. Now that I was rowing Stroke, the *swing* of falling into synchronization was more than a pleasure; it was my responsibility to lead.

We took slow pulls, warming up as we moved toward the racing area. The Varsity boat cruised ahead of us. Several of the seniors called out trash talk as they passed my Junior Varsity shell. The rest of the Varsity boat was made up of Juniors—my classmates and best friends. They made eye contact with me apologetically as their shell pulled away from mine. Their sympathy stung. As of the previous night's posted seating assignments, they were all now Varsity rowers. Nick and I were the only two still relegated to the JV boat.

"The seniors are still pissed after last fall," Nick said.

"Yup," I agreed, exhaling on my pull in time with the *clunk* of our oars. Everything in the boat was done according to a strict rhythm and cadence—even when we were just warming up.

I knew Nick's comment was intended to soothe both of our wounded egos by bringing to mind the epic race where our JV boat had smoked Varsity. I could still picture the big regatta that had been the culmination of our fall season. The Occoquan River, just outside Washington, DC, had been crowded with shells from a number of other colleges, in addition to the two boats from West Point. Army Varsity had been the favorite to win the entire race, but my JV boat had felt fast as we navigated the river course and passed other teams on our way to the finish. My thoughts went back to that moment— the yells from the viewing platforms; Nick's hoarse calls, urging us on; seeing us pull away from the trailing teams as we approached the finish line; the burn in my muscles; the rhythm of the oars.

When the results were posted, *Army-Junior Varsity* had topped the list, followed by *Army-Varsity*. It was a huge upset. And the people who'd been *most* upset were undoubtedly the Varsity guys and our coaches.

What else could I have done to convince them? I wondered. Nearly six months after I had led the JV boat to victory—after a winter's worth of gym workouts and the previous week of training—the memory of last fall's win caused me new irritation, mixed with regret. All week long during spring training, I'd given it my all, hoping to be assigned to the Varsity boat. I didn't care which seat I got; I just wanted to be on the Varsity boat.

Coach had posted the assignments the previous night. I'd searched the list under "Varsity," reading it over twice, sure I'd missed my name. It wasn't there. Then, I looked under JV. *Stroke: Sam Brown.* Same position as the previous fall.

No advancement.

I'd gone straight to bed, frustrated and confused.

Maybe JV's where I belong, I told myself, trying to talk down my ego. After all, I hadn't even been sure I would make the team the previous fall, after getting a knee injury that required surgery my sophomore year. In September, it had seemed like a miracle when the coaches assigned me as Stroke in the JV boat. "All that time in the rowing tank while you were healing made you a better rower," they'd remarked to me. "You've got better technique. Better control." And it was true—

our JV boat had killed it throughout the fall season, culminating in the upset where we'd beat the Varsity boat and everyone else in that final race of the season.

But that win hadn't been enough to earn me a Varsity seat this spring. And the senior Varsity rowers' trash talk didn't help. I pulled on my oar and clenched my teeth.

Doesn't matter, I told myself, not sure if I meant the JV assignment, the knee injury, the Varsity's trash talking, or all of the above. I tried to reorient my thoughts to my immediate surroundings. *Layer of fog on the water. Log cabins among the pines. The oars slicing in the water—listen.*

We rowed to the starting line. Given that it was Saturday, the last day of our training week, the coaches were racing our two boats against each other to establish a baseline. Typically, there was a wide gap between when JV and Varsity each crossed the finish line. Varsity always created a sizeable lead, which the JV boat would work to close all season.

Coach pulled up beside us in a speedboat and held out his stopwatch. Through his megaphone he lined our shells up with the bows even and called, "Ready…attention…*GO!*"

Our bodies exploded into action. I quickly found the rhythm that I'd practiced during all the tank sessions my sophomore year—the only rowing option available for me while my knee healed. What the coaches had said about me was true: the time in the tank *had* made me a better rower. I hadn't been able to exert myself at the same level as the other guys out on the Hudson; the only productive use of my time in the absence of strength was to focus on my technique. And that had made a huge difference.

The trick, I'd realized, was to establish a good ratio of speed in how fast I allowed my body to move toward my feet. Most people thought all the rowing power came from hauling the oar through the water: exploding backwards with your legs first, then following with your back and arms. But I'd discovered that the move *forward* on the sliding seat, with the oar out of the water, was equally as important. After such a powerful haul backwards, it was tempting for rowers to slide forward with little control, saving their energy for another pull. But when we didn't control our slide forward, we created backwards inertia. Eight rowers slamming forward in their seats at the same time decreased the boat's forward momentum.

My approach as Stroke was to create a more intentional slide forward to reset the oar in a compressed position, then explode out. It meant we had to sustain more energy on both the move forward and the pull back, but it also meant we were more efficient. The boat had more of a chance to run forward between strokes.

I could feel the guys behind me trying to rush the slide. I resisted their speed, knowing I had to control the pace. So long as I held steady, they would eventually follow me.

With a few more pulls, I could feel us start to move as one. The momentum in our slide began to feel uniform. The oars splashed into the water all at the same time. I could hear the oarlocks click in unison as we feathered the oars from vertical to horizontal, and felt our breath exhaling hard on each stroke.

"*Lengthen,* breathe. *Lengthen,* breathe," Nick called, matching the rhythm of his yells to the clicks of the oarlocks. All of us were moving in perfect synchronization.

"Two seats up on Varsity! Here we go. We're entering the second five hundred. Now, let's *really...set...*that *rhythm...*and *SWING!*"

We seemed to fly over those 2,000 meters. When we crossed the finish line, the Varsity boat was a full length behind us. A few guys in the JV boat whooped happily, but stopped as soon as they saw Coach's face.

Coach stared in disbelief between our JV boat and Varsity. "What the hell?!" he remarked. He scowled. Then, he cranked the wheel of his speed boat and moved it off a distance. We waited.

We couldn't hear what he was saying to the assistant coach, but it was obvious Coach was pissed. His gestures and tone all indicated he was angry by the unpredictable outcome.

He motored back. "We're going again," he said. "Line up for another head-to-head."

We rowed our boats to a new starting position and waited for the start. "Attention... *GO!*"

All of us hauled our oars back, this time finding our rhythm within the first few strokes. Despite the soreness we all felt from the week of hard training, finding our synchronized motion transformed our bodies. Just briefly, it was easy to forget the pain. We were flying.

"Thirty-four-and-a-half, *good*," Nick guided. We were right on pace. His voice got louder and more excited as he called updates that alerted us to our gains on Varsity. "Four seats up on Varsity. Last 750... Let's do a power ten in *three...two...one*, let's GO!"

Once again, our JV boat sliced across the 2,000-meter finish line—this time, an even larger gap ahead of Varsity.

Coach swore audibly and motored away from us again. He and the assistant coach took longer this time. We saw them staring at us, motioning back and forth between the two boats.

"Nope, it's not an anomaly," Erik said cheerfully behind me. "JV's just *that good.*"

"Coach doesn't know what to do with us," Nick said. "Bunch of underperformers beating his Varsity all-stars."

"All that work, perfecting his new lineup all week," I said. "Turns out it was a waste." I felt a grim satisfaction. *Guess my name should have been on the Varsity list after all, huh, Coach?* The thought was validating. I wasn't the strongest guy out there—not even close. But I knew what happened to a boat full of rowers when they followed my lead.

"I kind of like being the underdog," I mused. "People have minimal expectations of what you can do and then...you go out and perform."

Coach motored back over, scowling. Then he motioned to the Varsity boat. "I want Dan to switch with Jon. Dan, you take Stroke." Dan was one of the most aggressive type-A personalities on the Varsity boat—ruthlessly competitive. Coach stared at the rest of us. "The rest of the lineup stays as is. We're going again."

I could hear scoffs and muffled groans across both boats. After a grueling training week and then going all out on two head-to-heads, a third race felt especially ruthless. I also knew that Dan would give everything he had to beat us in an effort to earn the coveted spot as the Varsity Stroke. This third run was likely to be brutal.

"My hands are ripped open," Erik muttered as we rowed back into position.

"Mine too," I said, just as two other guys in the JV boat said the same thing. None of us had ever done three back-to-back-*to-back* races like that.

Coach called the starting, "GO!" We quickly locked into rhythm, ignoring the pain in our hands and our bodies. The morning chill had long given way to a warm March day, and all of us were coated in sweat.

Nick's voice was hoarse. "Let's *find*…our control, let's *find* our rhythm." I locked into our racing pace and the rest of the boat quickly followed. "Find that middle move! Let's stay long! I want *Varsity…* to *know*…that *they* can't catch us… That *we* are *elite*… That *we* are un*stop*pable…" Our oar locks smacked in perfect synchronization, making a cadence with the splashes of our oars slicing through water. Our bodies ached. The boat soared.

"We're entering *right* here! *Going* thousand, *middle* move! *Last chance* to black out, men! Right now, TEN—pick it up! NINE, that's it. EIGHT, good soldiers! SEVEN, let's go." I could see the Varsity boat's full length behind us and registered their coxswain's red, angry face.

Nick's yells intensified as we approached the finish line. "They're *eating…our…dust,* OPEN WATER! That's *three…two…*ONE, LAST PULL!"

For the last time, we flew across the 2,000-meter mark. As we crossed the finish line, it was clear to all of us that the JV boat had won by the greatest margin so far. We collapsed over our oars, exhausted, and dizzy with delight over our third consecutive victory.

Coach stared at us with a look of profound disappointment. He shook his head. "Take it in."

None of us spoke as we began maneuvering the boats back over to shore. It felt like we were kids who'd just been yelled at by a furious parent.

"What's this mean?" Erik whispered behind me. I shrugged.

On Sunday, we made the long drive back to West Point. Monday afternoon, we met at the boathouse near the banks of the Hudson River, just an hour's drive north of New York City. The sky was thickly overcast, matching the dark steel gray of the river. We began unloading the shells from the boathouse and fitting them out with our oars and shoe riggings. I glanced out at the water to see if there were whitecaps.

"Hold up on your riggings," Coach called gruffly. "We've got a change in the lineup. Sam Brown." Coach gestured to me. "You're now the Stroke of the Varsity boat."

My eyes locked with Nick's. He swore.

"Let's go, Sam. Get your stuff swapped over," Coach called. Quietly, I began pulling my shoe riggings out of the JV shell and walked over to the Varsity boat. I avoided making eye contact with the scowling senior who walked past me with his own riggings, demoted from Varsity to JV.

As I got closer to the Varsity shell, my buddies in the boat beamed. "There he is!" one called. I grinned and shook my head, still in shock at what just happened.

As soon as practice began, I found my stroke. The Varsity rowers behind me fought my rhythm longer than the JV guys had, wanting to rush the slide. I held my stroke and waited for them to fall in line. As soon as they did, we picked up speed.

In the head-to-head against the JV boat at the end of that first practice, it was once again my shell that crossed the finish line first. The Varsity team pulled far ahead to a decisive victory.

I never gave up that seat again.

Army-1, the Varsity boat, went on to have its best season in West Point's history. The next fall, during my senior year—this time, with Nick as the Varsity coxswain—we were invited to the most competitive autumn regatta in the country: the Head of the Charles, in Boston. We also qualified for the Intercollegiate Rowing Association's premier spring season national regatta in Camden, New Jersey—the first and last time an Army Varsity boat with eight rowers had ever been invited to compete.

Although I never said it out loud, I had the thought, plenty of times:

I'm the key variable. When people follow my lead, it makes them the best version of themselves. That's when the efforts of everyone else are maximized.

That's when we win.

* * *

At the combat outpost, reading about surviving combat in Afghanistan next to my "stretcher" cot. September 2008.

It felt crazy to turn my back on the man who had most likely planted the explosives intended to take the lives of my soldiers. Each step away from him seemed to sharpen the memory of his dark glare.

I breathed out heavily. Why did it suddenly seem even hotter than before? The desert sun beat down relentlessly.

"You okay, LT?" Anthony asked beside me.

"Fine. Just hot."

"I can't believe we're letting him go either," Anthony said grimly. We emerged from behind the wall of the mud compound. His tone changed abruptly. "Oh, *now* we're talking!"

I looked up and squinted my eyes in the direction Anthony was facing. While we'd been in the mud compound, the route clearance company had arrived. Their long train of vehicles gleamed in the harsh light, with the lead truck looking like something out of *Mad Max: Fury Road*. I felt a massive wave of relief.

A route clearance company is designed to detect and set off any buried landmines—thereby clearing a route. The heavily armored lead vehicle is equipped with what looks like a massive rolling plow on its front: a counter-IED package. Two long arms stretch out in front of the vehicle which hold either end of a wide horizontal axle. Attached to that axle is a line of thick, rolling tires. As the route clearance vehicle drives forward, that line of tires puts pressure on every inch of the road. If there's a landmine there, you can bet it will be detonated, and the vehicle is specially designed to withstand the blasts. That means any vehicle driving behind a route clearance vehicle is likely to come away unscathed—that is, so long as there aren't any bad actors hiding with a remote, ready to detonate a bomb *after* the route clearance company goes through. I pushed thoughts of the man with the black turban out of my mind. This route clearance company was exactly what we needed.

"Did they come here for us?" one of my privates, Winston, piped up behind me.

I shook my head. "They'd already been assigned to lead the last leg of the convoy's route back to KAF. But it sure is helpful that they're here."

I jogged toward one of the vehicles where I knew I would find the Company Commander. His towering MRAP had pulled up near the mangled remains of my own platoon's exploded MRAP, like a grisly "before and after" photo. I could see some of my guys still gathering equipment and cleaning up the debris.

"Make sure you're staying hydrated, men," I called to them. I made a mental note to chug a water as soon as I got back to my own Humvee. The heat was nearly unbearable this afternoon.

I slowed to a walk and trudged the final few steps toward the Commander's MRAP. "Captain?" I called.

After a pause, the Company Commander opened the door. Refreshing, cool air blew out from the vehicle. He lounged in the passenger seat and looked down at me.

"Lieutenant. How can I help you?"

"Sir, as you can see, our platoon has hit an IED. This was a concern I had to begin with, due to the fact that the convoy is coming back the same way it went to the Kajaki Dam. I came over to ask if you'll use your route clearance package to clear the rest of the route to the northern extent of our area of operation."

He didn't respond. Had he not heard me? I couldn't tell where he was looking behind his dark lens ballistic eye protection.

I tried again. "Sir—now that we've already hit one, can you just have your guys clear the rest of the route? We'll fall in behind and get into our secure positions, then your route clearance package can come back safely and stage where you need to be staged."

He turned his ballistic eye pro down at me. "Nah. I'm not going to do that."

What? I was in disbelief. I didn't think I was going to need to convince him to do this. Wasn't I making a commonsense request?

He started to close his door. I broke in. "Hey Sir, hold on. I just want to clarify—is there a *reason* that you can't do this? Clearly, the Taliban has taken the opportunity to plant bombs along this stretch and it's likely there are more. In fact, I just spoke to an Afghan in that mud compound over there who looks like he might have been the bombmaker."

None of this seemed to make any impression on the commander. He continued staring cooly down at me through his dark shades. I pressed on, growing increasingly frustrated by his icy countenance. "I didn't come over here just to be a pain or act entitled or anything. We've *hit* an IED—" I gestured angrily over my shoulder. "—And there are probably more. You and I both know the plan for the convoy's path of return violates the principles of security. Given that you have the specialized equipment necessary to clear and secure this route, would you please clear it?"

He smiled. His teeth were perfect and gleaming white. "Lieutenant Brown."

I nodded. "Yes, Sir."

"You're the one who was making all sorts of noise with Command about this return route. You and your squad leaders. Isn't that right?"

I tried to answer but he cut me off. "And now you're not getting your way. And that's upsetting to you."

"*Sir—*" I gestured to the smoldering MRAP behind me.

"My route clearance assignment is to stage at the intersection of *this* dirt road and *that* highway." He jerked his thumb over his shoulder toward the paved highway we'd come in on. "And then we're supposed to lead the convoy back to the airfield. *Your* job is to provide security for the area just south of the pass to the paved highway right here. So, why don't you do your job, and let my company do ours?"

"But—but, Sir—" I was sputtering. "You have the flexibility on the ground as a commander to make adjustments based on the circumstances. Clearly, we have a situation—how much more justification do you need? You have the unique assets to clear the route, and—"

"Thank you, Lieutenant." He flashed another gleaming smile at me and shut the door.

I stood there, stunned. My own arguments whirled in my thoughts: even if the commander thought I was entitled or complaining, what about the large multinational forces convoy? They would have to drive over the same terrain we were supposed to secure—terrain likely pockmarked with explosive devices. If his route clearance company's whole function was to clear the route for them—never mind his own fellow Battalion's units—*why* wouldn't he clear it for the bigger mission?

I wanted to wrench the door open and pull him down out of his air-conditioned fortress.

Instead, I turned around. There was nothing more I could do.

I took a few steps back toward the mud compound, planning to update Anthony and Steven, when my company radio popped again. "Comanche HQ, this is Ramrod HQ. Please update us on the status of the mission. Are you able to secure the route?"

The message had gone out to our entire company, but I knew it was mainly directed at me. I felt renewed frustration at the route clearance company CO's glib refusal. *We SHOULD be able to secure the route.* "Ramrod HQ, this is Comanche 3-6," I called back. "Stand by for an update."

I looked over at my platoon's destroyed MRAP. We were down one of our most heavily armored vehicles which made us more vulnerable. Being short a vehicle also meant that one of the squads had to be divided up and cross-loaded. And now that the route clearance commander had refused to clear the road, there was a chance that one of our four Humvees would hit another planted IED, further diminishing our platoon. Getting ourselves to the northern position did not look promising, either for our platoon or for the success of the mission.

I turned back toward the mud compound. A sight farther in the distance caught my attention—the glare of the harsh sun reflected off the vehicles of First Platoon, still idling on the highway.

I called through the company radio to Austin, my West Point classmate and the First Platoon leader. "1-6, this is 3-6."

He responded immediately. "3-6, 1-6. You want us to leapfrog you and secure the northern route?"

I felt relieved that he'd come to the same conclusion I had. "1-6, 3-6. How does that sound?"

"Makes sense," he said. "We're fully intact and have both our

MRAPs. We'll head north, and you guys can secure the southern sector."

"1-6, 3-6, there's something you should know," I said. "Let's sync in person before you head north."

The line of First Platoon vehicles turned off the highway onto the dirt road, one by one. Austin slowly drove his vehicle over to me, staying in line with his platoon. When he pulled up next to me, he hopped out. "What's up, Brown?"

I walked close enough that I could speak quietly. "The route clearance package is not going to go north. I requested it—I just spoke to their Company Commander. But he's refused to clear the road any farther north."

Austin didn't hold back his anger. "What the *fuck*? Well, that's a bitch move. I wouldn't have expected that from him."

I would have laughed if I hadn't been so angry. "There's a chance you may hit another one."

He nodded. "Understood. We'll lead with the MRAPs and call you if we need your guys to be a quick reaction force for us."

I shook my head, feeling disbelief over what seemed like a senseless risk. "Good luck. You guys be safe. Keep your eyes out for any more IEDs. I'll look forward to seeing you guys back at KAF tonight."

Austin gave me a fist bump and jumped back in his MRAP. His voice sounded again over the company channel. "Ramrod HQ, this is Comanche 1-6. We are taking the northern sector of the route and Comanche 3-6 will secure the southern portion." Austin's group of vehicles peeled off from the larger group and continued heading north, the two MRAPs leading. I watched them, trying to will their safety as they drove up to the northern pass between the mountains. How many more IEDs had been planted along this route?

Anthony and Steven walked up to me. "Route clearance isn't going first?" Anthony demanded.

I shook my head. "Requested it. Repeatedly. Got shot down."

"*Why?*" Steven asked.

"He didn't really give a reason."

Steven stared at the dust trail made by First Platoon as they drove north. "Well. We should hurry up and finish cross-loading then. Cause we're probably going to need to provide assistance if First Platoon hits an IED."

I nodded tightly. "Let's finish that up."

I strode quickly back to my vehicle, trying to control the rage welling up. The day's series of events seemed to compound, gather, and culminate in the commander's, "*Nah*—I'm not going to do that." First, there had been the warning signs we'd seen that morning, with the women and children fleeing the village and the "fighting-age males" darting between buildings. Then the first explosion. Then the lone Afghan man with the black turban, missing fingers, and glowering eyes—in my mind, I already thought of him as the bombmaker. And the multinational forces convoy's return along its same incoming route, flouting the principles of security. As an infuriating final straw—this grinning, flippant rejection from a higher-ranking officer of a legitimate request that was in the interest of preventing further injury and saving lives.

My mind raced with all the decisions I would have made differently, but none of that mattered. My job was to follow instructions, and lead my men to the best of my ability.

As I got close, I could see the crew had nearly finished cross-loading equipment off the destroyed MRAP. I called out to the platoon sergeant. "Once we're done with equipment, let's get new vehicle assignments for the guys from that truck."

I grabbed a water bottle off the back of my Humvee and slung myself into the front passenger seat, angling my legs out the door so I was facing away from Mike and Philip. They didn't greet me. They must have been able to read from my body language that I wasn't in the mood to chat.

Focus on the mission, I thought sternly. *Obstacles are a given. But at the end of the day, nothing outside of death itself needs to derail the mission.* I inhaled deeply, then exhaled slowly.

Staring out at the flat desert expanse, my mind suddenly conjured up a vision of flat, clear water. The lake in South Carolina. West Point rowing days. The memory filled me with a swell of pride that was instantly rejuvenating.

I'M the one who controls my outcomes. I missed a half season of rowing and had to stay on that JV boat longer than I wanted. But the outcome was only delayed. I still made Stroke on Varsity. I still accomplished what I set out to do.

I accomplish *what I set out to do,* I repeated in my mind. *I control the slide, and the others follow my lead.*

This was the pep talk I needed. With enough energy, with enough focus—nothing would permanently stop me. Not a bombmaker. Not an entitled commander. Not a poorly planned convoy route. There was no reason *any* of them should interrupt the pursuit of my goals and the execution of the mission, so long as I remained focused.

The company radio popped with Austin's voice. "3-6, this is 1-6. Thought you'd be glad to know First Platoon is staged in our position. Made it safe and sound."

I felt a massive wave of relief. "1-6, 3-6," I called back. "Very glad to hear it."

Good. First Platoon hadn't run into any more IEDs. *Maybe we hit the only one,* I thought. That seemed doubtful—more likely, First Platoon had just lucked out with their tire tracks. But for the sake of the returning convoy, I hoped First Platoon's successful drive north boded well for the whole mission.

My platoon sergeant's voice took over the radio as he began cross-loading the soldiers from the deadlined MRAP and calling out their new vehicle assignments. I watched him out the windshield; he was studying his vehicle seating roster. One by one, the soldiers gathered near him jogged to new vehicles.

I turned around in my seat to look at Philip. "Hey, Phil," I asked. "Would you be up for digging out those Canadian MREs? This is probably a good time to eat."

I peered back through the window at the platoon sergeant. Looked like he'd managed to cross-load everyone except for one guy. I squinted. Who was that? The soldier shifted and adjusted his gun. I grinned:

the only soldier with that small of a build and that large of a gun was Vincent Winston.

"We need one more seat somewhere," the platoon sergeant's voice came through clear in my headset. "Do any vehicles have an empty seat?"

We do, I thought. The seat right behind me where the interpreter normally sat was vacant. I started to speak up but then stopped.

For whatever reason, I didn't want Winston in that seat. I didn't want *anyone* in that seat.

The call came through on my headset again. "Please respond if you have any spare room in your vehicle. We've got to get Winston somewhere."

I remained silent. Out the windshield, I could see the platoon sergeant studying the seating roster. He must not have remembered that my vehicle was down our interpreter—and I didn't want to remind him. *There's got to be somewhere else that he can go.*

I didn't understand my hesitation. I liked Winston—everybody liked Winston. Anthony and a few others called me "the mind" of our unit, but everyone thought of Winston as "the heart." His childlike innocence made us all feel like he was our kid brother. Even watching him now, seeing his expression screwed up in a squint while holding that heavy gun, I felt a surge of affection. But imagining him loading into the seat behind me caused an intense feeling of uneasiness. Deep in my gut, I sensed that seat needed to remain empty.

The platoon sergeant's voice came through again. "We need one more seat somewhere," he repeated. "As far as I know, every seat that was open has now been filled. Putting out one last call. Did I miss something? Is there another seat left?"

One by one, vehicle commanders began piping up. "3-3 is full, Sarge."

"Full in 4 too."

"Our truck's full, Sarge."

Every other vehicle except mine called in. *What's your problem, Brown?* I wondered. *Call him over.* Still, I hesitated. Five seconds passed. Then ten. Finally, it felt impossible to wait any longer. I held up my platoon radio. "Hey, 3-7, this is 3-6. I don't have our interpreter. We left him at the FOB. You can send Winston over to me."

I watched Winston start to jog over us, his big machine gun juggling around in his arms. The feeling of uneasiness grew stronger, like a weight on my chest. I tried pushing it out of my mind.

Chill out, Sam, I told myself. *First Platoon made it to the northern end of the route without hitting any IEDs. My platoon is stationed where we need to be. The only people under threat now are in the returning convoy before they get to us, and once they get to us, we follow them all the way back to KAF. Our risk of IEDs from here on out is effectively zero.*

Philip hopped back in the vehicle, his arms full of the Canadian MREs. Winston arrived, sweating. He looked at the Humvee's doors, which had all been pushed wide open. "How's the A/C in this one?" he asked.

"Like shit!" Kevin called out from his turret. His drawl elongated the second word: *shee-at.*

"Yeah, but we've got a decent consolation prize," Philip said cheerfully. "Gourmet meals."

"Hop in, Winston," I said. "We traded some of our American MREs with the Canadians this morning."

"Aw, really?" He hoisted himself up into the seat behind me. "What are they?"

Philip studied the boxes. "Beef teriyaki…veal cutlet…meatloaf…"

"I call meatloaf!" Kevin hollered.

Philip passed out the rest, handing me the veal cutlet which the others had passed on. I ripped into the box. "You guys missed out," I called, starting to feel better. "I've got blueberry cobbler for dessert!"

Kevin started piping a new song into my ear: "Bubble Toes," by Jack Johnson. I relaxed into my seat, one leg resting on the floorboard, and the other hanging out the door. In the evening light, the easy melody made the harshness of the desert feel somehow more benign. A breeze blew through the vehicle. I took a deep breath. In a few hours, we'd be back at KAF. Showers, a real bed, air-conditioned rooms.

YOU control the slide, Sam, I thought. *Just keep it easy and controlled.*

The company radio popped alive with Austin's voice. "Comanche network, this is Comanche 1-6. We're receiving indirect fire from a ridgeline to our Northeast."

I paused, a bite of blueberry cobbler halfway to my mouth. Kevin turned off the music.

I spoke into the radio. "1-6, this is 3-6. Understand you're receiving indirect fire. Is it effective? Have you been hit?" I waited for Austin to respond and took another bite. This was probably a situation where the Taliban would shoot a couple of badly aimed mortar rounds and then bolt before we returned fire. That had happened to my own platoon several times already. It had always turned out to be a non-escalatory situation.

While waiting for Austin, I radioed the Battalion back at the combat outpost. "Ramrod HQ, this is Comanche 3-6. Did you receive the report from Comanche 1-6, regarding receiving indirect fire?"

The radio sparked with the voice of one of the platoon leaders back at the FOB. "Comanche 3-6, this is Ramrod HQ. Negative. We did not receive a message from Comanche 1-6 regarding indirect fire."

That meant Austin's platoon was out of radio range with the Battalion and possibly our company. I was the only one close enough to receive his messages. "1-6, this is 3-6," I radioed to Austin. "Your radio transmissions aren't going all the way back to Battalion. You're too far out."

There was a pause and then Austin's voice came back through—slightly louder than the first update. "3-6, this is 1-6. The indirect fire is now bracketing our position." I stiffened and sat up. The Taliban hadn't bolted, like I'd expected. Whoever was firing the mortar rounds was altering their aim, zeroing in closer on either side of the platoon. The situation was suddenly much more serious.

"Men, this is 3-6," I called on my platoon network. "First Platoon may need our assistance. Stand by for orders on driving north immediately."

"Guys—" I said to the group in my Humvee. "Gather your trash. We may be going somewhere quick."

"Time to finish your dessert," Kevin quipped.

In my mind, I was quickly trying to sort out how my platoon could maintain security over our own assigned sector, but also provide help to First Platoon. Our third squad—the men who had mostly been in the exploded MRAP, including Vincent Winston—had now been cross-loaded across all remaining vehicles. That meant Third Squad wasn't intact to drive up north and provide assistance. I looked at the MRAP parked in front of me. Most of those guys were Anthony's squad—and Anthony himself was in the Humvee behind me with the rest of his men. It would make the most sense for his squad to drive north with my vehicle if necessary.

I radioed Anthony, giving him instructions to prep his two vehicles for heading north. Then I radioed Steven and my platoon sergeant. "3-3 and 3-4, this is 3-6. I'm going to need your squads to work together to maintain security in this area. That might mean you need to spread out a little more." They would be fine—Steven, especially, was a gifted leader.

But where was Austin? I was anxious for another update. I used the company radio to relay Austin's updated status to the Battalion.

As soon as I released my own "talk" button, I heard Austin's voice bark through again. "3-6, this is 1-6. We're now taking direct fire from the village west of us!" His voice dropped off abruptly—a sign that he was delivering his updates to me as quickly as possible because he also needed to issue commands to his own platoon through their radio network.

"1-6, this is 3-6. Do you need support?" I asked. Mike stared at me, waiting for the command to start the ignition. Philip leaned forward from the backseat, staring at the MRAP in front of us. Nothing came through from Austin.

The radio sparked alive. "Comanche 3-6, this is Ramrod HQ." It was the Battalion. "Can you provide an update from Comanche 1-6?" Hurriedly, I called Austin's latest update back to the Battalion again and sent another message to the platoon, then waited for Austin.

"1-6, this is 3-6. *Do you need support?*" I repeated. Something was occurring at the base of the mountains that I couldn't see and couldn't hear, and my buddy Austin was in the midst of it.

"3-6, confirmed! We are now receiving direct and indirect fire from three different directions. We need support!"

"1-6, we're on the way!" I switched radios to speak to the platoon network. "3-1 and 3-2, this is 3-6. First Platoon needs our support! Your orders are to head directly to the northern portion of the route until we can visually assess the situation with First Platoon. 3-3 and 3-4, maintain security here with 3-7. Let's go!"

In front of us, the MRAP rumbled to life, but such a heavy vehicle takes time to get started. "Let's *go…*" I muttered impatiently. Finally, they lurched forward and then quickly accelerated—probably two to three times faster than they would normally go. We took off behind them, our vehicles once again kicking up the fine, powdery dust of the desert. The evening light slanted into the dusty swirls, causing them to glow and obscure our vision at the same time.

Mike carefully kept our vehicle in the lead MRAP's tire tracks, which I appreciated. If there were any more IEDs in our path, the MRAP would detonate them first. It would be another vehicle lost, but the MRAP was built to withstand those explosions, as we'd all just witnessed. So long as the rest of us stayed in the MRAP's tracks, we'd all make it to the aid of the other platoon intact. A few inches to the right or left, on the other hand—we'd be taking our chances.

The lead MRAP continued to accelerate. It became harder to make out the road with the clouds of dust. We hit a pothole and my knees banged against the dash. I gripped the radio, holding it up to my mouth as our Humvee bumped over the uneven ground, juggling the chaotic communication of calling directions ahead to the lead vehicle, receiving updates from Austin, and passing news to the Battalion. I had to yell to be heard. The Humvee's engine roared, underscored by the loud metallic clanging of ammo and machinery bumping around as we sped over the uneven ground.

Low in the sky, the sun's light was piercing. It was impossible to see ahead clearly, so I focused on the navigation system in front of me. We'd already gone 2,000 meters. Surely we were nearing Austin's platoon? I squinted through the window—I could see the ridges of the mountains through the dust. Dim shapes seemed to emerge—possibly the village that had been firing on Austin's platoon.

Over the roar of the engine and the clattering of ammo cans bouncing around the back of the vehicle, I suddenly heard Philip's voice yell over my left shoulder. "I love you guys!"

His words jolted me out of the frenzied radio communication and the mission at hand. For Philip to yell that out to a bunch of tough infantrymen running into battle—*I love you guys*—abruptly inserted our humanity into the war zone. With a shocking realization, it occurred to me that my platoon's survival might be at stake.

If it had been a stage play, everything else around us would have frozen. All other lights would have gone dark except for a spotlight on our own vehicle. The clatter and roar of the Humvee would have died away, leaving Philip's words to hang alone, suspended.

The rest of us were silent. Then, Kevin yelled down from his turret, repeating Philip's words. "I love you guys!"

"I love you guys too," I called.

"I love you guys!" Winston and Mike echoed at the same time.

Moments after Winston and Mike's words died away, the stage lights came back on. Everything was in a riot of motion and noise again, and we were hurtling forward.

Thirty seconds later, I could vaguely see the shapes of the vehicles from the other platoon through the dust and the low light. *Nearly there.* I held up the radio again and began calling out directions to the lead vehicle about where to go. "3-1, this is 3-6—"

I was interrupted—everything was interrupted—by the bright orange ball of fire that suddenly swallowed us whole.

CHAPTER 3

DEATH ITSELF

Getting ready to deploy. June 2008.

Tonight was the night.

I'd been meaning to do this ever since I'd arrived at Fort Hood to prepare for deployment. Now—with training at a lull, days before our departure—I finally had the space to conduct my own personal training checklist.

I dumped the medical supplies I'd gathered onto the coffee table. Thankfully, one of the medics had willingly gathered some for me, so I didn't need to break into my personal medical kit. I flicked on the floor lamp and perched on the edge of my leather couch, studying the array. What should I do first?

I pulled a package of bandages toward me and ripped it open, making a note of how the bandages unfolded so that I would feel familiar with the process in combat. I tried to put myself in the mindframe of battle—*imagine explosions around you, you've just been shot in the leg, you've got to hurry.* Quickly, I began wrapping my leg with the pressure bandage. It was important to get the pressure just right—too tight, I'd cut off circulation; too loose, it wouldn't do any good. I finished and studied my wrap job. *Good,* I thought, satisfied.

I practiced a shrapnel wound next. That involved packing loose bandages into the hypothetical bloody cavity, then doing the pressure bandage over it. I tried to mentally envision the pain I'd be in. Would I be screaming? *No,* I decided. *I'd stay focused on getting out of there.* Adrenaline would serve me until I could get myself to a medic.

I turned my attention to my arms next, assuming that my body armor would take care of my chest and abdomen. *Besides,* I thought, *if I get blasted somewhere in my abdomen, my own bandages aren't going to do much good.* Better to focus on what I could control.

I practiced tying a tourniquet, first on my right arm and then on my left. I was considerably more clumsy using my left hand, which didn't bode well for the IV practice. I made a mental note to start doing things left-handed more often.

Ideally, of course, someone would be there to help if I got wounded.

But there was no guarantee that anyone would be around in those initial moments. And the initial moments, I knew, could be critical. I remembered what our training instructor had told us: "If you ask someone to help you in the middle of a firefight, they're likely to become a casualty themselves. You owe it to yourself, your unit, and the mission to be prepared to provide yourself initial aid until someone can safely get to you. Do *not* ask someone else to put themselves in harm's way." It made perfect sense. I had to expect to operate alone if I got wounded.

Even so, I mentally rehearsed several scenarios where I provided rescue or aid to one of my soldiers. I practiced unrolling the bandages quickly, making the long ties needed for a pressure bandage, thinking through the different ways to create cover so that I could administer aid to my wounded soldiers.

Those mental drills brought me back to the task at hand: the best way to practice helping other people was practicing on myself. I examined the morphine syrettes and picked the place on my thigh I'd insert it. What if I lost a limb? I mentally rehearsed losing a hand, a foot, an arm, a leg—imagining the blood, envisioning the fear, reminding myself I would need to focus on breathing evenly.

The sun set without me noticing. I moved closer under the light of the lamp next to the couch. Once I was done practicing, I'd eat something.

I did the IVs last. I took a deep breath and clenched and unclenched my left fist. A large purple vein swelled under my skin. In training, we'd practiced starting IVs on each other, but I'd never done one on myself before. I needed the muscle memory though. It was hard enough to do my own IV sitting on my couch in my apartment. It would be a hell of a lot harder if I was under fire.

Sweat rolled down my forehead and I impatiently wiped it with the back of my sleeve. *Come on...* I picked a spot to insert the needle into my skin. *There.* Quickly, I attached the tubing. I studied my work, proudly. I'd done it! That excited me. I moved on to my right arm, working awkwardly with my left hand, but finally successfully getting the second IV.

Satisfied, I decided my work was complete. I began gathering up the trash and glanced at the clock. It was nearly ten. No wonder I was so hungry. But I felt pleased—I was now familiar with all the materials and prepared to administer my own aid, whatever scenario might unfold in battle.

I moved from the living room into the kitchen. Opened the fridge. Assumed I had covered all my bases.

The one scenario I never prepared for was the one in which I got burned alive.

* * *

KANDAHAR DESERT, AFGHANISTAN. SEPTEMBER 4, 2008. DUSK.

This is the last picture taken of me before the accident, from the morning's visit to the local village. The interpreter I worked with is on the right; he had been left back at the FOB. September 4, 2008.

How does one describe an inferno?

Everything went silent. The clattering of ammo cans and banging of equipment vanished. The engine's roar went mute. My own voice disappeared.

Sound was swallowed up.

Searingly bright flames engulfed what had been the dark cavity of the Humvee's interior. There was no horizon. There was no village. There were no other humans close beside me. There was only blinding, devouring fire.

I had the strange sensation of sinking down into my seat, like I was strapped into a roller coaster racing up an incline. I didn't realize that the Humvee had been hurled upward by the blast.

We've hit an IED—

A dim, horrific realization.

All of it in a millisecond, but time had slowed down—enough that I could register the strange horror of deafness, blindness, the sinking, the fire.

I was strapped in, with my seatbelt on. Trapped. Yet even as I tried to absorb the sensations of dying within the confines of my power—I was released. I felt the force of the vehicle being blown into the air, but I never felt it land.

Somehow, I was standing.

I was outside the vehicle. I was on my feet.

There wasn't time to register the strangeness of this, the miraculous improbability, because I was on fire.

The blinding orange flames had followed me. I was out of the engulfing inner space of the vehicle on fire, but now *I* was the tinder. The bright, orange light was inescapable—my face was burning.

There were horrible sensations—*searing heat—my flesh—the smell of it—agony—*

Almost worse than the pain of burning flesh was the sense of isolation. Everyone else in the vehicle must be dead. *How could they survive?* Any others were surely engaged in the fight. We had driven into the middle of gunfire and mortar blasts—I couldn't see how it might be developing—it might be escalating—even if someone else could see me, how could they get to me?

Panicked realizations hit: *I am burning—I am alone—I am dying—*

Instantaneously and for the first time in my life, I realized with utter certainty that I had encountered a situation where I had no control over the outcome. The severity of my circumstances was overwhelming. This man-made inferno was about to kill me and I couldn't do anything to stop it.

I had zero expectation that anyone, especially myself, could save me. The only hope I could appeal to was my Creator.

Surrender.

I threw my arms in the air and screamed out, "Jesus, save me!"

I dropped to the ground and began rolling, trying to extinguish the flames. But the powdery moon dust of the Kandahar desert couldn't compete with the fire's greedy consumption of my body. I smelled diesel and fertilizer chemicals. Realizations crashed against each other: *I was sitting directly in front of the fuel tank. The fuel tanks were full of diesel for the drive back to KAF. The homemade explosives of the bomb blew upward. I'm covered in diesel fuel and the residue of homemade explosives.*

All of it, burning. All of me, on fire.

Something pierced through my deafness—a primal, guttural scream. I realized with horror it had come out of me.

I got up again and ran, giving into a primal urge to flee the danger. It only made the flames more intense.

Desperate to see anything or to wrestle some relief, I ripped off my helmet. But that only fed the flames. They rose higher. Licking my eyebrows, too intense for my eyes—I had to close them. *Darkness again—*

I threw myself back down in the dirt, face first. The scream came again and it was terrifying. I was familiar with the sound of my own voice, but I'd never heard my voice in the midst of a traumatic death. It shrieked and wailed—repeated cries for help from God—repeated cries for my mother—

The voice was like something from the underworld. It shocked me to realize it was the sound of someone who believed he was about to die.

The pain was excruciating.

Pain so bad, it crushed my soul—

Pain so bad, I hoped death would come in seconds, not minutes—

Pain so bad, I wanted to die to escape it rather than survive and endure it—

Flames, yes, but the deeper gulf was fear: strength incinerating, abject vulnerability, total helplessness. It culminated in a complete loss of hope. Who could help me? Where was a defender, a protector, a healer? There was no one else.

I tasted ash and dust.

Was I already dead? Was this hell? It was total despair—cut off from every good thing—*there's no hope—I'm utterly alone—*

Memories raced, running out of time. Life had always been lived in the company of others. My earliest memories were with Daniel. High school meant sports teams. West Point was a shell of eight. Always partners, always brothers, always pushing each other to be our best, demanding excellence from one another. You couldn't take someone out of the boat. You couldn't take someone out of the family. And here, in Afghanistan—adversity was forged as a unit. We wrote each other's history. We knew our roles, knew each other's strengths and weaknesses—that's what gave us such offensive comradery—

But not now

No one is here

How long had I been on fire? Was it seconds or a lifetime?

The moment of death encroached like an enemy, and I lost the will to fight it anymore. Its defeat was inevitable. All I wanted now was for it to come quickly. *Let the pain and fear finish. Let it end.*

Face down. Eyes closed. I had been scooping the dirt over me as best I could, but as I waited for the end, I quieted down. It was impossible to catch my breath—with every inhale, I breathed in flames.

Three final thoughts suddenly emerged with crystalline clarity:

The first: *How long will it take to burn to death?*

I hadn't accepted that I was going to die—"accept" is too passive a word. I was searching for it, desiring it, *desperate* for it. Death couldn't possibly come quickly enough. Death was the only hope I had. In the absence of any influence or control over my own life, I was no longer an actor in my own story. I was a passenger with a one-way ticket to death, and all I wanted was for that train to plunge off the cliff and end the agony.

As quickly as the first thought articulated itself, the second tumbled on top of it:

What is the transition from this life to the next going to be like?

A terrifying realization hooked itself on the second thought: *I don't know where I'm going.*

I had grown up going to church, memorizing scripture, singing hymns. But in the crucible of those flames, a life's worth of pretense had burned away. Deep down, I was not convinced that I had done what I needed to do to have eternal life. I could not hope for heaven as an outcome.

"Get right with God"—I'd heard the phrase applied to deathbed moments, or foxhole fears in the midst of battle fire. It was a cliché. But now, it was my cross.

On the threshold between life and death, I knew in my heart and soul that I had fallen short. Jesus had never been the Lord of my life. *I* had been the lord of my life. Yet in my own self-idolatry, none of my accomplishments could render me atonement for my sins.

Every Sunday in church, every verse logged to memory, all the chapters I'd read in the Bible, every person I'd ever shared the gospel with—none of that mattered. They were diesel-soaked rags, already incinerated. The ultimate question was: *Is* Jesus Christ the Lord of my life?

No.

He'd never been.

The cry ruptured out of me again, though this time it was inaudible: *Jesus, save me.*

But I didn't expect that He would. I had lived my life. I had made my decisions. I had no right to ask for a literal last-second pardon.

The third thought followed this grim conclusion, and it was less of a thought and more of a decision:

I give up my will to live.

I had no idea what the Lord would do with me. But whatever God decided to do with me—either with the ashes of my current life or in the next life—was justified. I deserved whatever He had in store.

Never before had I been so aware of the truth of who and what I was. I was not invincible. I was no hero. I was completely crushed and humbled before my Maker, for the first time possessing a proper understanding of who I was, relative to Him. Every priority, every accolade I'd ever set my eyes on, all my toil, all the noble missions— none of it had earned me anything but pride. And the outcome of that was separation from God for eternity. It was me ignoring Jesus' invitation to be Lord of my life. It was me playing God.

But I couldn't save myself.

I was resigned. I had no ability or willpower to resist any longer.

Death was the only next thing.

PART 2

SURVIVAL

CHAPTER 4

ALIVE DAY

The wreckage of my Humvee after the IED exploded.

Certain death was arrested by four words.

"Sir, I've got you!"

Within an inferno of isolation and overwhelming despair, I suddenly heard Kevin Jensen's voice.

He was screaming. I would learn later that he, too, was on fire. But that didn't stop him from extinguishing the lie that I was alone, nor the flames that were eating me alive.

I had been utterly convinced I was already dead. Already ash. The encompassing darkness had buried me.

But then Kevin's voice cracked open the lid of my coffin. As his words broke through, death retreated.

"Sir, I've got you!"

I heard the thumping of boots hitting the ground as others converged on me. Each miraculous thump hit against despair and new realizations flooded in: *I'm not alone. Someone else is alive. Help is here.*

I felt dirt and dust being thrown over the top of my body. Other voices joined Kevin's—I heard Anthony. They were burying me, scooping dirt on top of me, smothering the flames. The crushing fear that was rooted in isolation gave way to hope. "Hang in there, Sir!" I heard someone yell. My soldiers, my brothers were actively fighting to save my life.

Only seconds prior, I had accepted death as a fact. The certainty of it went beyond knowing; I was *waiting* for it. The question hadn't been "if" but "when," and death promised to bring relief—it would be my escape from the pain.

But as Kevin's words shattered my sense of isolation and despair, they also shattered my certainty of dying. My position completely changed. I didn't want to die. In fact, I knew I *wasn't* going to die. Even if I had continued wanting to die—I wasn't about to.

I was going to live. I was certain I was supposed to live. And I knew I was meant to live for a reason.

With the same clarity that shaped my final three thoughts—or, what I assumed would be my final thoughts—a new conclusion formed. *My life has been spared for a purpose.* I didn't know what that purpose might be, or why, or what God might have in mind. All I knew was that this was a day that would be defined by living, not dying, and that life on the other side would look forever different than how it had before.

But that didn't mean surviving was about to be easy.

Under the thick layer of dirt, I became vaguely aware of the sounds around me. Roszko's voice was shouting directions amidst a rattle of gunshots. "Skotnicki! I want you working on the LT! Who's here, who's here? Kevin, Philip, Mike, LT—"

"Winston's still in the truck!" someone called out. Mike's voice.

"Cheney, come with me, we're going back for Winston—Skotnicki, you watch the rest of them—" Anthony's voice disappeared and Justin Skotnicki, one of my EMT-trained infantrymen, took top volume. His voice was a jumble of interrogations—questions to me, which I couldn't answer; questions to Kevin, Philip, and Mike, all of whom, I began to realize, had sustained burns of their own. He shouted instructions to the others; there were shouts of dismay; and over all of it, a cacophony of gunfire.

My eyes were still closed under the layer of dirt that had been my saving grace. But through my coated lids, I suddenly saw a flash and heard a boom. *Another explosion.*

"We've got to take cover!"

"Get him up," I heard Skotnicki order. Someone grabbed my hand and started pulling me to my feet. "LT, I need you to get up, if you can. He's shaking—help him, he's shaking. Clear his eyes—!"

"I'm still burning!" I said thickly. The heat of flames pressed hard against my back.

"You're not burning, Sir! We've got to take cover!"

How was it possible I wasn't still on fire? My back felt hammered by excruciating heat. Then I realized what must be happening—*my body armor. My kit—all of it was cooking along with me—*

"Get this fucking kit off me!" I pulled at the straps but my hands were useless. The soldiers around me yanked off the melted kit and let it fall to the dirt. They hoisted my body armor over my head and chucked that aside too.

I stood there, swaying on my feet—no helmet, no kit, no body armor, no weapon, no ammo, no radio. Everything I had relied on for safety, protection, and communication had either been incinerated or thrown away. I was a soft target, totally exposed in the middle of an ambush.

"We've got to *fucking take cover*! Run, Sir!" Mortar shells exploded nearby. Machine gun fire rattled on every side of us.

"This way!" One of the guys pulled me into a hunching run and directed me toward the vague shape of a mud wall nearby, on the outer side of a small compound. As soon as we reached it, we collapsed down against the berm. My consciousness was suddenly horrifically absorbed by everything causing me pain. Being alive *hurt*.

As I'd tried to run, each movement had caused friction with the environment around me. Even the air on my raw nerves was anguishing. Every contracted muscle created new signals everywhere, flooding my brain with the recognition that something was hurt, something wasn't right, something was very, very wrong. The flames that had burned me were gone, but it still felt like my body was on fire.

Sitting against that mud berm, I winced as the different parts of my body each demanded attention. My legs were bad. Although my boots had protected my lower legs, everything above them had been burned. But the pain in my legs was nothing compared to the throbbing pain in my arms, and more intense still was the agony concentrated in my face and hands.

My hands. The pain centers in my brain decided my hands deserved the bulk of their attention, and sent waves of torment through my nervous system, crashing into my wrists, fingertips, and the backs of my hands. I stared down at my gloves. They looked half melted. Through the fog of the pain, it occurred to me that I had been trying to beat the flames out with my hands—that's what I'd used to scoop dirt on myself, and take off my flaming helmet. The charred leather of the gloves was coated with dirt and sand. I wanted them off.

I tried to take off my left glove and immediately realized that was impossible. I had lost all dexterity and strength. More concerning still, the gloves appeared to have fused with my skin.

I called Skotnicki over next to me and once again tried to speak. "Take my gloves off." My tongue felt like cardboard.

Skotnicki reached down to comply but then hesitated. "They look melted on," he said.

"Pull it off," I repeated.

"I don't know if that's—"

"Get them off!"

He grabbed one firmly and tugged. The gloves were tight to begin with and made of thick material—leather and fire-resistant Nomex. The left one didn't move.

"LT, I think I'm going to pull skin off if I—"

I nodded my head violently to urge him to *do it*. He pulled again, hard, and the glove started peeling off. "Pull harder," I said thickly. He yanked. The glove came off.

My flesh peeled off with it.

Underneath, what was left of my hand looked like raw meat. It was shiny and oozing. Amidst the blood and shreds of melted fabric that still clung to the tissue, I could see exposed muscle and the thick strands of my tendons. He stared down in horror. I looked away.

"Do the other one," I commanded, but he shook his head violently. I thrust my right hand toward Hayes, another young private. "Pull my glove off." He stared at me in disbelief and began to protest. "Pull it off, Hayes!" I repeated and put the glove in front of him.

He gave the second one a hard pull, seeing how hard it had been to rip the first one off. The right glove came off halfway. He looked at me, his eyes pleading. "Are you sure, Sir?" His plea may have been more for his own behalf than mine—who knows what sort of nightmares followed him after this moment. But I was desperate. And I was incapable of helping myself.

"Yes! Take it off!" I yelled.

He finished ripping off the second one. Once again, my outer layer of flesh peeled off along with the glove.

I had hoped for some relief, but there was none. My raw nerves, now exposed to the air, radiated pain with even more intensity. I squeezed my eyes shut, but that only sharpened my awareness of my body's pain. My forearms ached with a deep throbbing as though they'd been crushed—like someone had pulverized them with a hammer. The pain in my hands and face was sharper and more piercing. I opened my eyes again and tried to focus on something else—anything else.

Anthony had rejoined us and was barking communication into the radio, then shouting instructions to all of us. His presence was a relief. I'd always known that, if anything had happened to me, my squad leaders would be able to assume command, and Anthony was proving me right. At the same time, I again registered the fact that I now had no radio, no weapon, no pack.

No command.

No authority.

As I waited for instructions from Anthony, my attention was caught by the flaming wreck in the distance, which illuminated our surroundings. With a shock, I realized it was my own vehicle. The top had split apart like an opened aluminum can and several of the doors had blown off. Suddenly, I remembered something—Mike's words. *Winston's still in the truck.*

"Roszko—where's Winston?" I asked.

He ignored me. I could hear him communicating via the radio with Austin. We'd been on our way to help First Platoon. From the sound of it, First Platoon was now sending help to us.

I stared helplessly at the flaming vehicle. "We need to go get Winston!" I said. No one responded. Who could help me get him? Kevin, Philip, and Mike all crouched near me, looking dazed.

Over the booms of mortar rounds and gunfire, Anthony yelled for some of the soldiers to go into the mud compound behind us and clear it. Several of the soldiers beside me peeled off and ran, following his instructions. I stared at my Humvee. It was completely engulfed in fire. I could feel the heat emanating from it, even though it was thirty or forty yards away.

"Roszko, *where's Winston?*" I repeated.

He turned toward me, his face crestfallen. "Sir—" He began to speak and then stopped. When he spoke again, he struggled to get the words out. "Sir, he didn't get out of the vehicle."

"We need to go *get* him—"

"I already tried!" Anthony said huskily. "Cheney and I already tried. The ammo started going off." As if on cue, an enormous blast suddenly shook the vehicle, the flash momentarily blinding us. A detonated grenade. "There's a couple hundred of those in the ammo crates on the back," Anthony reminded me. "The heat of the fire is setting them all off."

I stared in horror. *Winston's still in the truck.* "There's nothing we can do," Anthony said. "It's suicide to try to get him out, and I'm not about to lose anyone else." His voice faltered.

Anyone else. I didn't want to register the meaning of what he'd just said.

Lose anyone else.

We'd lost Winston.

Another blast went off, leaving a crater around the vehicle; each grenade had a kill radius of five meters. Winston couldn't possibly be alive, and there was nothing anyone could do to change the situation. But the futility of trying didn't change the overwhelming sense of failure I felt.

I had lost one of my troops. Vincent Winston—the heart of our unit, everyone's little brother—was dead.

Anthony began calling into the radio again with renewed force. "Mud compound is clear!" he yelled. "Let's go!"

The few of us still sitting against the berm struggled up and ran, following Anthony into the compound. I tried to register which direction the gunfire was coming from. We'd been taking fire from the east initially, but now, as we moved around the south side into the compound, I could hear gunfire from behind us. Were we approaching exposure to a new direction of attack? I shook my head. It was hard to think. I focused on keeping up with the soldiers in front of me.

At the last corner on the west side, we found the compound's entrance and ducked inside. Immediately, behind the thick mud walls, the volume of the gunfire fell. Anthony motioned us into a smaller enclosure, and we dropped down. Inside these walls, I felt secure for the first time since the explosion.

But that created a new challenge. As adrenaline ebbed away, pain once again demanded all my attention. My hands still clamored in agony. A close second in discomfort now was my thirst.

I had never been so thirsty in my life. I learned later that, physiologically, the flames hadn't just charred my skin—they had literally burned up most of the moisture in my body. I had been thirsty plenty of times before, after a good workout or after being out in the sun. But this was thirst on another scale, at a *cellular* level. My body was so depleted of fluid that every cell screamed for water.

On top of that, the powdery moon dust of the Afghan desert covered me. When I'd been on fire, I was screaming face-first in the dirt, scooping that dust all over myself, inhaling it, trying to smother the flames. As a result, the dirt now covered my face and coated my mouth. The rattling noise from the machine gun fire, the threats we still faced, the excruciating pain I felt in the rest of my body, even Skotnicki's physical manipulation of my body as he examined my wounds—all of it seemed to shrink into the background. I became consumed with one myopic obsession: *I need a drink of water.*

"Hey," I spoke hoarsely to the soldier next to me. "Can you put the straw of my CamelBak into my mouth? I can't use my hands." He lifted the hose of my CamelBak water bladder to my charred lips, and I tried to suck through the dust-covered mouthpiece. But there was no relief. No water seemed to be making it through the hose. Frustrated, I muttered, "Something is broken or blocking the hose."

The soldier pulled the hose close to him in the dark. "The plastic's all burned! The whole thing is burned, all the way through to the water bladder. It's empty."

That's when I started to feel not just the pain of the burn, but the *life energy suck* of the wounds. My body was slowly shutting down.

My soldier hurriedly pulled out his own CamelBak straw and held it up, but Skotnicki called out, "NO! Don't give him water right now!"

"Do NOT give the LT water!" Anthony repeated. His attention, which had been diverted by the firefight, suddenly turned on me. "He needs an IV. Get him prepped to transfer." Just as quickly, he faced back out toward the window and fired off his gun.

"In EMT training, they taught us—" Skotnicki's eyes were wide with regret. "Burn victims can't drink water—"

"I'm *thirsty*," I said, nearing desperation. I was going to die if I didn't drink something.

My young soldier put his CamelBak straw in my mouth. "He can have a sip, at least!" he insisted to Skotnicki. I sucked. A small amount of water leaked into my mouth. He quickly pulled the straw away.

That single sip was so far short of what my body needed. It did nothing to alleviate the anguish my body was in—not even to cool or clean my mouth. All it did was turn some of the dust I'd inhaled into a little muddy trickle down my throat. My craving for water intensified. The world contracted even more.

Clearly, there was intense activity happening all around me, but I struggled to process any of it. Later, I learned that Philip was lying beside me and had gone into shock. Kevin, like me, was pleading for water. Another soldier was bouncing back and forth between the two of them, trying to help, while Skotnicki was working on me. Mike was in a rage, trying to take weapons from the other soldiers to go out and fight, even though his face and arms were burned. Anthony was yelling at him—"Sit down! I don't want to worry about you getting hurt more! You need to *calm down* and stay here. Let us do the fighting!" Meanwhile, soldiers were firing off their guns. Gunshots were firing at us. Anthony was yelling into the radio again. "He is in the room—he's barely speaking. He's covered with burns from head to toe. He's only asked for two things: he asked for water, and he asked about Winston... Listen, *I need to get him out of here*, I need someone to come get him!" He began cursing. He didn't like the response he'd heard.

These were the sorts of things that, only an hour earlier, I would have felt deeply interested in. But paying attention to them would have meant keeping my senses on high alert, and the pain was too intense to allow any sensory information to penetrate. I shut my eyes. Maybe I could hide from the pain in a place deep inside myself. I imagined emptiness—something void, something dark.

Everything except the pain receded as though I was in a fog. The rattle of gunfire, Anthony's hoarse calls on the radio, the scrambling activity of the other men—all of that faded into the background as I tried to hide from the physical agony. My senses were consumed entirely by the pain. It defined reality. It overwhelmed everything else.

Finally, a familiar rumble brought me back to the present. I felt the ground vibrate and opened my eyes. "Wait for the signal," Anthony commanded. I tried to peer out from behind the mud wall. The dim light from the fire, which still burned around my vehicle, just barely illuminated two Humvees pulling up. A third Humvee followed them, parking itself horizontally behind the other two as a shield. They were American vehicles—from First Platoon, by the look of it—the very platoon my troop had intended to aid. Their lights were off so as not to draw fire.

Skotnicki pulled me into a crouch. My body tensed, preparing to run. A new wave of adrenaline coursed through my system, and the increase in awareness once again amplified my brain's recognition of pain. My sensory nerves were burnt to full exposure across my arms, face, neck, and upper legs. I had managed to run into this mud compound, unassisted. Now, I didn't even know if I could stand.

Anthony gave the signal. "LT, I want you in the third Humvee with First Platoon's medic. Now everyone, go! Go! Go!" The guys around me exploded to their feet and darted to the Humvees, firing their machine guns in the direction of enemy fire. The guns on top of the Humvees joined in, rattling with the increased rapid rate of fire to try to provide cover for us.

I got up out of my crouched position, feeling my entire body violently protest. As painful as it had been to hold still, it was infinitely worse to move. I had once been the fastest runner in our platoon but now, doubled over in pain, my movements were horribly slow.

The guys ahead of me jumped into their Humvees and slammed the doors, with Anthony leading them in the first vehicle. The first one took off in a cloud of dust, followed quickly by the second.

I forced myself to traverse the open space toward the Humvee. Each step required me to stretch and contract my muscles beneath the raw, burned skin that only delicately covered most of my body. It was impossible not to register the fact that I was starting to succumb to the severity of the burns.

My stumbling finally brought me to the Humvee, and someone wrenched open the back door. I clumsily slid into the back passenger side seat, registering a young private at the wheel and a medic in the front passenger seat.

I leaned back, too pained to try to sit up straight. Somehow, I sensed I was coming to the end of whatever I had left. It was like seeing a "low battery" signal on my phone—I had just a little juice left, but didn't know how much longer I could hold out until the screen went black. As shock began to set in, the ability to do anything beyond just breathing was escaping me. I felt an ominous feeling. I'd been so confident I was going to live—I was *still* confident I was going to live—but I was running out of energy and time to be able to do anything for myself.

Up above me, I could see the vehicle's gunner. He was firing the huge M2 .50 caliber machine gun, still at a relentless rapid rate of fire. Despite the noise thundering over me, time suddenly seemed to slow down. Almost in slow motion, I could see the large, brass shell casings rain down through the turret hole onto the metal floor area next to me, could hear their metallic jingle as they hit each other, the clank as they hit the floor. For the first time since the explosion, I felt some relief. I felt protected by superior firepower.

The door slammed shut. I could feel the Humvee lurch forward. "Hang on tight, Lieutenant," the driver called back. "We're not taking our chances on any more IEDs in the road, so we're going through the poppy fields."

The poppy fields in Afghanistan consist of a large grid of mounds in roughly ten-meter squares, about eight inches high, with irrigation ditches that hold water when the fields are flooded. In other words, we were driving over a series of floral speed bumps.

It was agony, bumping along like that—but it was a *steady* state of agony. The pain was less piercing than it had been earlier. And it wasn't anywhere near the horror of fear and isolation I'd been consumed with when I was still on fire. I knew I was going to safety. We were headed to the Helicopter Landing Zone, the "HLZ." Soon, I'd be MEDEVACed—I had a destination to look forward to. That made the pain—even as the Humvee rocked up and down—somehow easier to bear.

Suddenly, the truck stopped. No one spoke to me. Up front, the driver and medic exchanged a few quiet comments to each other.

It was terrible to feel the vehicle stopped, to feel the idle of the motor. *Why aren't we moving?* I wondered. I didn't have much longer before I was deadweight to the people around me.

Painfully, I pulled myself up and tried to look out the windshield. The dust kicked up by the vehicle curled in a cloud around us. I called up to the gunner above me. "What's going on? Why'd we stop?"

The young private driving the Humvee turned around and looked back at me. He hesitated. "Sir, I don't—I lost sight of the vehicles in front of me."

"You don't need to see them," I said. "Just go to the HLZ."

The driver must have known we didn't have time for anything but the painful truth of our situation. I could hear his fear as he spoke again. "I don't know where I'm going! I was just following the other guys."

I tried to force my brain to focus. At any moment, the enemy could spot our vehicle and converge their fire on us, and I was minutes away from being no help to anyone. We had to figure this out fast.

Sensing that the driver's panic would soon become its own threat to our survival, I turned my attention to the gunner. "Can you see any better? Do you see any signs of the vehicles ahead of us?"

"No, I can't see either!" he called down.

I couldn't clearly hear the exchange of machine gun fire anymore—that meant we were far enough away from the engagement area that we weren't under fire. But now, we were in no man's land. I peered through the windshield into the dark. The other vehicles had completely disappeared. The driver and medic looked back at me nervously.

"Do you know where to go, Sir?"

I tried to pull my thoughts together. Somehow, I had to summon enough focus and strength to help direct our next move. Our survival hung in the balance: *we* didn't know where we were, but there was a good chance the Taliban did. Even if they didn't find us, I knew my life span was hanging by tenterhooks; each passing minute was a more tenuous hold.

Less than an hour ago, I'd completely surrendered my will to live. Now, that will to live was in full force. *We are not going to die here.* I forced myself to fully sit up and block out the pain.

I said, "Look—get on the radio and find out where the HLZ is. Get the eight-digit grid."

The medic picked up the radio and called back to the First Sergeant, asking for the location. The First Sergeant rapidly read off eight digits. "Good," I spoke to the medic. "Plot the digits into the navigation grid and you'll see our position. Then you can get us there."

"I don't know how to operate it," the medic said, panicking. I wanted to fire back, *Yes, you DO.* Surely he had been trained on this system. But then I registered his breathing—he was taking short, shallow, fast breaths. Was it possible his panic was putting *him* into a state of sympathetic shock? I tried to force my brain beyond my own pain for a moment and recall what I knew about the young man in front of me. This was his first deployment. Most likely, my burns were his first serious casualty. Who knew what kind of anxiety my own charred presence was stirring up in him? In this moment, his memory was failing.

From the back seat, I was the only other person in the vehicle who could see the navigation screen. *Pull yourself together, Sam,* I thought. *These guys need you more than you need them.*

The First Sergeant on the radio had read off the eight-digit grid location rapidly, but—bizarrely, miraculously—I realized I could recall the numbers with total clarity. They seemed seared into my brain. Normally, I would have to write something like that down, but I *knew* what they were. Maybe they stuck in my head because the stakes were so high. Our lives literally depended on us getting to that HLZ, fast.

I pulled myself forward and leaned over the back of the seat in front of me. I studied the map grid on the touch screen. "Look," I said. "We're right here—" I pointed to the screen. "The HLZ is right here," I said, and touched the screen. "That means we've got to go due south for about 1,800 meters, maybe 1,900. So, just go south a couple kilometers. You'll get there."

I collapsed back against the seat. *This is not my day to die,* I reminded myself. I thought back to the certainty I'd felt, just after Kevin Jensen had finished extinguishing the flames. I knew then I was going to live—that my life had been spared for a purpose.

But what would be left?

A sinking realization dawned on me: survival did not necessarily mean I would get to return to my old body, my old capabilities, my old authority and strength. It was impossible to inventory all the ways my body was shutting down. The thirst alone was about to undo me. Would it be a life I returned to, or a half life? Would it be anything like it was before?

What would remain of *me*, when all was said and done? What would be left of the life I'd known?

I glanced at the medic to ensure he'd understood what I'd said. He was staring in horror at the grid. Where I'd touched it, there was a thick smear.

I had left my charred flesh on the screen.

CHAPTER 5

BLIND AND BROKEN

My platoon in C-Co, 2nd Infantry Regiment, 3rd Brigade Combat Team of the 1st Infantry Division. I'm standing at the far right, and Steven Smith is just to the left of me in the middle row. Standing next to him is Kevin Jensen, my gunner. The head just to the left of Jensen's shoulder is Philip Kopfensteiner. Vincent Winston is kneeling in front on the far right. Anthony Roszko is standing, second from the left. Mike Debolt is in the back row, fifth from the right.

"Aw, man, I knew we should have left earlier." Austin shaded his eyes as he looked at the long line snaking into the KAF chow hall. We'd walked over together from the containerized housing unit we shared with another platoon leader. "I'm so hungry."

We took our place in line, tucking ourselves into the thin stripe of shade cast by the semipermanent structure. The midday desert sun beat down. "Hey, are you guys missing anything from your trucks?" I asked. Both of our platoons were preparing to head out from KAF in the next few days. "We've got a busted radio that's going to have to be repaired before we leave."

He nodded and we began trading notes about prepping for the journey out. Slowly, the line moved forward. As we reached the hand-washing station, a cool breeze wafted out from the entrance. Once we crossed the threshold into the shaded, air-conditioned interior, we let out a collective "*Aahh.*" I took off my hat.

Austin grinned. "Smells like spaghetti."

The mess hall was noisy with the voices of service members from all over the world: Brits, Canadians, contractors from Sri Lanka, Afghan interpreters, plus the mixture of accents of soldiers from the US. Long tables stretched from one end of the large cafeteria to the other. Allied soldiers and workers, wearing a variety of uniforms, were all digging in.

"Hold up—isn't that Bauer? From West Point?" Austin said. He pointed to a young woman dressed in Aviation fatigues.

I squinted, trying to catch a glimpse of her face. "It looks like her. It's 'Emmy,' right?" Austin nodded. "Hey—" I waved. "Emmy Bauer! Emmy!"

We pushed our way through the crowded tables. Emmy heard our voices and glanced up from where she was filling her tray. Her face broke into a wide grin. "*What?* Some familiar faces! Austin Wallace and Sam Brown! So good to see you guys!" She reached up and gave us both hugs. "Come sit by me once you have your food."

"Yeah, we've got to catch up! Are you a pilot now?"

She nodded as she moved toward the tables with her tray. "Hurry up! I'll fill you in!"

It had been over two years since we'd all been together at West Point's graduation. "Didn't Emmy join the Medical Services Corps?" Austin asked as we moved through the buffet. "Kinda badass that she's a pilot now."

"Maybe she's doing MEDEVACs," I mused. We pushed our trays along and headed over to Emmy's table.

"Emmy Bauer," Austin said, delighted. "Catch us up on what's been happening since West Point."

Emmy had just recently arrived in Kandahar and confirmed that she was serving as a MEDEVAC pilot. While we dug into our spaghetti, she told us about several harrowing evacuations that she'd participated in.

"No way," I said, impressed. "You know, I almost joined Aviation. Hearing you talk makes me wonder if I made the right choice."

"What made you do Infantry instead?" she asked.

I shrugged. "It was a close call. But I figured I could have the greatest impact as an Infantry Officer."

She smirked. "You Infantry Officers seem to think us MEDEVAC pilots make a pretty significant impact when we're rescuing your wounded asses out of the battlefield."

I laughed. "Touché. But also—I didn't want to get soft, joining Aviation," I ribbed back. "You pilots get the cushy life. Always around hot chow, and real beds, and showers. Mandatory rest periods."

"You say it like it's a *bad* thing," Austin retorted at me, his mouth full of spaghetti. "Now you're making me wish *I'd* gone Aviation."

Emmy laughed again. "Yeah, I'm not going to apologize for getting eight hours of sleep every night. You Infantry guys can sleep in the dirt and eat your MREs and feel plenty tough. Then, when one of your soldiers gets his leg blown off, you're going to decide *I'm* the most heroic person in the Armed Forces when I carry him to safety. And trust me, you'll be glad I'm flying on a full night's sleep."

"You know, there's a good chance we might be seeing you in the next couple months," I said ruefully. "Although I hope not."

"Our Battalion is standing up that new FOB Ramrod on the far West side of Kandahar," Austin explained. "So we'll be going out to the Maiwand district. We'll be right in the area where Kandahar and Helmand meet."

"That's a pretty hot spot, isn't it?" Emmy asked.

I nodded. "The intel on that area is that there's a lot of potential enemy activity. Guess that makes sense, given that it's the birthplace of the Taliban." I grinned, readying an attempt at humor. "So, you know…if you get a call for a MEDEVAC flight out there in the next couple of weeks, there's a good chance you're coming to pick me up."

She rolled her eyes at my joke. "Doubtful. I don't get called for Lieutenants. I get called for their soldiers: Infantrymen, at the tip of the spear. But I hope, for both your sakes and for the sake of your soldiers, I don't get called out there at all." She smirked again. "But if I pick up a soldier who's too tall to fit across the fuselage, then I'll know it's you, Sam."

"Ha!" I laughed at the thought. "Well—if you can't get the door shut, don't get pissed at me when a bunch of dust blows into the cockpit from the rotor wash. I know how you pilots hate to get dirty."

Her expression darkened. "I don't care about dust when I'm doing a MEDEVAC. I care about getting soldiers out alive."

KANDAHAR DESERT, AFGHANISTAN. SEPTEMBER 4, 2008. NIGHT.

"There it is." The relief in the driver's voice was palpable. I felt the Humvee accelerate.

"Almost there, Sir," the medic said. "I can see the secure perimeter. Sergeant Roszko's waving us in."

By now, whatever sustaining power I'd experienced from the adrenaline had exhausted itself. It was hard to even hold myself up. I reminded myself I wasn't about to die—if it had been my day to die, I would already be dead. But with every passing second, there was less battery power. My body was rapidly shutting down.

We braked quickly and someone wrenched the door open. Steven and Anthony, my two right hands, began pulling me out. The company medic was with them, calling out instructions. Steven was staring at my arms, then glanced at my face. "Shit," Steven said under his breath. "Shit. *Shit, shit.*"

"Stop trying to do it yourself," Anthony ordered me. "You need to let us help you right now."

A few other guys ran up—soldiers I recognized from the route clearance unit. "I need a stretcher!" the company medic barked at them. One of them ran over to a vehicle standing by and pulled a stretcher off the roof line.

"Where's Winston?" I heard Steven ask Anthony.

"Everyone's over here," Anthony said. Then he spoke to the First Platoon medic climbing out of the vehicle behind me. "I want you working on Kevin, Philip, and Mike with Doc Brun! Sergeant Medina is going to work on Lieutenant Brown."

Two soldiers ran over with a stretcher. Steven and Anthony began lowering me down, and I didn't fight them. I was incapable of doing anything other than following their lead. *My bed,* I thought wryly. *Putting me to bed.*

"Where's Winston?" Steven asked Anthony again.

Hearing Steven's question broke my heart. Winston was in Steven's squad—he was one of his guys. At the mention of his name, an image suddenly blistered my mind: the Humvee on fire, the grenades exploding in the heat. Winston's body still buckled in his seat.

Then I remembered Steven's words that he'd spoken to me months ago: "All I care about is getting everyone home."

It was a gut-wrenching thought.

The conversation had happened at Fort Hood, just a couple months before we deployed. I was in charge of leading some training exercises out at one of the ranges. Ahead of the training, I planned to spend a day going out and evaluating the terrain of the range, recording grid coordinates for planning purposes, and figuring out where to put the different elements. I wanted to take someone else along as a second set of eyes, someone who had the insight to consider variables I might miss, someone to help take notes.

That was my excuse, anyway.

Really, I just wanted to have a reason to get to know Staff Sergeant Steven Smith better.

Steven and Anthony had both quickly established themselves in my mind as highly impressive individuals, guys who were worthy of my respect. Rather than try to throw my weight around as their platoon leader, I learned to lean on their wisdom. They were both more experienced on the battlefield than I was, with previous deployments under their belts. They often raised questions in our strategy discussions around points I'd never considered—a habit of questioning I learned to embrace, rather than get defensive about.

Plus, Steven was just a *good* guy. When I'd arrived at Fort Hood, I'd made up my mind to be the last person to leave the training area. There was always more work for me to do—and I figured it was important for my soldiers to see their leader demonstrating the same kind of work ethic I was asking from them. That was my resolution: to be the last guy gone.

I couldn't do it. Steven always stuck around longer. I'd finish up the last of my work and start to head out, but when I walked by the squad leader area, Steven Smith would be in there—still working.

"Sergeant Smith," I called to him, the first time it happened. "You've got to get out of here, man. There's nothing so urgent to get done that you need to stay any longer."

He sat there and argued with me, justifying his tireless work. "No, LT—I've got to do this. I've got to do that."

I finally learned that it was pointless to argue with him, and I gave up my goal of being the last to leave. The last guy gone was *always* going to be Steven Smith. His work flowed out of the fact that he genuinely loved his guys, like they were his own family. He was intent on being the most prepared he could possibly be, so that *they* were the most prepared they could be, and that collectively, his squad could accomplish the mission safely. It didn't take long for me to develop tremendous respect for him.

That's why some one-on-one time appealed to me.

"Hey, Steven. I could use a second set of eyes on the ground while I'm doing my leader's recon. Want to join me?"

It was an enjoyable drive out to the range. We chatted about a number of things—the upcoming deployment, our training, his experiences in Iraq. About ten minutes from the training location, he shared something that I often thought about afterward.

He spoke solemnly. "Sir, on my previous deployments, I was blessed to bring everyone home that was in my charge. My greatest fear with the upcoming deployment is being unable to do that." I glanced over at him. His expression was earnest. "That's really my only desire in this upcoming deployment—that I'm able to bring everyone home."

I nodded, absorbing the gravity of what he'd said. "So…your greatest fear *isn't* that you'd get wounded or be killed…but that you would lose one of your guys?"

"That's right, Sir."

His remark validated all the respect I'd already developed for him. "Well, I feel blessed to have a leader like you in my platoon, Sergeant Smith."

The memory twisted like a knife.

"I'm sorry," I gasped out loud. There was so much noise and activity all around me—the company medic shouting out for help and supplies, Anthony hurriedly unrolling gauze, a number of others crowding around me, staring down with horrified expressions. Steven hovered above me too, but he wasn't looking down. His eyes roved, looking at the soldiers who had just returned. Counting who was there. Registering who wasn't.

"Steven, I'm sorry," I gasped again. "I'm so sorry."

I knew Steven's worst nightmare had been realized. And for the rest of his life, he would never get an opportunity to live the moment himself to see if he could have changed the outcome.

"I'm sorry," I repeated. Steven looked down at me, seeming to finally register what I was saying. My voice came out in a croak, but I couldn't say it enough. "Winston's gone. And I'm so sorry."

Steven looked at Anthony with dismay. Anthony nodded bleakly, confirming what I'd said. "I'm sorry, buddy," Anthony said. "We tried to get him out. There was nothing we could do."

Guilt overwhelmed me. I hated that I'd lost him—that Winston had died while riding in my vehicle. I hated that Steven was realizing his worst fear. I hated that I was hurt so badly I had to be MEDEVACed out.

In my mind, I was letting my guys down. I was failing them by not being strong enough to stay.

Sergeant Medina, the company medic, interrupted us. "The helicopter's going to kick up a lot of dust when it gets here, Lieutenant Brown, so we're going to cover your eyes." He spoke quickly, keeping his voice low and quiet as he began wrapping gauze around my head.

I tried nodding. Moving was hard—all my joints felt stiff. I didn't realize that, as my skin cooled, it had begun to contract, tightening itself around me like a vise. I had been freed from the blinding flames, but now, my body was becoming its own cage.

Lights dimmed with the first layer of gauze. I shut my eyes. A deeper darkness set in as the medic circled my head with a second layer, then a third. Blind once again.

Sounds sharpened. So did the pain.

And there was still that unbearable thirst.

"I need water," I said hoarsely. "Can someone give me a drink?"

"If we gave you a drink of water, it could send your body into shock." I could feel Medina cutting off my sleeves. "Water doesn't know where to go with a burn victim. It doesn't know where to start. The only way to hydrate you is with an IV." He ripped my sleeve up my arm. "Damn it." He ripped up the other sleeve and swore again in frustration. "Both of your arms are charred, Lieutenant."

I knew I would need an IV, and I knew it wouldn't work in my arms. I'd already thought this through. "My arms are burned but my feet aren't," I croaked. "Get my boots off. Cut up my pant legs."

"We don't have time." I felt the tug of my shirt collar and heard the metal scissors begin to bite into the thick cloth. "Get me a Fastı!" he called.

I'd never heard of a "fast one." *What's a fast one?* "Listen, I have good veins, you can find one in my foot. Get my boots off." I tried to speak authoritatively, but my voice was raw and weak.

"I can't do that," he said.

"Yes, you *can*. Just do it!"

"No, sir, I can't do that. It's too risky." Around me was the sound of people tearing open packages. I felt Medina move so that he was hovering right over me.

"What do you mean, 'it's too risky?'" I wasn't used to soldiers disobeying my orders. "I wasn't burned below my knees. Just cut up my pant leg and put in the IV down there."

Medina was now pulling open my shirt, exposing my chest area which had been protected from the flames by my body armor. "I've got to use a Fastı," he repeated. I felt him touching the center of my chest, right on top of my sternum. Something cold pressed on top.

"Sir—" he hesitated. "This is going to hurt a little bit. Hold still."

The pressure changed as his weight bore down on that spot in the center of my chest. Something sharp shot into my sternum—a ring of metal pins. I gasped. "Hold still," he repeated. "That's the anchor." The pain was like having a cat dig its claws into my chest, but it was nothing compared to what followed.

As Sergeant Medina pressed down on the device, a large gauge needle punched a hole through my sternum. There was an audible cracking sound. It felt like getting shot.

He was speaking quickly but I could barely focus through the pain. "—*push a lot of fluid... Flushes out the bone marrow... Anchored medication delivery site... Right to the heart—*"

I struggled to breathe. "I'm not experiencing a great deal of pain relief."

"Get me morphine!" the medic yelled. "We'll hit you with intravenous morphine, Sir," he said. "Give me five minutes."

The pain in my chest was unbearable. The sound of boots running over. "We already hit him with a shot of morphine," someone panted.

"Intramuscular?" Medina demanded. "That's like putting a bandaid on a broken leg. You think that's going to help? How much did you give him?"

"*Look* at him!" the other voice said. "What were we supposed to do? We were getting shot at, we couldn't hook up an IV! He needed *something.*"

"How much did you give him?" the medic yelled. They began arguing back and forth—grams, dosage limits, adverse side effects. "You want to kill his respiratory drive on top of the smoke inhalation?!"

Someone knelt down. "LT." It was Steven's voice. "LT. They can give you just a little more morphine intravenously, but that's it. You just gotta hang on through the pain. Helicopter will be here soon, and once we get you back to the airfield, they'll have better stuff for you."

In spite of the excruciating pain, Steven's voice brought me back to the most pressing concern. *All I care about is that I bring everyone home.* "I'm sorry," I said to Steven again. I could never say it enough.

Steven spoke firmly, but his voice was ragged. "LT, there was nothing you could do about Winston."

That's what made me feel worst of all. *There was nothing you could do.* There was nothing I *could* do, which was another way of saying *I could do nothing.*

"I'm sorry," I kept repeating to Steven. The importance of the words pushed themselves past my dust-coated tongue, forced themselves beyond my cracked and swollen lips, bubbled out beyond the excruciating pain.

One of my soldiers had died; three more were wounded. And now—too destroyed to continue—I felt like I was abandoning my platoon.

I'm the first guy gone, I thought.

But then another thought countered the first, as though some larger Truth were pressing into me. *I was saved for a purpose.*

I wrestled, internally. If I couldn't stay and lead my guys—what purpose did I have? I couldn't answer that. I couldn't *begin* to fathom an answer.

Truth pressed again and a new thought bloomed in my mind. *The life I live is not my own.*

It repeated itself, the thought growing in power and clarity. *The life I live is not my own.* In the ash of failure, it felt like a seed of hope.

Maybe I couldn't imagine what was next. But maybe Someone could.

For a while, it got quiet around me. The medic might have told people to give me space. But the quiet made it hard to think about anything other than the pain. Not far away, I heard Steven speak quietly: "So...what happened?" I fixed my attention on his voice, hoping for a distraction that could distance me from my physical suffering.

Roszko's deep voice responded, though I couldn't catch everything he said. "Mushroom cloud...crazy bright, blinding... Thought *we'd* been hit at first... Then we realized it was them."

Lying there on my stretcher, I tried to imagine the scene through Anthony's eyes as he described what he'd seen. "We reversed... Opened our doors and jumped out... I stand up and I look... One person running... Flames from his boot all the way up... Entire body is on fire... I knew it was Lieutenant Brown... I see Kevin Jensen climb out of the top—he had to unclip himself... He's running... Arm and his leg is on fire... Debolt gets out of the driver's side and drags Philip out..."

Steven asked a question, which I couldn't hear. "No idea, man," Roszko responded. "No idea how the LT got out. I just saw him running."

The remark confirmed my memory of being violently lifted up inside the vehicle—then suddenly being outside of it, for no apparent reason. Everyone else had climbed out. How had I ended up out of the vehicle without anyone helping me? *Could that have been some sort of supernatural intervention?* I wondered.

My thoughts were interrupted by an unfamiliar voice. "Can I help you, Sir?" *That's not one of my soldiers.* A vague face swam into my mind. I made the connection: it was the Drug Enforcement Agency guy who had been assigned to join our platoon after we'd arrived. He'd tagged along on several missions, taking notes about the opium trade to pass back to his superiors at the DEA.

He spoke again—apparently to me. "Sir. Is there anything I can do for you?"

The question irritated me. *I'm covered in third-degree burns, in excruciating pain, my medic just punched a hole in my sternum, and I lost the soldier who was the heart of our platoon. I'm not going to be able to stay with my soldiers. We failed to complete our mission.* What did he think he could do for me that would help at that point?

Then, I had an absurd inspiration. "Yeah," I said, grimly. "There is something you can do for me."

He paused and waited. "Well, what is it?"

I tried licking my lips, tasting dust and ash. "I want you to take a picture of me," I said.

He let out a fast breath. "Uh, Sir…you look pretty bad right now. I'm not sure that you really want a picture of this."

This irritated me even more. An hour earlier, I was the guy that everyone took orders from. Now, I couldn't even get this DEA civilian to snap a picture. "No, I really do. You asked what you could do. I told you, take a picture of me."

"Sir…I'll take a picture of you," he said. "But before I do, I have to know—why do you want a picture?"

I didn't have the wherewithal to break down any complex emotional processing with this guy. Even short phrases were a challenge.

"I want a picture of what I look like when I'm being a bitch." I couldn't help but crack a smile—which hurt.

"Okay, Lieutenant. If you say so."

Why did I want a picture? Even I didn't fully comprehend the reasons behind my request. But beyond what I could articulate, I sensed that what was happening to me on that stretcher—lying there, blinded by gauze, in the dusty sands of the Kandahar desert—was a defining moment of my life. This night, this very hour, was the threshold of the "Before" and "After." It began in the moments right after the flames were extinguished, when my certain expectation of death gave way to impossible hope: the realization that I wasn't going to die and the understanding that I had been spared for a purpose that went beyond me.

"Before," the journey had been predictable: if I put in this effort, then I would get this outcome. I was at the peak of human performance for a young combat leader. Highly autonomous, influential in leadership, operating from a place of command and control. "Before" meant the power to influence and dictate outcomes. God was my co-pilot, the benevolent force that blessed me so long as I threw up my obligatory prayer for protection before each mission.

"After" was unknown. Forget my ten-year goals; I had no idea what the next ten minutes would look like. "After" was surviving in real time: enduring every next moment of pain so intense it seemed impossible to withstand. "After" was being physically crushed, permanently scarred. It meant total blindness: I could see nothing around me, and I could see nothing in my future. It meant slipping into a life of wrapped gauze and forced IVs, where I was a passive participant in a whirlwind of circumstances beyond my control. I did not get a voice. I did not get to bark orders. It was a version of life that I could never have imagined—and so far, it was a nightmare. There was no escape, no way to wake up. No ability to influence or direct it.

God, in the "After" was an overwhelming force. He was Lord, Maker, Creator—One I was wholly dependent on, fully surrendered to. Before this God, I was weak, wounded, and traumatized.

Yet I also wasn't alone. This God had saved me—and, as part of the deal, had apparently set me on a path that I could not foresee or predict. It was a life that no longer belonged to me; I couldn't find any redemption in all of it for myself. But the simple miracle of survival gave me confidence that I wasn't in this alone, and that there *was* a reason behind it. Dependency and trust had been thrust upon me; I'd been forced to accept this surrender. Somehow, bizarrely, that was comforting. It was a strange, awful, painful, beautiful new reality.

And in the same way that parents want to capture photos of their newborn child, I wanted to memorialize the beginning of whatever *this* was. I wanted to capture the moment I emerged from the dust of the ground, when the breath of life filled my nostrils, when I became a living soul. The "After" signified the starting point for the rest of my life.

I wanted to be able to refer back to this moment—not just in my memory, which seemed dangerously unreliable at the moment—but with tangible evidence. A photograph.

And, perhaps, morbid curiosity was also at work. How bad *did* I look? Was it as bad as I felt? Was it worse?

"You want to see?" Without waiting for an answer, the DEA agent lifted the gauze around my eyes and thrust the screen of a small digital camera into view.

Waiting for the MEDEVAC at the HLZ. This is the first photo of me after being wounded.

The person on the stretcher was hard to detect, initially. Underneath a shiny green army thermal emergency blanket, you could just barely make out a dirt-colored face emerging out of it. Only the gauze stood out—a bright, white rectangle in the midst of a nearly monochromatic jumble of gray dirt, gray stretcher, gray head, gray face. As my eyes focused on that white rectangle, I began to see it stretched across the vague shape of a human head. The hair looked dusty—devoid of color. A streak of red blood signified the parting of a mouth. Sand on the side of the face was crisscrossed with streaks. There were shiny patches of pink on the chin and cheek, the plasticky sheen visible even underneath the coating of dust. Next to the face, an IV tube snaked out from beneath the blanket.

Looking at the picture, I decided I didn't look nearly as bad as I felt.

The low din around me was suddenly broken by the rhythmic thrum of the chopper. The DEA agent dropped the gauze and patted it back over my eyes. "Looks like your ride's here, Lieutenant."

I felt dust pick up around me. The noise of the whirling blades seemed to churn up my own panicky questions. I was about to leave my soldiers for good—I was going back to the US. What would happen to them? What was the status of Kevin, and Philip, and Mike? How badly were they injured? Would Steven and Anthony be okay? How had the mission resolved? Did Austin's platoon make it out?

I couldn't ask and I couldn't see. The questions would remain unanswered.

I heard shouts to get ready. Wind picked up—I felt the blanket on me whip up, then someone tugged it back down. The chopper grew louder, nearly drowning out all other sound.

Abruptly, I felt the jolt of being picked up and carried on the stretcher as the thunderous noise grew still louder. I heard a clang of metal against metal, then something solid slid beneath my back. Yells—nearly impossible to hear over the noise of the whipping blades—then, a lifting motion. I imagined the helicopter rising above the floor of the desert, curving in a wide arc toward the KAF airfield. Yet—even after getting airborne—nothing eased up. There was still the overpowering noise, still the rotor wash sweeping in terrible wind.

A yell from the pilot—hard to hear. "*Why'd you—the door—take off?*"

Yells back. "*Patient—too tall—hanging out—what are we—?*"

"SIR! SIR?" The flight medic leaned close over my head to yell in my ear. "Sir, can you please bend your knees so we can shut the door?"

With an effort, I managed to bend my legs.

Someone shut the door. Things got quieter and less turbulent. Next to me, I heard murmured greetings from Kevin, then Philip, then Mike.

"Hey, LT."

"We're with you, LT."

Dimly, it occurred to me that their voices seemed to be coming from above me, a sign they were sitting up. That meant I was the only one who needed a stretcher; they had been able to move into the chopper on their own power. The thought brought relief. Suddenly, I felt so tired.

"Who is that?" A woman's voice spoke from the cockpit—a familiar one. "Who is that on the stretcher?"

Kevin responded. "First Lieutenant Sam Brown, Ma'am!"

She swore. "Fuck! Sam Brown?! Hang on, buddy!"

I tried to remember how I knew that voice—it seemed to belong to a recent memory, but also connected to a different time. Who was it?

I could feel myself slipping away and welcomed the approaching unconsciousness. I gave up trying to place the voice. It didn't matter.

Everything "Before" was already a lifetime ago.

CHAPTER 6

VALLEY OF THE
SHADOW OF DEATH

Mother and me, during West Point's graduation weekend. May 2006.

As dusk turned to darkness over the Kandahar desert, my mother was on the other side of the world, driving down green Virginia roads. She had just dropped my father off at work.

Mother had just gotten a new worship CD and put it in the player. The lyrics were about God's presence, His sovereignty, His love. The country roads of Southern Virginia swept by as she drove. Tall, old trees stretched out their green canopy over the road. She felt her body relax.

It relieved her that my father, Scott, was finally well enough to be back at work. When she'd first heard the news of his accident, she was afraid he might not make it.

She'd gotten the call from the hospital—*Tanya Brown? Your husband had a motorcycle accident. He's in the ICU.* She'd rushed there, her heart in her throat, terrified with the thoughts of how bad it might be. X-rays showed a broken hip, broken hand, and broken foot—but no head trauma or internal bleeding. Not life-threatening, they assured her. Still, rehabilitation could take months.

That wasn't even the worst part. The worst part came when he nearly died on his hospital bed from a pulmonary embolism, caused by complications from the accident. She could recall the madness in the hospital room, people rushing around, yelling orders. The horrible beepings from the machines, the alarm in their voices. All she could do was silently pray: *Please God, please God, please God, no.*

He'd pulled through—she thanked God for that. And now, two months after she'd first rushed to the ICU, he was home. She was starting to get used to the new routine. In her opinion, she'd become a halfway decent at-home nurse. "In sickness and in health," they'd vowed, and she supposed sickness included injury; so, now was the time for that kind of love.

He couldn't drive himself anywhere yet—not with those casts on. But he was starting to work again. That was a relief.

Driving down those country roads in the late summer sunshine, with peaceful music playing, it felt possible to think of the traumatic events of the past several months as receding into the past. Mother relaxed. It was going to be okay. All would be well.

Suddenly, a bizarre picture appeared in front of her—slightly to the left, seemingly obscuring the oncoming traffic. The image was oval-shaped, like a mirror or an old-fashioned window.

It's Samuel, she realized, shocked. *He's in a hospital room. Wrapped in bandages.* She watched herself enter into the frame and walk through a glass door toward me—her oldest son.

After a moment, the image disappeared. The plain stretch of asphalt returned.

Uh oh, she thought, her sense of calm giving way to unease. *What was THAT?*

I'd better pray for Samuel, she resolved. That's what she did for the rest of the drive: she prayed, letting the words of her worship music CD guide her meditations.

When she arrived home, she registered the time: 9:30 a.m. Afghanistan was 9.5 hours ahead of her. She did the math: it would be evening there—around 6:00 p.m. *Hope Samuel's doing well,* she thought. *Wonder what he ate for dinner. Maybe he's doing something fun with his buddies.*

The light blinked on the answering machine. She made up her mind to listen to the messages in a few hours. There were too many things on her to-do list needing her attention right now.

It was only later—after she'd gotten the frantic call from my grandmother—that Mother finally pressed play on the answering machine. The voice she heard coming through sounded weak and tired—even raw. The words arrived slowly, as though each one required a great effort. Despite the message's attempt to reassure, she knew instantly that something was wrong:

"Mother and Father, this is Samuel. My truck was hit. I'm okay… They're flying me back through Germany. I think they'll be in touch with you. I love you."

I wasn't awake for much of what followed, but I do remember a few things.

First: the hellish return of consciousness when they began the debridement process of cleaning my wounds at the Kandahar Role 3 hospital—the combat equivalent of a Level One Trauma facility. I have no visual memories of this because I'd shut my eyes tight to deal with the pain. All I remember is the agonizing sensations of my raw flesh being scraped, cut, rubbed, irrigated, peeled, and scrubbed. It was a frightening preview of the months and years of "healing" still ahead of me.

Finally, I was left alone, doing my best to breathe and block out the pain. A Sergeant Major from the Battalion came to check on me. I remembered that I'd seen him use a satellite phone before and asked him to call my parents.

He hesitated. "I'm really not supposed to do that…"

"Come on, Sergeant Major. I want to let them know I'm alive."

He called.

They didn't answer. I left a voicemail and tried not to alarm them.

The only other number I had memorized was Meemaw's. The Sergeant Major held the phone up next to my head. "Meemaw?" I said when I heard her answer. "It's Samuel."

"Oh *hey*, Samuel! It's so good to hear from you!" Meemaw's drawl was full of delight. "How're things goin', honey?"

"Well, Meemaw—I've had an accident, but I'm okay. They're sending me home early. I need you to get in touch with my parents and let them know that I'm coming home."

"Oh my gosh, Samuel! You've gotten hurt? What happened? How bad is it?"

"It's not too bad, Meemaw," I lied. "I can't really talk right now. Can you let Mother and Father know?"

She said she would—I think. I don't remember how the conversation ended or what happened next. That's about when my memories just cease.

Roughly eight hours after the explosion, I stopped breathing. My body succumbed to the trauma-induced exhaustion. Because I had breathed flames down into my respiratory system, I had scarring up and down my trachea—something called "inhalation injuries." My oxygen levels plummeted and my system crashed. I had an emergency intubation, was put into a medically induced coma, and given strong dissociative painkillers.

Soon thereafter, I was flown out to a ship to keep me stabilized for the journey back to the United States. My mother, seemingly answering the summons I'd shouted out while being burned alive, was flown out and joined me onboard. I was so relieved to see her. Mother had always managed a nurturing duality in how she cared for me: she was both a comforter in my pain and a challenger, prompting me to toughen up and endure hard things. She sat with me in the ship's common area and told me that she was proud of me. "We're going to get through this, Son," she repeated quietly. At times, she read scripture: "... *Though I walk through the valley of the shadow of death...*"

I didn't have a room on the ship, so there was never a secure place to go. I got the sense, in fact, that I wasn't welcome there at all. The crew seemed to treat me with hostility, as a wounded deadweight who couldn't even manage to move his own wheelchair. I overheard their mutterings: "We had to be taken off our mission for *this* guy?"

"Can't believe our new mission is escorting this wounded soldier back home."

"Isn't there someone else who could take care of him? Why are we stuck with it?"

It was painful to feel like such a burden, especially when I had been used to leading soldiers like this. I didn't want to be the one that had to be supported or taken care of. I had no control: not over others' perception of me, not over my movement, not over my own destination. I was wholly dependent on other people moving me around, a loss of self-determination that seemed exacerbated by the fact that I was on a ship in the middle of an ocean. And the servicemembers in uniform—men and women I'd always thought I could trust and lean on like family—had turned against me.

A few days into the journey I ended up in a sailor's cabin, deep inside the recesses of the ship. As I looked on, shocked and horrified, several sailors tangled themselves in a drug-fueled orgy. One looked up, saw me there, and shouted at me, "You're going to tell on us!"

My shock switched to alarm—how was I supposed to defend myself? For a minute I was speechless, but my thoughts violently protested. *I'm just here to get better! All I'm focused on is healing. I don't care what other people are doing around me.*

Finally, I managed to say something out loud. "I can't do anything," I said. "I'm stuck in this wheelchair."

One of them walked up menacingly. He held up an aerosol can of hairspray in one hand and a lighter in the other. He flicked the flame and began spraying through it, creating a flame thrower. I writhed as he came closer, but couldn't escape. Then he was spraying it on me, burning me, re-burning me, I was on fire again. I cried out but couldn't move, once again powerless against the flames.

The torture was interrupted by the Commanding Officer. He burst into the room, demanding to know what was happening. The sailors lied, making up a story about something I had done. Once again, my thoughts protested but I couldn't make a verbal defense.

"We didn't hurt him *that* bad, Captain."

The Captain looked at me. Even in the belly of the ship, he wore dark sunglasses. He smiled, revealing teeth that were perfect and gleaming white.

I felt panic. Couldn't he see I was incapable of doing anything to anybody? Yet, as he smiled down at me, I sensed there would be no fair evaluation of the facts. Even though the evidence was clearly on my side, I was still deemed to be in the wrong. Were the officers of the ship just there to protect their own? Were they afraid I'd expose their bad leadership culture? Better to accuse the outsider who couldn't muster a defense, and then get rid of me as soon as they could.

The senior officers took me down to the very bottom level of the ship, the keel. There was a makeshift torture room down there with a metal table. I was strapped onto it, naked and face down. Along the wall were cut sections of fire hose, each about four to six feet long. All the officers of the ship came down and gathered around the metal table where I was trapped. One by one, they took strips of the fire hose and beat my back with it, whipping me, lashing the only part of my body that hadn't been covered in burns.

Through the pain, I felt fury. I was being tortured for someone else's failure. I'd lost a soldier, saw three of my men badly wounded, and had experienced life-threatening burns because of someone else's decision. Now, I was bearing the entire cost of that? And what were their consequences? They stood, whole-bodied, and jeered.

I passed out. In my unconsciousness, I dreamed of falling into a dark, deep, cube-shaped pit. The darkness was so encompassing, no light could penetrate. There was no bottom or sides—I was suspended deep inside it, unable to move. On scaffolding above the pit, demonic figures moved and prowled. Surely this was hell—I was in hell. *I'm in hell.*

When I regained consciousness, I found myself in another Forward Operating Base, similar to the one where my unit had been stationed in Afghanistan—only this FOB was in Mexico. This was confusing to me. Hadn't we been trying to make it back to the US? I'd nearly made it there, but wasn't yet safe. Even more confusing was the fact that Afghan terrorists were roaming the streets of Mexico, almost as if the war in Afghanistan had moved to the US's southern border.

My Battalion was with me though—that was a relief. I observed small teams of my guys going out on patrol. I felt a mixture of resignation and disappointment watching them leave. I knew I wasn't in a position to join them, but my inability to engage was depressing.

Despite not going into the field, I was captured anyway. The Taliban broke through all the security that had surrounded me—my guys, our armored vehicles, our weapons—and I was taken hostage. For several days I was held as a prisoner of war inside a mosque, guarded by Congolese mercenaries. The mixture of characters and places was bewildering: Where was I? Was I alone? Who could I trust? Would rescue ever come?

At one point, a conflict occurred in the mercenaries' camp outside the mosque—some sort of big firefight. I pulled myself out of my wheelchair and escaped, doing my best to maneuver through the streets, moving with the grace of a zombie. But I stepped in the wrong spot. An explosion erupted underneath me. When the smoke cleared, I saw with horror that my lower half had been entirely blown off.

I was now half a man, impotent and emasculated: cut down to only a badly damaged torso, battered face, and tortured mind. Soldiers nearby—Americans, though not my soldiers—picked me up and threw me into a dumpster. Inside the dumpster, I found myself surrounded by other mutilated body parts.

Was this where I belonged now? I was a horror, a grotesque—fit to be thrown away, discarded, and left for dead.

But *I* wasn't ready to be left for dead. A frantic need to survive took hold of me. How could I escape? I tried looking for a way to climb out, but instead began sliding down toward the bottom of the slanted dumpster. There was nothing to grasp onto—nothing but other mutilated body parts. As I slid past bloody arms and wounded torsos, I spotted someone else's lower extremities near the bottom. Before I could stop myself, my exposed lower torso had merged on top of the foreign legs.

The sensation was mortifying. I felt contaminated on the deepest level. But I also realized I was able to animate the foreign legs beneath me. Disgusted and appalled, I accepted that this severed corpse was my way out.

Pieced together like Frankenstein's monster, I climbed out of the dumpster and found my way to a field hospital. The hospital was in Mexico—I was still beyond the safety of the US—but at least the hospital bay felt secure and spacious.

Here though, the isolation was profound. Despite the multiple beds in the ward, there were no other warriors—there weren't even nurses or doctors. No one came. I felt increasingly uncomfortable, yet there was no one to provide relief, or answers, or help. I also was once again immobilized: I was back in a wheelchair, my brief mobility terminated.

Days passed. Eventually, a nurse showed up, then left almost as quickly. My mother occasionally looked in, then disappeared.

The fear and frustration were consuming. When would I ever start healing? When would I be taken to the security of American soil? When would there be safety and help?

One day, I was taken somewhere, then almost immediately brought back. From my wheelchair, I stared at my bed in shock. The corpses of two young Marines had been set in my cot. Somehow, I understood the nature of their demise: they were from a Battalion of Marines that had redeployed from overseas and landed in San Diego. On their first night back, several of them had crossed the border into Mexico to party. These two had ended up drunk and lost, stumbling down a dirt road in the middle of the night. They'd gotten hit by a car and brutally killed—their carnage, if possible, even worse than mine.

Horrified, I tried calling for help. "Can someone move these Marines? There are other beds around me!" I called. "I'm the only living guy here!"

The nursing staff entered the room and assessed the situation. They picked me up out of my wheelchair and tossed me into the same bed with the dead Marines. Then they left.

There was no word about who the young men were, no mention of their deeds, no mourning, no celebration of their courage. They were simply discarded, a casualty of war, no longer any use to the war machine.

"I don't *belong* here!" I called. "Why are you putting me in the bed with these guys? I'm not dead! I'm still alive!"

I could smell the dirt and dust on their bodies. It seemed to coat the inside of my nostrils and mouth, like the sand and ash I'd inhaled in Afghanistan. They still smelled of exhaust fumes and spilled diesel gas. I felt sickened by their company and grief-stricken by our collective loss.

Perhaps I lost consciousness again—I must have started dreaming. I imagined myself floating above the earth, almost as though I *had* died. My viewpoint started at ground level, then zoomed high through the lower atmosphere with a view of Earth like a satellite. Far below on the surface of the earth, I could see a series of coordinated explosions—a choreographed global attack on major cities around the world. Mushroom clouds and the echoes of massive detonations bloomed in succession, first across the Middle East, then into Europe, and then in the United States. Sleeper cells all over the world—undetected and unseen—had waited until that certain day, that certain time, to detonate bombs in major cities.

With a sickening realization, I watched the dream tell a story of utter failure. Terrorism was widespread. Winston's death, my injuries, all the other casualties of war—it had all been in support of a higher mission, a noble cause. Yet, even so, the world seemed to be going up in flames all around us.

When I woke up, I found myself in a madrasa, an Islamic school for children—though, strangely, we were still in Mexico. The teacher was a man with a black turban who was missing several fingers. His eyes glowered like a storm while he instructed the students on how to be suicide bombers. This was alarming enough, but even more unsettling was what I noticed hanging in the back of the classroom: an American flag.

The door burst open. The President of the United States came in, along with the Secretary of Defense. "We are proud of you!" the President spoke. "You've completed your training to become undercover terrorists for the United States. Your reward is US citizenship." The instructor began to guide the students through a citizenship ceremony, the President personally shaking each child's hand, congratulating them.

"You will each be sent to infiltrate a known terrorist cell somewhere in the world," the Secretary of Defense explained. "Using your training, you will assess the optimal moment to do maximum damage to the terrorist group. Then, you will detonate yourselves. Hopefully, you will kill as many other people as you possibly can. In doing so, you will be supporting the ideals and values of this country—a noble cause."

Stunned, I watched the President as he left the madrasa and boarded Air Force One. As the plane lifted off into the low evening light from the remote airstrip near this desert oasis village, I suddenly heard sharp shots. The enormous 747 was being shot down. Flames shot up from the plane's engines. The nose dipped toward the ground and the whole plane crashed into the earth, flames erupting from its center.

The flames grew bigger and all-consuming. They filled my view.

Then, out of the fire, I heard a familiar voice.

"No wonder he hasn't been able to sleep! All this time I thought he'd lost his mind, in addition to being nearly burned alive!"

Mother? I opened my eyes. Fluorescent lights glared harshly above me, reflecting against sterile, white walls. I smelled disinfectant.

"I could have *told* you to take him off the ketamine if anyone had bothered to tell me he'd been on it! He thought he was in danger. He thought we both were in danger!"

Why was Mother so angry?

"I've been trying to calm him down to get him to sleep, and meanwhile, y'all have been giving him hallucinatory drugs that have kept him trapped in a war zone!"

Someone was arguing with her—"Dissociative drugs…help a patient disassociate from their pain—"

"Maybe that works when the patient isn't dealing with PTSD! I've been trying to reason with him, telling him that we're in San Antonio at the hospital, and meanwhile he's telling me that we're surrounded by enemies and we've got to get on the helicopter, and yelling for his Sergeant. No one thought to tell me that he was *hallucinating*? No one thought to mention to his mother that he wasn't *actually insane*, that he was just on hallucinogens?"

The other voice was protesting again. Mother wasn't having it.

"He's been running in his bed, trying to climb up into the helicopter! It broke my heart! You think moving like that is good for his healing? And y'all told me he had to stay intubated until he calms down and sleeps—so, I've been reading him stories and showing him pictures from his West Point crew days, and counting sheep backwards… Meanwhile, he thinks he's in a life-or-death situation because of your dissociative drugs! That's why he's on superdrive!"

"Mother?" I spoke. My throat hurt.

She didn't hear me—the other person had interrupted. "He's off it now, so—"

"Even after y'all took the tube out, he's been acting crazy. If I had *known* that he was on hallucinogens, I could have told you to take him off a long time ago. Do you have any idea how sad it's been, to watch Samuel go through all that trauma while he's been in the safety of a hospital room? And all from the freaking ketamine?! I tell you, I am pissed off. I am seriously pissed off."

"Mother," I croaked again, louder.

Both Mother and the medical professional looked down at me.

"Is the President still alive?" I asked. "Were there a series of explosions and bombs going off?"

She sat down next to me and took my hand. It was thickly wrapped with gauze—like a paw.

"No, Samuel," she said, in a steely and much quieter voice. Her eyes flickered up angrily to the medical professional. "None of that happened."

"Did the Taliban attack? Where are the dead Marines?"

"You're safe, Son. You're in a hospital in San Antonio. You've been… living in an alternative reality for days now. All those horrible things you're describing—that was all just in your mind."

This was inconceivable to me. I had *lived* it. Those experiences had been far more real than any dream I'd ever had. So real, in fact, that I had dreamed *inside* of what she was describing as hallucinations.

I pushed back, reminding her of our journey on the ship, the torture room, the hospital in Mexico, the dead Marines.

"None of those things were real," she insisted. She began explaining a different version of reality—but it wasn't my reality. It was *their* reality.

In anyone else's reality, I had spent thirty-six hours in Kandahar at the airfield. Then I was transported with other wounded veterans—including Philip Kopfensteiner, Kevin Jensen, and Michael Debolt—to Bagram Airfield in Northeast Afghanistan. After another thirty-six hours passed, we flew with a larger collection of wounded soldiers to a major hospital in Landstuhl, Germany.

At that point, many of the wounded were checked in for treatment and rehab at Landstuhl. The location was close enough to the combat zone theater that soldiers with more minor wounds could be quickly treated, quickly healed, and quickly returned to battle.

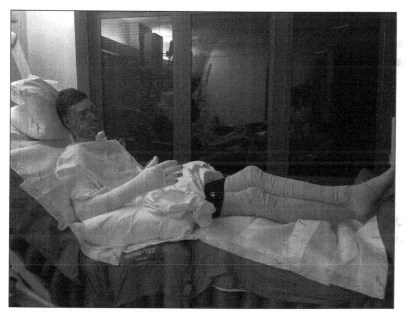

Recovering in US military burn unit at Fort Sam Houston in San Antonio, Texas. October 2008.

I did not meet that criteria. They determined the burned First Lieutenant was ineligible for a quick return to combat, and I was put on another flight, this time to San Antonio, Texas, with a final stop at Brooke Army Medical Center. BAMC, with its formalized burn unit, was the final stop for the most badly burned soldiers in the Department of Defense. Apparently, that was my new category.

At BAMC, I was kept in a medically induced coma while initial treatment began, including preliminary skin graft harvesting from the healthy skin off my back—an experience which, in *my* reality, took place in a torture room in the belly of a ship.

In *their* reality, there was no ship. There was no torture room. There was no dumpster, no madrasa, no series of worldwide explosions.

It was all in my mind, Mother reassured me. A result of the ketamine. "You're safe now," she kept insisting. "It's all right. Healing can begin." She opened her Bible and flipped it to the center.

"The Lord is my Shepherd. I will have everything I need. He lets me rest in fields of green grass. He leads me beside the quiet waters. He makes me strong again. He leads me in the way of living right with Himself which brings honor to His name. Yes, even if I walk through the valley of the shadow of death, I will not be afraid of anything, because You are with me..."

I didn't hear the rest. The phrase circled in my head—*valley of the shadow of death. Shadow of death. Death.*

Healing can begin, she'd said.

I hoped she was right.

PART 3

LEARNING TO LIVE

CHAPTER 7

PAINFULLY AWAKE

First time at an Army–Navy game as a member of Corps of Cadets. December 2002.

"Bone graft? I'm going to need a *bone* graft?"

The doctor perched on his swivel chair in front of the computer. He looked at me patiently, as though he were used to explaining the frailty of a human body to West Point cadets who—like me—largely believed in their own invincibility.

"That's right. You sustained a hairline fracture at the base of where your femur meets the tibia." He pointed to an anatomical poster on the wall. "That fracture cut off your blood supply to an area of the knee...here. And part of your bone tissue has died." He moved over to his computer screen, where there was an X-ray of my knee. "See this dark hollow space?" He tapped the screen with his pen. "That's supposed to be dense white. That's how we can see the bone has died."

"But...I don't even remember getting *injured*. How could I have gotten a fracture?"

The doctor shrugged. "It's not uncommon for high school athletes to sustain an injury that they push through. My guess is you got the fracture at some point during high school and the unhealed fracture ended up cutting off the blood supply, which over time, led to the bone dying. That's likely why it's been hurting you for so long."

I was still skeptical. "I've never heard of anyone else having this."

The doctor smiled. "Yes, you're very special. ACL injuries are much more common. Your knee injury is rare. It's called osteochondritis dissecans, OCD for short."

"OCD? I thought that was obsessive-compulsive disorder."

"You know, the psychiatrists and the orthopedic surgeons are always fighting over who gets that particular three-letter combo." He smiled, attempting a joke. I scowled.

"Well, how long until I'm healed?"

"First, let's talk through *how* you'll be healed. In surgery, we'll need to scoop out that dead tissue. Then we'll take a bone graft off the front top end of your tibia—that's your shin bone—where the bone is extra thick. We'll pack the crater where the dead tissue was with the live bone tissue, and use screws to hold that little bone cap in place."

"I'll have screws in my knee?"

"Not forever, no. It will take about three months for the bone graft to integrate into the rest of the bone around it. Once it has, we can take out the screws in another surgery—"

"*Another* surgery?"

"…That's right, and then you'll need additional time for that to heal."

I stared at the doctor bleakly. I was thinking of all the training exercises, my long runs, playing pickup basketball games with my friends on the weekends. Most of all, I was thinking about crew. "So… how long until I'm better?"

"You need to stay off of it for three months, until the graft heals. And when I say stay off of it, I mean absolutely *no* weight on it. You'll have to get around with crutches."

I hesitated before asking my next question. I didn't want to know the answer, but I suspected I needed to. "What about crew? I'm a rower. When I row, I'm not standing on my legs, but I use them to push back when I pull the oar. Can I still do that?"

He stared at me as though the answer were obvious. "If you put *any* strain whatsoever on your knee while it's healing, the graft is likely to die, and we'll have to start the whole process over again."

My face returned to its scowl. "I'm going to miss the entire spring season."

He nodded, matter-of-factly. "Looks like it." He stood up cheerfully. "We've scheduled your surgery one week from today. Lots of ice and ibuprofen until then. And *no weight* on the knee."

That was a depressing spring. As West Point woke up from winter, daffodils bloomed and the cherry trees were covered with pink blossoms. All the other West Point cadets seemed high on life. On good days, I sat in the sunshine on a bench and watched my friends throw the football around. On bad days, I stared out my window as the members of the crew ran together in front of the barracks toward the boathouse.

Being injured sucked.

After three months, the doctor confirmed the bone graft had "taken," and I could start doing gentle activity. I was allowed to walk, but *no* running, *no* lifting, and *no* rowing.

"Can I row in our indoor rowing tanks, at least?" I asked, desperate for some way to maintain my spot on the crew team.

The doctor didn't know what I was talking about. I explained that the West Point boathouse had a couple of huge water tanks with sliding seats in the middle, simulating rowing in a single shell. "I wouldn't be hauling hard on the oars, like I'd be doing if I was in the boat with all the guys," I pleaded. "I could go easy and just work on my technique?"

He agreed—but warned me to stop if I felt pain.

The tanks became my saving grace. When the JV team left for practice, I went with them. They all climbed in the shell; I climbed onto the sliding seat between the tanks. They cruised down the Hudson; I rowed in place. But being back in the boathouse meant I was part of the team again—now, I just had to get good enough to earn a spot back on one of the shells. I'd lost nearly all my strength, but I still could work on form. In that solitary tank, I drilled technique without force: over and over and over again, all by myself.

Occasionally a coach or a coxswain would come in and watch me for a few minutes. They'd provide a few tips or suggest an adjustment. Then, I'd drill that new adjustment, isolating technique away from everything else. Focusing on form while still babying my bad knee made me realize the importance of controlling my slide forward—and that ended up being the big game changer.

I was still weak from the muscle atrophy that had occurred over the past six months when the fall season started, at the beginning of junior year. Following the doctor's instructions, I hadn't put real weight on my right leg or exercised it. But my technique had gotten so good, the coaches still put me in the stroke seat in the JV boat. We rowed to victory that fall, even beating the Varsity team. The next spring, I won the Varsity Stroke seat and we had one of the best seasons West Point crew had ever seen.

The lesson became internalized: *Temporary setbacks are opportuni-*

ties to create even bigger wins. When I push through adversity, I come out stronger. I've got more to contribute. I'm an even better leader.

Years later, in another hospital room, I circled back to that lesson. I repeated it to myself, again and again, with the same repetitive force of rowing on a sliding seat in a stationary water tank. The repetition got me nowhere: there was no discernible progress.

But there was still that hope: *Maybe I'm changing. Maybe I'm getting stronger. Maybe soon, I'll be back on the team.*

BROOKE ARMY MEDICAL CENTER, MID-SEPTEMBER 2008.

Mother had printed off a number of pictures for me, and taped them up where I could see them from my hospital bed.

She'd chosen happy pictures, meant to cheer me up: a picture of our family at Christmas time. A picture of me at graduation. There were several pictures that she'd found on my digital camera from Afghanistan: me, reading *Lone Survivor* by my stretcher-cot at the FOB. Me, with a group of smiling kids in one of the villages. She'd also taped up pictures of me with the West Point crew team: holding up the shell. Pulling the oars in unison just after the starting pistol.

The guy in the pictures was good looking. Tall. Strong. It was me—at least, the "me" I'd always been.

He didn't look much like whoever I was now.

I lay in my hospital bed, wrapped in bandages from the crown of my head, down to my lower extremities. The parts of my body that hadn't sustained burns, like my back and thighs, had all been used as donor sites for skin grafts. It felt like there wasn't a single part of my body that hadn't been either burned or harvested.

I had escaped the ketamine-inspired war zone and was finally, painfully awake. But reality was brutal.

Time moved with agonizing slowness. Hour after hour, I lay in that hospital bed.

Stuck.

At one point, I'd been the fittest soldier in my Infantry company. Now, I was so weak it was difficult to stand. The initial period when I'd been intubated and on a ventilator had resulted in a significant decrease in my caloric intake. I'd never had a ton of body fat to begin with, but during those early days in the hospital, I became emaciated. I lost body fat, and I also lost muscle. That, plus the pain of the burns, grafts, and contracting scar tissue, made me feel trapped inside my own wrecked frame.

Even if I *had* been capable of getting out of my bed, I couldn't have. I was literally tied down. Because my arms had been so badly burned, they were in danger of becoming immobilized by the contracting scar tissue. In order to stretch the skin and try to keep it flexible, the nurses had attached my arms to a wing-like structure, stretching off each side of the bed. Whenever I woke up, I was lashed in a crucified position. They quickly detached my arms once I was conscious, but the sense of freedom was short-lived. We had more painful healing to get to.

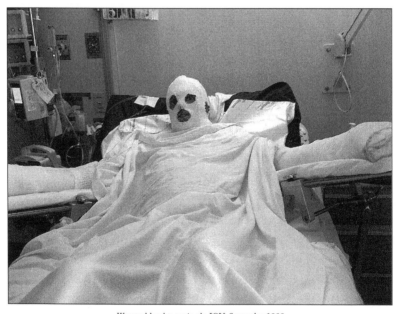

Wrapped head to toe in the ICU. September 2008.

The day's activity began with the long process of wound debridement. I'd had my first experience of wound debridement at the KAF airfield, when medics and military nurses had worked to clean the dust, dirt, pieces of melted uniform, and dead tissue off of me, to create a clean environment for the skin to heal. In the hospital, wound debridement was Priority Number One for burn victims. Only in this stretch, it wasn't dust or charred uniform fabrics the nurses were scrubbing off. It was dying tissue—the parts of my body that had shown themselves to be past the point of ever being able to heal. If that dead tissue remained, it could rapidly lead to infection and bring down the other healthy tissue surrounding it.

It started off gently enough. Every morning, two nurses would come in and very, very carefully begin to take all my bandages off. It took hours: they were basically unwrapping a mummy. Once I had been stripped of all the bandages and was mostly naked, they lifted me onto a metal gurney. Just before leaving the ICU room, the nurses gave me two milligrams of a strong painkiller, Dilaudid.

The first time they gave me this painkiller when I was lucid and *not* high on ketamine, I asked about it. "Why do I need a painkiller when I'm just taking a shower?"

"You're going to need it," one responded grimly.

The nurses wheeled me into the shower room: a big, tiled room with multiple shower heads and handheld spray nozzles. As we approached it, the screams of pain which were ubiquitous on the burn unit floor grew louder.

"Is someone being murdered in there?" I joked, nervously. The nurses looked down at me, then made eye contact with each other. One of them clenched her jaw. Neither responded to my joke. It occurred to me that they seemed more apprehensive about the whole thing than I did.

Standing in the shower room, one of the nurses reminded me of the drill. "You're only allowed two more milligrams of Dilaudid. Last as long as you can, then tell us when you need the second hit."

Bracing themselves, one of them reached for the spigot. There was no point in asking if I was ready.

With a rush, the shower heads were turned on. Water sprayed down with force. The nurses began scrubbing.

And I began screaming.

Using debridement scrub brushes with thick, stiff bristles, the nurses scrubbed my burns to remove dead necrotic tissue. My skin had been burned severely enough that all my nerves on the burn sites were exposed—and those raw nerves were being forcefully scoured. It was necessary, but it felt like torture.

I lasted as long as I could until it was impossible to endure any longer. Finally, I cried out, "I need more pain medication!"

The nurse nodded, gave me the second hit. "That's all you get now!" she called over the noise of the water. "You just have to deal with the pain until it ends!" Each second was a minute. Each minute was an eternity.

Finally, the shower spigots were turned off. I was wheeled back to my room, still reeling from the pain. The long process of being rewrapped began.

Visiting hours usually began around the time the nurses were finishing up my rewrapping process, which meant Mother joined me after I was back in my mummy get-up. Once I was rewrapped, the next "healing" task was to sit. Literally, my first Physical Therapy exercise was sitting in a chair for four hours. I'd been burned on the backs of my legs, burned on my butt, and wherever I hadn't been burned, doctors had taken large slices of donor skin grafts. On top of those raw nerves and exposed flesh—that's where I rested all my weight. Sitting was agony.

Similar to the wound debridement, sitting was *necessary*: I was rebuilding core strength and the ability to sit up. But no one explained that to me at the time.

Maybe because I'd acted so insane at first, none of the medical practitioners ever bothered explaining *why* I had to sit in the damn chair. No one walked out the process for me, to spell out the duration or purpose or goal. I was just told, "Do this. It's part of your therapy."

The first day in the chair, I sat there for about thirty minutes—which, to me, felt herculean. After a half hour, I said through my gauze, "Okay, I'm ready to be put back in my bed now."

"No, no, no. You need to stay sitting. This isn't voluntary."

For four hours, I had to sit—although "four hours" were words they never said. I had no idea how long this sitting needed to go on; I only knew that every time I asked to go back to bed, I was shut down. There was no way for me to count down the minutes or measure how much longer. After another eternity, I was finally carried back to my hospital bed and immediately passed out.

The next day—after the shower and the debridement and the rewrapping—they said it again: "All right, time to go sit."

"No, no, no," I begged. "I did that yesterday."

"No, no, no," a nurse mimicked me, feigning cheerfulness. "You've got to do it today too."

"*Why?*" I demanded. "How long?"

"We're keeping track" was the chipper answer.

Mother tried to make things easier. On the second day, she turned on a football game and wheeled me in front of the TV. I was angry about everything—angry about the stupid showers, and the stupid gauze, and the stupid pain, and the stupid chair. Angry that I wasn't with my guys, angry that my body wasn't healing. I was angry at the nurses, and the doctors, and Mother.

I stared at the TV, miserable.

"I love you, Son," Mother said to me quietly.

I glared at her. "If you loved me, you wouldn't let them make me sit like this."

She looked shocked. "Samuel," she said, clearly hurt. "You have to do that."

"No, Mother," I said. "You could change it if you wanted to."

It wasn't fair of me to say that. But from my perspective inside that mummy shroud—stuck in my own skin, incapable of an activity as basic as *sitting*, overwhelmed with the stabbing pain of sitting on my burns—no one seemed to understand how hard it was to do the things they were asking of me. I felt like I was giving everything I had and it wasn't enough.

Mother set about proving her love to me. After I'd fallen asleep, she went to find the medical staff and do battle.

"I don't know how other families deal with the recovery of a loved one, but I can't just passively watch when I think there are things that need to be done better. You're having him sit on a *wooden* chair. His butt is burned! You need to give him a cushion to sit on. He can still do his PT and get whatever benefits you're after if he's sitting on something soft instead of a rough wooden platform, can't he?"

They started to answer. She cut them off.

"Of course he can. Tomorrow, things are going to look a little different."

The following day, during my chair sitting time—which had improved accordingly, thanks to the provision of a cushion—Mother explained her new outlook to me.

"Well, Samuel, after I realized they'd had you on ketamine that whole time, I just said to myself, 'Tanya, you've got to be your son's advocate. They're not going to do anything beyond what's necessary to make him comfortable. They're not taking care of the details. They're just going for the easy approach, not the best approach. And the only way they're going to take care of the little things is if I complain about it.' So, I complained. And they changed it."

"Thank you, Mother," I said, chastened to think of my meanness the day before.

Even still, after days of this routine—the unwrapping, the shower, the debridement, the rewrapping, the chair—I was tempted to despair. *I hate this,* I thought. *I don't see any progress. How long is this going to go on?* It took several days for me to wake up to the fact that this WAS my recovery reality. This was what I had to go through.

Even through the layers of gauze, Mother could recognize my discouragement. Once again, she took matters into her own hands.

"Samuel," she told me one day. "Look. I know you don't like to be in this situation, but they've got their requirements of what they expect. And we've just got to do it. So, I think we should set a goal."

I perked up my ears. I've always been goal-driven. *Was* there a goal?

"Let's make a backwards plan, Samuel. When would you like to be out of the hospital?"

I thought about that. Could I *ever* get out of the hospital?

She spoke up, having already decided. "Your birthday's coming up pretty soon. Would you like to shoot to get out of the hospital by your birthday?"

"Yes." I felt incredulous that such a thing might be possible. "October 15?"

She nodded, firmly. "Let's shoot for that. We're going to have that as our goal."

"What do I have to do?" I asked, muffled by gauze.

Mother got a list from the medical staff. Before I could be discharged to the outpatient clinic, I first had to graduate from the ICU to the step-down unit, in another wing of the hospital. My graduation was dependent on three things: one, I had to drink from a straw. Two, I had to feed myself. And three, I had to walk.

Goals! Having something to work toward was a light at the end of the tunnel. The shift was so energizing I couldn't believe I hadn't thought of it sooner. Mother knew me—she knew I had always been goal-driven. But, as I considered the cards I'd been dealt, I decided I needed to think even bigger.

October 15 was a step on the ladder. The *real* goal was to get back to Afghanistan. We had been early into our deployment. If I could recover fast enough, I could go back there—lead my guys again. Complete our mission and finish the deployment. That became my singular focus for pushing through every bit of pain. The harder I pushed myself, the sooner I could go back.

The *real* goal was to step back into leadership with my guys.

I didn't say my new goal out loud. I suspected, if I did, I'd get hit with negativity. The doctors and nurses would tell me it was unrealistic. But they didn't *know* me. They didn't know I'd come back from a crippling knee injury at West Point and had gone on to win the stroke seat. They didn't know what I'd overcome at Ranger School. They didn't know what kind of fitness I'd had before the accident—what fitness, I was sure, I could achieve again.

What had I learned after the knee injury at West Point? I'd learned that adversity could be a blessing in disguise. So long as I pushed through it, looked for the lessons to be gained, and applied them diligently, I could come back *even stronger*. I could be a better leader! If I just focused on healing and hit every goal they put in front of me—forget that, if I *blew past* every goal they put in front of me—then they'd see that I deserved to get back with the team. I could be given the leadership spot again. I could lead my guys to victory.

When I woke up now, I had a purpose. I had something to prove!

We worked on the straw first. Because my entire face had been burned, the contracting scar tissue around my mouth had closed it to a tiny opening. But it was big enough for a straw. Mother held up the cup for me. I managed to close my lips around it—at least, what was left of my lips. After a few messy attempts, I was able to suck liquid down.

BOOM. *One step closer to drinking from a CamelBak in the desert.*

"Now he's got to feed himself," the ICU nurses reminded her.

"How is he supposed to manage that?" Mother asked. "His hands got burned. They're covered in bandages. He can't hold anything."

"He's got to learn if he wants to go to the step-down unit," they said. I agreed with that. If I expected to tear open MREs and pass them out to my team at the FOB, I needed to learn how to use my hands.

Feeding myself took much longer than the straw. It wasn't just the bandaged paws that posed an obstacle—it was also my tiny mouth. But we worked at it, and worked at it, and worked at it. Every time I got frustrated, Mother would remind me of the goal. "October 15," she said. "We're going to get out of this hospital for your birthday." I nodded, thinking even further into the future: *I'm going to share a meal with my soldiers.* Finally, by using a padded fork and taking very small bites, I was able to use my left hand to get food inside my mouth.

Walking: the final goal. My ability to run great distances had always been one of my strengths. Walking sounded painful, but it was also the goal I felt most excited about. Plus, they told me that if I could walk, I could do shorter stints in the chair. Anything, to get out of that chair!

The first day I tried to walk, I managed three or four steps away from the bed. At that point, I started to collapse. I had to be half-carried back.

The next day, I was determined to beat my record. My goal was to double it, but I did better than that—I took around ten or twelve steps. I went far enough to escape my ICU room! For once, the screams from the shower room that reached me as I ventured into the hallway felt like a celebration, rather than a reminder of the next morning's torture. Ten steps was a far cry from the distance I used to be able to run, but it was a heck of a lot better than sitting in that chair.

Finally, I could see *progress*. It was addictive.

Each step brought me closer to the step-down unit, and getting discharged by October 15.

Each step brought me closer to redeployment: getting back to Afghanistan with my soldiers.

At the end of the day, I would study the crew pictures from West Point that Mother had taped next to my bed and remind myself: *This is the slog in the rowing tanks. This is working on technique, without force. It doesn't feel like you're getting stronger, but you are. This is going to make you a better leader. This is the work that gets you back with the team.*

I measured my days according to how much further I had gone than the day before. I made it my personal challenge—a competition with myself. Moving my limbs in any capacity meant moving and stretching melted skin, subjecting my nerves to new agonies. Every inch was painful, but the progress kept me motivated.

On the third day, I managed to walk partway down the hallway *and then back*. My nurses looked at me dubiously, as though expecting me to collapse. "I'm exploring!" I said through the bandages. "I want to see something different!" How far could I get?

I loved seeing the surprise on the faces of the medical staff. All the therapists and nurses seemed incredulous by how far I was going, which egged me on. *If they were impressed by that yesterday, how much farther can I go tomorrow?!*

It was the first moment I had felt anything positive. Painful—but positive.

"You keep at it, you'll walk yourself right out of this ICU," one of the therapists quipped.

Walk out of the ICU. Why *shouldn't* I walk out of the ICU? The next day, that's what I set my sights on. With each painful step, I stared at the double doors leading into the main hospital corridor, eager to see what was beyond them. For the vast majority of my life, I had *explored.* I'd explored the wilderness around our property in Arkansas. I'd explored new wildernesses as a soldier. Since the accident, I'd been an object lesson in immobility—but not anymore.

"Let's keep going," I said to the physical therapists walking beside me. They pushed open the doors. It was a hallway. A hallway! Something new! Mother—following behind me—let out a little cheer.

I walked farther. This was not territory that would have excited Lewis and Clark: the corridor was long and bland. I passed storage closets and offices. But it felt thrilling to have taken myself beyond the confinement of the ICU; each new discovery felt exhilarating.

The corridor opened to a large, central, open area. "Sam, you're doing great!" one of the therapists said. "You ready to turn back?"

I was exhausted, but the thought of returning to the ICU was terrible. Suddenly, I had an idea. "Where's the step-down unit?" I asked, muffled by the gauze.

The two therapists locked eyes. "Is that a good idea?" one of them asked the other.

"It's a good idea!" Mother answered. "Come on, Samuel. He can do it," she told the therapists.

They led me down another long corridor, stretching into a different hospital wing. I began to wonder if I'd overestimated my ability to keep going—I nearly felt ready to collapse. But walking this far had resurrected a shred of my old self: the guy who could control his own outcomes. *Keep going,* I thought. *You're one step closer to doing village work again. One step closer to running with your pack on.*

"There it is," one of the therapists said, pointing to another set of double doors. "That's the step-down unit."

"That's where we're going!" Mother crowed behind me. "Today is ICU graduation day!"

They held open the doors, and I managed to step over the threshold. My legs wavered. The therapists quickly moved to support me on either side.

"It's Patient Samuel Brown!" Mother called to the medical staff on the step-down unit. "You've got a new patient, it's Lieutenant Samuel Brown! Please point the way to his room!"

The nurses opened a door halfway down the hall. By the time I finally made it to the room, I needed to collapse. Mother propped me up. "He needs to lie down!" she called urgently.

Two nurses rushed in behind us. "His bed isn't made up yet," one protested.

"No one expected him to just *walk over here,*" the other nurse said.

"Here, put him in the chair. He can do his chair time now," they concluded. "Three hours of chair time."

I let out a muffled groan. *To hell with chair time!* I thought. The walking was supposed to earn me a break from chair time! I looked at Mother in distress.

"He can't do his chair time!" Mother protested. "He's just given everything he has to get here. He needs to rest!"

"Well, we don't have his bed made up yet," a nurse repeated.

"You need to *get* his bed made up, and he needs to lie down!"

The medical staff had identified a course of action and did not intend to deviate. "No," they responded to Mother. "He needs to do his three hours of sit-up time in the chair and eat."

Fuming, but seeing no alternative given that the bed wasn't made, Mother guided me to the chair. I could barely hold my head up. *Wasn't that enough?* I wondered. *Didn't I show them what I was capable of? Do I still have to do more? What do they need to see?*

One of the nurses brought me lunch. I wasn't able to pick up the fork to eat. "Mother, I can't do this," I muttered.

"You have to, Son," she said apologetically. Then she seemed to change her mind. She addressed the nurse again. "He can't even eat."

The nurse was unsympathetic. "Well, he's got to eat before he lies down."

"I want to talk to the head nurse!" Mother spoke loudly and authoritatively, her lilting Arkansas drawl firm as steel. For the first time, I realized how *I* must have sounded giving orders to my troops.

It was Mother versus the Head Nurse. One smiled brightly and cheerfully, offering platitudes of hospitality and polite refusals. One was a bulldozer, refusing to take no for an answer, ready to throw open every hallway door until she found bed linens herself and had managed to tuck in her grown-up son.

Mother won. A hospital worker dragged in a mattress. In short order, a bed was made up and I was finally allowed to lie down.

"I don't believe that being a Christian means I'm supposed to lie down and let people walk all over me or my son," Mother reflected after they'd cleared out of the room, considering the moral implications of her victory. "That's not the kind of Christian I am." She looked down at me. "But it's probably a good idea to get back to the Christian aspect of it, anyway." She pulled her Bible out of her purse and flipped to a passage.

"Second Corinthians 4. *'We never give up. Though our bodies are dying, our spirits are being renewed every day. For our present troubles are small and won't last very long. Yet they produce for us a glory that vastly outweighs them and will last forever!'*"

I was asleep before she finished.

On the step-down unit, everything kicked up a notch.

All the therapies increased. I had to move my joints more to keep the scar tissue from contracting. Walking was supplemented with doing stairs. Each joint had to be moved and stretched. Sometimes, I had the rare experience to interact with other burn patients in the physical therapy room. It was difficult to talk through my mask of gauze—but we were there. Together. Working side by side toward the common mission of healing.

The medical staff was paying particularly close attention to my respiratory system. The inhalation injuries I'd sustained had produced scarring all down my trachea, so there was an aggressive lineup of medications to try to calm down the scarring in that affected area.

Another point of concern was my left index finger. "I don't like the look of it," one doctor told me.

I hadn't seen it. Usually, when the nurses wrapped or unwrapped me, I shut my eyes and tried to go to that quiet place in my mind to block out the pain.

"Obviously, both of your hands were badly burned," he said. *No kidding,* I thought, remembering the agony of when my soldiers pulled off my gloves, tugging off a layer of skin with them. "But this particular finger doesn't appear to be getting good blood flow. I'm concerned it may never regain function. We'll need to keep an eye on it."

This struck me as funny, given that I'd never actually looked at it beneath the thick layers of bandages. "Okay," I agreed, nodding. "I'll keep a close eye on it."

The wound debridement showers still punctuated every morning, but—on the spectrum of pain and bodily trauma—the showers had moved to the lower end of the scale. I wouldn't have believed it if someone had told me those showers would *ever* take on "minor" significance, or that I would have to endure anything much worse.

But: they did, and I did.

The surgeries to harvest donor skin for grafts effectively replaced the showers on the upper end of that spectrum. I'd had skin grafts already, but the grafts had either been taken when I was in the medically induced coma or, later, when I was on ketamine. In the ketamine nightmare, I'd interpreted the skin grafts as taking place in a torture chamber.

Now, lucid—I still sort of felt like the skin grafts belonged in a torture chamber.

Here is how skin grafts work. (Feel free to skip this paragraph if you have a weak stomach.) Picture a cheese slicer with an electric blade. Using a tool like that, a medical professional runs that slicer over the burn victim's healthy skin to harvest a thin strip about three to four inches wide, and anywhere from six to fifteen inches long, at about half the depth of the epidermis. In my case, they collected that skin from my sides, my back, and the unburned parts of my legs. That thin strip is called a partial thickness skin graft. In order to maximize the healing potential of that strip of skin, it's perforated, using a device that punches holes in it like a meat tenderizer. Then, the graft is able to be stretched out onto a larger surface of the affected burn area. Ideally—provided the graft site has proper blood flow and the patient is getting the proper nutrition—the graft eventually reintegrates into the body and grows back over the wound.

The only trouble was that my body's epidermis wasn't healing *or* scarring the way it was supposed to. The trauma of getting burns on most of my body had kicked my scarring response into hyperdrive.

"It's called hypertrophic scarring," the doctor explained to me. "It means your scarring response doesn't know how to turn itself off, so it keeps adding layers of new scar tissue. Sort of like your skin doesn't know when to quit." He smirked. "Have you always been this much of an overachiever?"

His comment caught me off guard. "Yes," I said, with a chuckle.

"Well, I think we can expect your burn areas to continue piling on tissue until we can get grafts to effectively 'take.' That's why these areas are getting thicker and more red—" He pointed to an area of my face. Instantly, I felt self-conscious. *IS my face getting thicker and more red?* I wondered.

"Do you have a mirror I could use?" I asked. It was a rare moment when my face was unwrapped. I hadn't seen myself outside of my mummy-wrap in weeks.

"Let's go look in the bathroom," he prompted.

In the bathroom, under the bright fluorescent lights, I stared at my reflection. I was leaner than I'd ever seen myself—my cheekbones jutted out and I noticed sharpness around my collarbone. I could also see my shoulders had narrowed. Much of the muscle I used to have was gone. My face, as he'd pointed out, was red in parts, and the skin seemed slightly thicker than before.

But I still recognized myself. Beneath it all, I still looked like *me*.

That's not SO *bad,* I thought. I remembered my goal and felt a thrill wash through me. *A few more months of therapy and I could be ready to put on a uniform again.*

The next day, I decided to inform my doctors and the medical staff about my goal. They should understand how motivated I was. "I'm planning to discharge by or before my birthday, October 15," I told them.

"It's ambitious, but you're doing well," they agreed. "It's worth shooting for."

"Then, I'm planning to redeploy," I continued. "I'm going to get back to my platoon in Afghanistan. Step into my leadership role again."

This statement was met by an awkward silence. Two of the nurses looked at each other uneasily, then looked at the doctor.

"I think you should plan on a lengthy healing process," this doctor said. "It's highly unlikely that you will ever be able to return to your duties as an Infantry Officer. And it's impossible to think you would be able to return to your current deployment. Most burn victims are looking at a healing timeline of *years,* not months."

I didn't say it out loud, but my thoughts shot back at this. *I'M not most burn victims.* This doctor didn't know me. He didn't know what I was capable of.

"I'm hitting every goal you give me," I pointed out. "I'm beating everyone's expectations."

"Yes, but... Well." The doctor smiled patiently. "I just think it would be wise to temper your expectations."

I made up my mind to do the opposite. I had done it at West Point. I had overcome injury in Ranger School. This was the exact same, only bigger: bigger injury, bigger adversity, steeper learning curve, greater potential for coming back even stronger.

That evening, Mother brought a rented DVD for us to watch: *Ratatouille*. I'd never seen it before. The antics of the animated mouse and the hapless human chef he controlled made me laugh out loud.

"You just laughed," Mother said. I looked over at her. She had tears in her eyes. "That's the first time I've heard you laugh since the accident."

"It's funny," I said. Inside, I felt energized. I was blowing past healing milestones. I had a goal. I still recognized myself—my old self. I *could* laugh.

"Hearing you laugh makes me feel like things are going to be okay," Mother said warmly. She reached over and patted my bandaged paw. Then we turned our attention back to the movie.

The next day produced a dimmer outlook.

They'd asked Mother to come in earlier than usual. "If Sam hopes to check out by October 15, we'll need to train you to be his non-medical attendant," they'd informed her. "You'll need to take over the wound debridement and the bandage wrapping and unwrapping." She agreed to come the next morning after they'd unwrapped me, to practice the debridement process.

I don't think it occurred to anyone that Mother hadn't ever seen me without my bandages on. I'd gotten so used to being unwrapped and wrapped up again every day that I forgot she'd never seen it. Apparently, none of the medical staff thought to warn her either.

As soon as she entered the room and saw me mostly naked, she began crying. I heard her sobs even before I saw her. When I turned around, she had sunk into a chair and was covering her mouth with her hands, staring at my body in horror.

I felt terrible. "I'm sorry, Mother," I said. Inwardly, I felt a stab of disappointment. *It's not SO bad, is it? Can't you still recognize me?*

"Your back, Samuel…"

I hadn't seen my back, but that's where they'd taken large grafts from. Did it look terrible? A voice inside reassured me: *That won't be visible under your uniform. No one needs to see that part.* "I'm sorry, Mother," I repeated.

"You shouldn't be sorry," she sobbed. "I'm just…I'm just so sad to think of the pain you're in." She covered her eyes with her hands, folded into the chair, and wept.

Finally, seeming to steady herself, she rose up and walked over to me. Her eyes were still wet, but she seemed determined to face reality. She rested her fingertips gently on my shoulders. "Right here, where they put the grafts… They kinda look like my mother's ten-minute steaks," she said, gulping out something between a laugh and a sob. She gently touched my back. "I can see where your normal skin is, between your shoulder blades…and under your arms."

She smiled at me, her eyes shiny. "I'm just… It's hard for me to not think of my baby boy. Your perfect, smooth little baby skin." Her voice caught with another sob.

"I'm sorry, Mother," I repeated.

She made herself firm. "I guess this is the clearest visual so far of the fact that you were on fire. Now I see how much damage it did to your body."

Her words were sobering. I didn't *want* people to see me as this damaged. I wanted them to see how I was getting stronger.

"Mrs. Brown?" I heard a tentative voice from a nurse behind us. "Do you feel ready to try the wound debridement? It's time for Sam's shower."

Mother looked at me again, her voice wavering. "Back up in the ICU, Samuel explained about the showers to me," she said, apparently speaking to the nurse. "He said it made him feel like a slab of meat on a meat counter. He cried just thinking about going in there, getting sprayed and scrubbed to get the dead skin off." She stopped and shut her eyes tight. "It's just hard to think of what my son has endured."

The nurse looked from Mother, to me, then back to Mother again. "We can try this a different day."

"NO," Mother said loudly. "No. I've got to do this if Samuel's going to be discharged by his birthday. Isn't that right? It's on me." She turned to the nurse and nodded her head. "Show me what to do."

They gave Mother a water suit to wear and a scrubbing brush. Just before exiting the room, they gave me the two milligrams of Dilaudid. On the way to the shower room, we could hear the screams from other patients.

"Samuel, we can do this," Mother said, raising her voice to be heard over the screams. "I'm just going to turn off being your mother for the next little while and be your medical attendant."

In the shower room, the nurse beside Mother called out instructions. "You've got to scrub his skin, like this," the nurse said. Mother scrubbed. I knew it was too gentle. "You've got to scrub harder than that!" the nurse called.

She pressed down and dug the brush into me. I began crying. "Please, Mother—please don't," I begged.

"Samuel," she said firmly, "This must be done, and we have to do it." She moved the brush in great, hard circles. "Am I doing it right?" she called to the nurse.

"Yes, that's right!"

Mother managed to endure my screams and pleas that she stop. And I managed to endure her scrubbing.

Back in the room, they taught her how to rewrap me. As usual, the process took several hours. "You'll need to do this every day," they reminded her.

She nodded, her mouth tight.

At last we were through both the shower and the wrapping. As the medical staff filed out, Mother turned off the lights.

Much later, we were awakened by a cell phone ring. Afternoon light shone laterally into the darkened room—we must have been asleep for several hours. Mother squinted at the phone. "It says 'Unavailable,'" she said. "Hello?" Her eyes brightened and she smiled at me. "It's Steven Smith. Here." She held the phone up to my ear.

"Steven?! Buddy!"

"How are you doing, LT?" he asked. "Man, it's good to hear your voice!"

I tried to sit up. "I'm doing great! I'm healing fast. I'm beating everyone's expectations."

"Aw, man, that's awesome, Lieutenant! We're thinking of you every day. It's great to hear you're healing fast."

I felt a rush of adrenaline. "That's right. I'm working to get back with you guys. You need your old Platoon Leader!"

Steven's voice changed. "Well…actually, LT…we were assigned a new Platoon Leader."

The words felt like a punch in the gut. *Assigned a new Platoon Leader.*

I couldn't speak. Mother continued holding the phone to my ear, but I just sat there, dumbfounded. My thoughts boiled. *How could they do that? Those were MY guys. Has the military given up on me already? Doesn't anyone believe I'm coming back?*

After a long pause, Steven spoke again. "Don't worry, LT, we like you better," he said awkwardly.

"Well…" I tried to unscramble my thoughts. "Well—tell him not to get too comfortable. It's just a temporary assignment. I'm going to get my old job back."

Who can I call? I wondered. *What high brass do I phone to say, "HEY, here I am! I'm recovering fast. I'm sorry I had to be gone for a little while, but I'm coming back just as fast as I can. Don't give up on me yet!"*

Steven changed the subject. He talked more about the guys, how everyone was doing. He filled me in on how the rest of the night of the explosion had unfolded. "Once your Humvee exploded, all the Taliban left First Platoon alone and headed to attack you guys. That's how Lieutenant Wallace was freed up to send you all his vehicles. The Taliban put up a pretty good fight, even though Anthony and the others were giving it to 'em good too. The Air Force ended up taking care of business with a couple of 2,000-pounders. That took out the rest of them."

I only half heard his words. I hadn't thought of the mission once since that night. How was that possible? Even stranger, I found I didn't care. All I cared about was the fact that I'd been replaced. *Assigned a new Platoon Leader.*

Mother seemed to notice my distraction. She pulled the phone away. "I think we'd better say goodbye," she said to Steven. "Samuel's looking a little tired."

That frustrated me. "Let me say goodbye," I said. She brought the phone over again. "Tell the guys I say hello. And tell them I'll see them soon. I'm healing fast and I'm coming back."

"Sounds good, LT. We're rooting for you."

The call went dead. A long silence filled the room. Mother finally broke it. "You doin' okay, Son?"

"Fine."

Another long pause. *Assigned a new Platoon Leader.* I couldn't believe it. Was I that easy to replace?

"Do you want to pray togeth—"

Mother was interrupted by a doctor's entrance. He pushed open the door and flipped on the lights. I blinked in the harsh brightness.

"Sam Brown. I'm Dr. White, one of the staff surgeons. I think we need to make a decision about that finger." He grabbed the room's second chair and pulled it to the bed. "I'm recommending amputation."

I stared at him, in disbelief. "Amputation?"

"We could leave it alone and hope for the best, but it's starting to show signs of infection. And there's no sign of its increased blood flow, which means it's unlikely to ever regain its function. If it gets infected, the infection could spread quickly. Then we might be discussing amputating much more than just your finger."

"Such as?" Mother asked.

He looked at her. "Several fingers, possibly. Or the entire hand."

I stared down at my left hand, feeling something like betrayal. *You giving up on me too?* I wanted to demand of my finger. *What's the matter with you?*

I looked back at the doctor. "Do you know if an amputated finger would disqualify me from military service?"

He stared at me for a moment, unblinking. After a pause, he said, "No. Soldiers can still fight even if they're missing a finger. But Lieutenant, I think your expectation to return to military service is highly unrealis—"

I cut him off. "Do I need to make this decision right now?"

He paused again. "No. You can take the evening to think it over. I'll come by again in the morning. We should make a decision by tomorrow." He stood up to leave, then paused. "Keep in mind, Lieutenant, you can choose to try to keep the finger and it might be okay… But it also might get a lot worse." He made eye contact with me. "Trying to deny the gravity of what your body is experiencing could end up leading to much more serious long-term consequences."

I was sick of the negativity. "Okay. Let's make the decision tomorrow."

He nodded and left. The door closed slowly.

There was a long pause. I stared down at my left hand. In the corner of the room, I heard Mother digging into her purse. She cleared her throat and began to read.

"We never give up. Though our bodies are dying, our spirits are being renewed every day. For our present troubles are small and won't last very long. Yet they produce for us a glory that vastly outweighs them and will last forever! So we don't look at the troubles we can see now; rather, we fix our gaze on things that cannot be seen. For the things we see now will soon be gone, but the things we cannot see will last forever."

"Samuel…" she said, and hesitated. "Even though parts of your body are dying, your spirit is being renewed."

I didn't answer.

"The real battle is on the inside," she continued. "It's the battle in the mind. Scripture says the physical injuries are just a *'small trouble that won't last long. But they produce a glory that will last forever.'* So—we've got to lift our eyes past the physical. There's an eternal purpose for this. God's preparing you for something that has greater value than what we're going through right here and now. So, we've got to take care of your soul, first and foremost."

I remained silent. I found comfort in her words—but I also struggled with them. This affliction didn't feel light or momentary. In my opinion, it had already gone on far too long. They'd found a new Platoon Leader. My finger needed amputating.

But, I supposed, when compared with eternity—these things felt smaller. I sighed.

Mother seemed to take that as permission to continue. "Samuel, we need to pray and forgive the Taliban for what they did."

I looked over at Mother. "What?"

"The battle's for your mind, Samuel. I want us to make sure we've done everything expected of us to be right with the Lord. Because, Samuel, if you're carrying around anger and bitterness, that can affect your body."

"My body is already affected," I pointed out. "I've had skin cut off—both good and bad. And, they want to cut off my finger."

"I mean it can make it harder for your body to heal. A clean conscience will help you move on. It will help you walk this road." She paused and looked down at her Bible.

I waited. "Do you have another scripture you want to read?"

"Yes. This is from the Sermon on the Mount." She began reading to me out of the book of Matthew. *"Forgive us our sins, as we have forgiven those who sin against us... If you forgive those who sin against you, your heavenly Father will forgive you. But if you refuse to forgive others, your Father will not forgive your sins."*

Forgiveness. That was a hard word. It was easy to feel angry at any number of people—the nurses assigned to my wound debridement showers. Whatever military higher-ups had assigned the new Platoon Leader. The new Platoon Leader, for that matter. The Route Clearance Commander, who hadn't agreed to clear the road.

The Taliban.

I thought of him—the bombmaker. I remembered his face, his angry expression. The black turban. The missing fingers.

It goes back earlier than that, I mused. I thought of the terrorists who had planned 9/11, how many of them had been harbored and hidden among the Taliban in Afghanistan. Memories from the ketamine nightmare swam back: how the war in Afghanistan had seemed to follow me from Kandahar to Mexico—my nightmare of being held as a prisoner of war inside a mosque run by the Taliban.

I guess I am harboring anger, I thought. Anger felt so easy. Maybe it *was* making it harder for my body to heal. "Maybe anger's the thing infecting my finger," I said aloud, trying to joke.

Neither of us laughed. I shut my eyes and leaned my head back against a pillow.

"Look, this is a terrible thing that happened to you—" Her voice caught and trembled. I waited.

"But if there's any spiritual warfare that's going on, based on what happened over there," she continued, "I want to cut those dark powers off right now, in the mighty name of Jesus."

I opened my eyes and looked at her. The sunlight through the window had gotten lower, more golden. It made the bed and chair cast dark shadows on the walls. "Samuel, it may be hard, but would you be willing to forgive them? Maybe they're led by evil to do the things they do. If it's evil that's controlling them, we can forgive the people. Scripture says to 'overcome evil with good.'" She waited. "Will you pray to forgive them, Samuel?"

I felt too tired and too disappointed to resist. "Yes," I said.

We prayed together. When we opened our eyes again, the sun had set. Visiting hours were over.

After she left, I struggled through dinner, the nurses prompting me to grip the fork—"Use your thumb—try again." I tried to remember my goal: redeployment. *I need to grip my fork if I expect to hold a gun.* Somehow, the goal didn't feel as energizing as it usually did, even when I reminded myself that I didn't need my *left* index finger to pull a trigger, just my right.

Mother's Bible readings circled in my head. *Though our bodies are dying, our spirits are being renewed every day.* Was that really the case?

After the medical staff had cleared out of my room, they turned off my lights, but I didn't feel ready to sleep yet. I turned to look at the pictures which Mother had printed out—she'd taken care to remove them all from the ICU room and tape them up again in the step-down unit. My eyes rested at first on the pictures of me rowing at West Point.

You could come back stronger, like you did before, a voice said inside.

Tonight, the pep talk felt like an empty boast.

My eyes landed on the picture of me with a group of Afghan children. It was a picture of me squatting next to a passel of Afghan kids—maybe ten of them. They had huge grins, especially the boy standing right next to me. Even the oldest boy on the end of the line, wearing a turban as though he was already a man, had a small smile, as though he couldn't help himself.

I remembered that day. After every picture, the kids had demanded to see their faces on the digital screen of my camera, and then they laughed like crazy. Few of them had ever seen their reflection in a mirror. They were excited to get their picture taken—they wanted to see their digital images, again and again.

With Afghan children in a small village. We were using my digital camera to take pictures so they could see themselves on the screen. August 2008.

I studied the picture, noticing the two older men in the background. They were smiling too. One wore a black turban.

The night before the picture had been taken, we'd received rocket fire at our FOB. We knew what direction it had come from and roughly how far the rocket would have been able to travel. When we'd driven out to the area the next morning to investigate, a little family compound was the only thing we'd found.

We'd called out a greeting, entered the compound, hoping to determine if they were friendly or if we'd need to worry about them shooting rockets at us again.

They'd waved us in as though we were friends. Showed me into a small house. Offered me tea and some candies. Through an interpreter, they explained the Taliban had driven up next to their compound in the middle of the night and launched the rocket. It had nothing to do with them, they insisted.

I didn't know if they were telling the truth or not. But I drank the tea and ate the candies. We made small talk. I remember wondering, *Am I talking to someone who genuinely appreciates the help we're trying to provide? Or is this someone who wants to destroy me?*

Maybe they were only being polite because they weren't in a position to fight us at that moment and survive another day. It occurred to me that when we rolled up thirty-strong, wearing body armor and carrying machine guns, they might have the same questions about us: *Are these soldiers here to help us? Or destroy us?*

We gave them information about how to contact us if the Taliban showed up again, then finished the tea and headed back outside. That's when the kids surrounded us. That's when the laughter began.

They were just like any other kids in the world. They were running around, some were playing make believe, some of the other ones were playing hide and seek. When they got too rambunctious, one of the adults checked them with a stern remark—just like my mother had with my brothers and me when we were growing up.

Now, in the step-down unit room—nearly two months after that photo—I stared at the kids' faces in the picture. A six-year-old with gaps in his smile from a newly lost tooth. A serious-looking toddler in her big brother's arms, her head bent under his protective hold. A taller boy with a fresh, open, eager smile. A shorter child with curious, probing eyes. The boy standing next to me, mid-laugh.

What's going to become of you? I wondered. *Are you going to grow up and try to support the Afghan government? Are you going to become members of the Taliban? Are some of you going to die young? Will some of you try to escape Afghanistan and live somewhere else, less plagued by war?*

Somehow, thinking of the kids I'd met took me to an emotional place that went further back than anger, that was deeper down than grief. It took me to something resembling basic humanity. I thought of Mother's comment earlier—"I just remember my baby boy." All of us started off playing make believe, playing hide and seek. We all were susceptible to doing the wrong thing, on both an individual and collective level. Each person was responsible for their own actions, yes—but also, each person made mistakes. None of us were perfectly objective about what was right.

The lines of scripture came back to me. *If you forgive those who sin against you, your heavenly Father will forgive you.*

I thought of the bombmaker: the man who'd likely planted the explosives that had killed Winston, wounded three of my other soldiers, and changed my life forever.

He'd been a kid once. Maybe he'd been brought up to fight foreigners, to defend his country.

Now he was missing fingers.

And tomorrow, I was likely to lose one too.

A part of me pushed back against any inclination to humanize him. *He is a murderer. Even if we're all human, there should still be consequences,* I considered, lying there in the dark. *People still need to be held accountable if they commit evil acts.*

But the philosophizing exhausted me. I felt too tired to be angry anymore, too discouraged to hang on to bitterness. *Maybe I can just trust that God will bring the justice that he deserves.*

Wrapped in gauze in that hospital bed, my job wasn't to hold anyone accountable at that moment. My job was simply to heal—internally and externally. *I* wanted God's grace and forgiveness and love. The Bible said He'd given it to me. In return, He asked me to give grace, forgiveness, and love to others.

It seemed like a fair request.

I prayed for God's help to forgive the people who'd been responsible for my pain. And I prayed for the kids in the picture—that they would be safe and blessed.

As I fell asleep, I was still thinking of their faces.

The next morning, the surgeon came back.

"Well?" he asked.

Saying yes to the amputation meant choosing to permanently remove a part of myself, to acknowledge that part of me had become so damaged—so beyond repair—that it now posed a threat to other, healthier parts of me. It meant recognizing that a full recovery would never actually occur. It meant my physical body would be permanently altered, permanently changed, permanently disfigured.

Mother looked at me. I could guess at her thoughts. *Though our bodies are dying, our spirits are being renewed every day.*

I looked at the surgeon and gave a quick nod.

"Cut it off."

CHAPTER 8

LIFE CONTRACTED

Airborne Ranger aspirations took hold early. Me, around the summer of 1986.

We started in the dark, before sunrise.

Scrambling through bushes and peering through dim moonlight in an attempt to get my bearings, I'd gotten off course somehow. The contours of the terrain looked so much different than the lines on the map. Had I already passed the ridge? I studied the map's depiction of landmarks with a red-lens flashlight, then erased my pencil lines. This wasn't good.

I needed to reset. I needed to reorient myself to the physical reality of my surroundings. After another long glance at the map, my compass, and the shadowy curves of the land, I set off again—hoping I'd recalibrated successfully.

It was no use. When the sun finally came up after 6:00 a.m., I was lost. My mission had been to complete the Land Navigation course within five hours. At 8:30 a.m., the five-hour mark, I knew that I had spent too much time searching for one of my points.

It was a failure.

I'd done Land Navigation courses before, but this was the first time I'd failed one. I was a strong navigator, and even in those rare cases when I got off, I was able to use my speed to catch back up. Physical endurance and speed were my calling cards. In a short sprint, I was easily bested, but over long distances, I was unbeatable. Even with an eighty- or hundred-pound pack on my back, I could move quickly and even run. But this time around, I didn't have that advantage.

Instead, I was nursing a painful knee injury.

That right knee was turning out to be my Achilles' heel: it was the same knee that had been an issue at West Point, but it felt like a different injury—the pain was in a different spot. In the couple of weeks before Ranger School officially started, I'd been doing a group workout with a bunch of other Lieutenants and a Staff Sergeant who had already completed Ranger School. The sergeant was leading it, taking us through high-intensity plyometric exercises. We were jumping up and down off a small, elevated platform when I landed badly. I felt a shooting, burning pain along the outer side of my right knee.

I figured it would be fine. Infantry soldiers don't complain about injuries. You grit your way through. You don't whine, you don't go see a doctor, you don't even bother with ibuprofen. You just trust your body to tough it out and heal on its own.

Except my body didn't seem to be doing much healing. The knee didn't get any better in the remaining three weeks before Ranger School started. If anything, it seemed to get worse.

On the first day of Ranger School, we had a physical fitness test: push-ups, sit-ups, pull-ups, and a five-mile run which needed to be completed within forty minutes. In my training up to the knee injury, I would complete that run at a 6:10 minute/mile pace with over nine minutes of spare time. But the pain of this injury forced me to slow down. I limped my way through the five-mile run, finishing just under the forty-minute deadline.

Day Two was the Land Navigation test. I had never failed on a course like this, normally finishing in the top five percent. So, despite suffering terrible pain in my knee, I had no concerns until I found myself struggling to find the second point of my map and validate it with the unique stamp tethered to a post at that precise location. I lost almost an hour scouring an area I was convinced it was at. Finally, I realized I didn't have enough time to get my remaining points.

I had failed a Land Nav course for the first time in my life, and now my knee was the worst it had been in weeks.

I got one chance to retest. Just one. If I failed again, I could be kicked out for failing to meet the rigorous Ranger School standards. My only hope would be to appeal to the Battalion Commander directly.

Day Three of Ranger School, like the previous day, started before 4:00 a.m. There were only a few of us that hadn't passed and needed to retest. As we congregated around the Ranger Instructor for a repeat of the same guidelines we received just twenty-four hours ago, I glanced into the dark night sky and registered the cloud cover. No moonlight this time.

And my knee was killing me.

I was moving too slow to risk getting lost again—there was no chance of catching up if I made any errors. I decided there was only one way I was going to finish the test on time: using my compass, I'd plot a straight line to the point I was trying to get to. I would force my way through whatever terrain was on that straight line. I wouldn't attempt to follow certain terrain features, or use some other technique to get there quickly. I was just going to go *straight*, bush-whacking and stream-fording as needed.

About an hour into the course when it was still dark, I was staring down at the glowing compass, pushing through dense woods. I wasn't looking up or paying attention to the gaps in the trees; I was focused on staying true to the azimuth that would lead me to my next point. Suddenly, I caught a stick in my eye.

Mother fu… I rubbed my eye, trying to get out the grit that I could feel under my eyelid. Why did it hurt *so bad?*

I closed the hurt eye, trying to squint down at my compass with the good one. But that eye, in apparent solidarity with the other one, had started watering profusely.

I hobbled forward, feeling increasing desperation. I couldn't see clearly and I could barely walk. I thrashed through the trees, plunging forward, knowing that I was likely forging ahead in futility.

The sun finally rose, but that made things worse. Both eyes reacted to the light with severe sensitivity. The realization dawned on me as the sun's rays intensified: I was going to fail again. I had no chance of meeting my goal. I was too blind, too hurt, too lost.

The Ranger Instructors confirmed this. "Failure," they said out loud when I finally reached the rendezvous point.

Later that day—after I was informed at the infirmary that my bushwhacking had led to a severe corneal abrasion—I stood before the Battalion Commander. Embarrassingly, my eyes were still watering.

He sized me up and down. "Well, Lieutenant Brown. You failed."

"Yes, Sir."

"Am I to believe your poor performance over the past three days should be considered an exception?"

"I believe so, Sir. I'm dealing with an injured knee. I was much slower than usual on the course. I'm sure it will heal up if you allow me to recycle, Sir."

He looked down at his desk. "We have high expectations of all Infantry Officers, Lieutenant Brown. You appear to have performed well in your prior training. And your previous PT test results are exemplary."

"Thank you, Sir."

"Your performance thus far at Ranger School has been very disappointing."

"Yes, Sir."

He took a long look at me. I straightened up and pulled my shoulders back, trying to make the most of my height. Before the knee injury, I'd been in the best shape of my life. I had more muscle on my frame than I'd ever had before. I was young, strong, fit, and good-looking. If any part of him was making this decision based on my physicality—surely, I'd get his approval.

He finally nodded. "I'm approving your request to recycle, Lieutenant. You can start again with the next class in three weeks. I don't want to see you in this office again."

"Yes, Sir!"

I had failed—but it wasn't the end.

My military ambitions hadn't been shut down yet. I still had every opportunity to go on and become the leader that I'd set out to become. It was a *momentary* failure, not a missional failure.

Now, I just had to make sure I never failed again.

* * *

Mother and I during the early days of my recovery.

On October 10—five days before my twenty-fifth birthday—I was discharged from the hospital.

It was a bit anticlimactic. I would be living in the Extended Stay hotel, just across the street. And going to the hospital would still be my full-time job.

But we told ourselves it was a victory. "You did it!" Mother cheered as we exited the hospital lobby. "Five days ahead of schedule!"

We entered our hotel room. There was a kitchen off to one side and a stiff-looking couch in front of a TV. The couch was gray; the paint was gray; the light filtering in through the window was gray. On one wall, there was a generic black-and-white picture of some sort of plant. One door led into the bedroom, which had two queen-sized beds and contained the bathroom. The whole apartment felt dark and sterile.

"Home sweet home," I remarked.

"Be thankful." Mother batted me with her hand. "It's better than the hospital."

The new routine began. My first appointment was physical therapy in the morning. These PT tests were a far cry from my military training. Mainly, we worked on building back my ability to just… move. My range of motion, due to the contracting scar tissue, needed constant attention. We stretched my scar tissue and tried to keep my joints moving. This was more labor intensive than it sounds: every single joint was at risk of becoming permanently stuck if I didn't stretch and work it every day. Since my hands had gotten burned, for instance, each finger needed to be stretched, moved, and exercised so that my hands weren't permanently contracted into immobile claws.

The splints helped with this, which was usually appointment number two. The splints were intended to help during the times I slept or relaxed—those times when the contracting scar tissue would otherwise have a chance to set in and undo whatever progress had been made in PT. By sticking my hands and arms into various splints, my limbs were held in a position that maintained some stretch even while I was relaxing or sleeping. These splints were tailor-made, built by technicians working with the therapists to correct my particular warping.

"This reminds me of that time we went to the tailor to get you a suit for prom," Mother said cheerfully one day as the PT assistant measured off a piece of plastic that would be molded for a new arm splint.

I thought about that. "I'm not sure which get-up is less comfortable," I said.

After getting fit for a new splint, I would usually head to the hospital cafeteria for lunch. The first appointment of the afternoon was the burn clinic, either to do pre-op work or post-op wound care. I needed reconstructive surgeries and skin grafts basically everywhere, so I was always either recovering from surgery or preparing for the next one.

Then came another hour of therapy, this time with the occupational therapist. We did cool things like add padding around the handles of my silverware so I could more easily hold them and not drop food all over myself. (I still dropped food all over myself.) Sometimes, they introduced me to a new tool to help me bathe more effectively. Dwelling on how *easy* it used to be to lift a fork and put food in my mouth, or how *easy* it used to be to get ready in the morning—ten minutes, from waking up to running out the door—only depressed me. So, I just didn't think about how far removed all this was from my pre-explosion days.

Instead, I focused on the next goal: straightening my fingers. Graduating from a bandaged face to pressure garments. Walking a mile on the treadmill.

Life required accepting small, incremental gains. But it was easy to lose patience with that—I wanted a breakthrough. I wanted something impressive to report to the guys, the next time they called from Afghanistan. Perhaps because of that, once I saw progress in a certain area, my temptation was to push harder for continued progress *there*. But given that I had a very finite amount of energy, when I favored one part of my body, I ended up neglecting other areas. My left elbow, for instance, was the most stubborn of my joints. Even as I was regaining function, mobility, and strength in other areas of my body, that left elbow was a challenge. It just couldn't get unstuck.

Eventually, I grew impatient with my left elbow. I stopped focusing on improvement there and directed my energy to drive for more range of motion in other joints where I *could* see progress. Years later though, I had many moments to regret that I didn't push harder. I never did regain full function over that left elbow which also meant I never regained full strength in that arm. A failure.

Scattered throughout the day were other appointments: if I wasn't with occupational therapy, I would be in another clinic or appointment for a range of things like evaluating my brain for Traumatic Brain Injury, talking to a psychologist to keep up on my mental health, meeting with my nurse case manager to go over my upcoming week or review past appointment and test results, or waiting for the pharmacy to hand me another bag full of narcotic pain killers and other medications.

Once this new daily grind at the hospital was done, I headed to the hotel. Mother and I ate dinner—usually something we'd bought from the hospital cafeteria. Meal time, for her, must have been a flashback to my baby days. She had to help feed me and clean up my mess afterwards.

We spent an hour or two unwrapping my bandages. Then it was time for the wound debridement shower. We spent several more hours *re*wrapping me.

And then we both passed out: another day gone.

I missed the days defined by a clear mission, with set objectives. I missed having my team around me. What was my mission now? "To heal." It felt non-specific and also kind of impossible.

"You're making *such* good progress," Mother said one night at dinner. "Everyone at the hospital says so."

The bite of penne pasta I was aiming toward the tiny opening of my mouth couldn't fit through. It pressed against my face and fell onto the plate.

"I know it may not feel like you're making a lot of progress." Mother watched me grip the padded fork and go after the noodle again. "But… you really *are*," she repeated.

I nodded, pretending to agree with her.

On the morning of October 13, Mother announced that she had made plans for us to celebrate my birthday.

"What? What do you mean?" I asked.

"We're having a special guest!"

"Who?" I asked.

"His name is Cliff," she answered.

I stared at her, confused. "Who is *Cliff?*"

"Your Battalion Executive Officer put me in touch with him. Major Ruth."

Major Stephen Ruth had been a professor at West Point, and ended up being the Executive Officer of my Battalion as well. Like Austin Wallace, he'd been one of the few people to see me through both my West Points days and my deployment. Hearing his name made me miss him. "But...who is Cliff?" I asked again.

"Cliff is his old friend. They were both at Texas A&M together and he lives right here, in San Antonio. Major Ruth called him up and told him that one of his soldiers and former West Point grads was at Brooke Army Medical Center, and he asked Cliff to come see you since he couldn't be there himself. So, he's coming for your birthday!"

"Oh," I said.

Spending my birthday with a stranger didn't sound like the best time. But I wasn't about to reject someone Major Ruth had sent my way.

That evening at dinner, Mother got a call from Cliff. She pulled the phone away and turned to me. "He wants to know what you want for your birthday," she said.

I stared at her. What did I *want?* There were a lot of things I wanted. Most of them couldn't be brought to a birthday party. "He said he could rent you a video game console?" she asked. "Would that be fun?"

I shook my head. I wasn't interested in a video game console. I stared down at the take-out containers from the hospital cafeteria. "A home-cooked meal," I said.

The night of my birthday, I met Cliff Dugosh. He showed up

with two brown paper grocery bags: one full of ingredients, and the other containing a filled casserole dish and a spatula. He wore a sweater vest, stood with a slight stoop, and had thinning hair. He smiled warmly when Mother opened the door. His eyes found me. I appreciated that he didn't flinch at my appearance. "Happy birthday, Soldier," he said.

"Thank you, Sir."

Mother waved him in. He headed for the kitchen and turned the oven on. "It's not 'Sir.' I'm a civilian. You can just call me Cliff."

"What is it you do, Cliff?" Mother asked.

He beamed at her. "Well, I do my best to serve the Lord and serve people. That's my main mission in life."

"Are you in the ministry?" she asked.

"I certainly hope so!" he said, smiling again. It struck me that I hadn't seen him *not* smiling since he walked in. "But not at a church. Well—not in a paid capacity, anyway. I don't *work* doing full-time ministry, but I tend to think about life as full-time ministry. I'm not married and I don't have children, so I do my best to just give all my time to the Lord. I do a fair bit of volunteering. I spend most of my working hours as a substitute teacher." He beamed again.

"A substitute teacher?" Mother asked. "For…children?"

"I'll go wherever the district needs me, but mostly, I'm at the high school. It is a real privilege to get to interact with young people. I also do a little bit of motivational speaking and leadership training on the side. That helps supplement my income." He looked at me. "But I think I'm talking too much about myself. It's not my party. Sam, I'd love to hear more about you."

I cleared my throat uneasily. I'd never had any trouble answering this question before the accident—I had plenty of things to share about myself. But none of my old distinctions seemed relevant anymore. These days, when people met me for the first time, their immediate question was "What *happened?*" I didn't want to talk about Afghanistan—not tonight, on my birthday. What was there to talk about? Did he want to know my therapy routine?

He looked me right in the eyes and grinned warmly. "Tell me what kind of instructor my buddy Stephen Ruth was at West Point."

I relaxed. If my mouth could have grinned back, I would have. "He was great," I said. "He wasn't even my professor, but he still invested in a relationship with me. I got to know Major Ruth when I'd visit one of my best friends from the crew team in his class. Major Ruth didn't ignore me, like other professors might have, since I wasn't his student. He asked me questions and acted genuinely interested in getting to know me. Plus, I thought it was cool that he was a Texas A&M grad, not a West Point grad like a lot of the other profs."

"That's right!" Cliff beamed. "An Aggie, like me. That's where we became close."

As I shared about West Point and Major Ruth, Cliff continued to prep dinner, putting the casserole he'd brought into the oven and washing lettuce for a salad. He asked me questions periodically, getting me to elaborate. Sometimes he pointed out connections between things I'd said. His questions conveyed genuine interest—like he cared to know more about my experiences and understand more about my thoughts.

In his company, it became somehow possible for minutes at a time to forget I was a burn patient. With Cliff, I was simply a young man.

Mother prayed for our meal when we all sat down at the table. Cliff's casserole was cheesy and warm—good, classic, comfort food. He didn't ask me questions about my padded fork. He didn't seem to notice when I spilled food. Instead, he wanted to know about some of the other soldiers I'd met on the burn unit. "How are they doing?" he asked.

"They're doing okay… Well, I guess it depends on the soldier," I said. "Some guys have more minor wounds and others are in much worse condition than me. My injuries are pretty bad. But I'm progressing better than a lot of them."

"Huh. What do you credit that to?" he asked. He looked at Mother and his eyes twinkled. "Good genes?"

Mother straightened up. "I think it's because of his faith," she said.

Cliff looked back at me. "Is that right, Sam?"

I nodded. Suddenly, I wanted to tell him a bit about the accident—at least, about the part that mattered. "When I was on fire in the desert, I thought I was all alone. I couldn't see through the flames, and I thought I was going to die. I threw up my hands and yelled, 'Jesus, save me!'" Cliff nodded intently, but didn't interject. "In the hospital...Mother has been reading a lot of Scripture to me, and it's been encouraging. I guess..." I hesitated.

"Go on," he prompted.

"Well, I believe my life was spared for a reason. Like I'm supposed to live for something bigger now. My life isn't my own anymore—it belongs to God. But I don't know what I'm supposed to do."

He looked at me thoughtfully. "These other soldiers on the burn unit ward," he said. "You said most of them aren't seeing your level of progress?"

I nodded. "It's easy to feel angry or bitter. And I think that can make it hard to engage with the therapies sometimes. It's hard to work at building your life back when you don't think your life is going to be worth much anymore."

"But that's not your problem?"

"No," I responded. "I trust my life has a purpose, even if I don't fully know what that is yet."

Cliff studied me. "Seems like God might have a mission for you right where you're at."

His use of the word *mission* struck me.

A *mission*. Right where I was at.

I watched Cliff clean up our meal after we'd finished—insisting that he do so without any help from Mother or me. As I reflected on our conversation and watched him continue to serve us, it occurred to me that I could serve people around me too, whether I knew them or not. My mission was not simply my own healing—keeping my head down, working on my therapy, seeing the other patients in a competitive light and trying to outpace their progress. If I were to take Cliff as my example, I could be someone who actively sought to engage and serve others, providing them hope, right where I was at.

It didn't require a platoon of soldiers; it didn't require a trip across the world. Cliff hadn't gone far from home at all to find his mission field. He'd found people to serve all around him—and maybe I could too, if I was willing to see them.

Maybe there's an aspect of my mission that's changed, I thought. *Maybe it's not just returning to battle. Maybe there's a new temporary mission assignment: leading and encouraging others right here—like Cliff.*

Before Cliff left that evening, he hugged me. "By the way," he said, "if you ever want to share your testimony of how God met you in the desert, I'd love to invite you to speak at one of the groups I work with. I lead a Christian men's retreat for Texas A&M students during the summer, and another one for professional alumni too. I think they'd be inspired by your story."

Inspired? Yeah, right, I wanted to retort. How could my wrecked body inspire someone?

He hugged Mother goodbye too. "'A woman of valor'," he said to her. "I'll be praying for your strength." He looked back at me. "And praying for your healing and your mission, Sam. And praying for encouragement for you both."

Then he left.

I had the sense that I'd just met a great man.

* * *

The next day, on the burn unit ward, I paid closer attention to the people around me.

Every soldier getting wheeled to the showers, or in a therapy context, or walking down the hall had their own story. They had people who loved them, who were checking in via text or calls to see how they were doing. They had families—some of them, spouses and children. Their plans for their future had been altered, like mine. Most of them had a date on the calendar that was *their* Alive Day.

I wasn't the only one going through a life-altering crisis.

I started to see them in rough categories: some patients were ahead of me on my own path to recovery. They were further along in their surgeries and in their treatment, closer to a finish line, such as it were. Sergeant Adam Clark, for instance—a young Marine Sergeant who'd gotten injured roughly a year before me and had similar injuries. Among the burn unit patients and staffers, Sergeant Clark was considered the model patient. He'd made great progress, engaged with the therapies, and was nearing the end of his treatment. I often saw him on the step-down unit when he came in for therapies, and he inspired me to step up my efforts.

Maybe I can be that kind of example, I thought. *Maybe that's my purpose.* There were plenty of other patients in my same stage of healing, or behind me in their journeys. Maybe I could show them life was worth working toward. I survived. Now I was trying to live. Perhaps I could encourage them to do the same thing.

I didn't have to wait long before trying out my new resolution. That afternoon, I heard yelling from one of the therapy rooms. I couldn't make out exactly what was being said, but a few curse words came through loud and clear, and the interjections seemed to interrupt the voices of the medical staff. The person yelling was obviously being hostile.

One of the nurses hurried out of the room. It was Betsy, who'd become close enough to Mother and me that I called her Auntie Bet. She had tears in her eyes.

"Auntie Bet. You okay?" I asked.

"Sam." She impatiently wiped a tear from her cheek as it spilled out of her eye. "I wonder if you could talk to Captain Ortiz. Maybe you could get through to him. None of us can."

"He's a Captain?" I asked.

"Special Forces Captain, I think." She lowered her voice. "And he's being an *asshole.*"

"Special Forces is what I want to do. That's my dream job in the Army."

"Well, I hope this gentleman could aspire to be a little more like *you,* than you aspire to be like *him.*" She put a hand on my shoulder. "So. Will you talk to him?"

I nodded.

That afternoon, I knocked on his door and slowly opened it. Captain Paul was lying in his bed, scowling.

"Hey, man," I said. Based on what I could see, his burns were similar to mine—except his face wasn't as bad. "I'm First Lieutenant Sam Brown. First Infantry Division."

He gave me a once over. "Captain Paul Ortiz."

"What unit were you with?"

He sighed, as though the question irritated him. "Tenth Special Forces Group. Alpha Team leader."

"Right on," I said, impressed. "That's my dream job." He stared straight ahead at the blank wall, his face still in a scowl. "Looks like we both got pretty well torched. IED?"

He nodded, silently.

"Except your face is better than mine," I pointed out.

He glanced over at me, then looked back at the wall. "Probably because of my beard," he muttered.

"You had a beard? Ah, because you were Special Forces. Yeah, I was clean shaven. Look at me now," I cracked. I touched my scabby, swollen face. "Not exactly as smooth as a baby's butt."

He didn't answer. I tried again. "So…what was going on this morning? I heard some yelling out of your room."

His scowl deepened. "Yeah, because they're not giving me the pain meds I need. I'm not about to do their fucking therapy when I'm in so much fucking pain and they won't give me any more fucking pain meds."

Now *I* felt irritated. But I tried to remember my new mission—to encourage. "I know it hurts. *Clearly*, I know it hurts. I'm not much further ahead of you. But if you refuse to engage in your therapy, that's a disservice to yourself as well as everyone around you who's trying to help you reach your full potential." I stood up and held out my left elbow. "Look." I bent my arm. "That's as far as it goes. Which means I'm probably never going to regain full strength in that arm. You know why? Because I stopped doing the therapy on that joint. I got tired of it. Now, I'm kicking myself. That's what happens if you don't take full advantage and push through with your therapy."

He briefly glanced at my elbow, then slid his eyes back to the wall. "None of them have any idea how fucking painful this is."

"*I* do," I retorted. "I know exactly how painful it is. You think you're avoiding pain right now, but you're actually decreasing your long-term potential for a full recovery. Besides—dude, we can *handle* pain. We made it through Ranger School. You did all the Special Forces training on top of that! We dealt with the pain because people depended on us and we needed to lead them through the mission."

"No one needs me now," he muttered.

"What about your family?" I asked. "Are you married? Do you have kids?"

"Yes, *Lieutenant*," he hissed. "I'm married and my wife stopped coming to visit, thanks for bringing it up." For the first time, he made eye contact with me. "She said all I care about is getting more pain meds. And she doesn't want to 'enable an addiction.' Her words." He shook his head, angrily. "She doesn't get it."

I sat for a moment, sobered by his confession. "Well, I get it," I said. "And *she* needs you. You've got to view healing as your mission. People are depending on you. You can push through this pain to get better. If you don't do the therapy, and you keep sucking down the pain meds, you're just ruining your future. And you're ruining *her* future." I stared at him, feeling admiration, despite his attitude. "You're *Special Forces*, man. Alpha Team Leader!" I urged. "You've got this."

He didn't respond. I wasn't sure if anything I'd said made a difference. I sighed and stood up to leave. "Do me a favor—" I added, before walking out. "Be nicer to the staff. They're just trying to help you."

Weirdly, I felt invigorated by the conversation with Captain Ortiz, even though he hadn't given me any indication I'd been helpful. It still felt good to try to encourage someone. For that window of time, I'd oriented my attention toward someone else. I hadn't been thinking about my own struggles or injuries; I hadn't been indulging in self-pity. I'd used my limited bandwidth to attempt to encourage a fellow wounded soldier who was struggling to find the internal strength to fight for his own recovery. Ironically, it hadn't sapped me; it had given me a boost.

With a shock, I realized that I'd mainly been healing in isolation. Yes, I'd been surrounded by therapists and medical staff—but my focus had mostly been on myself. I had kept my head down and focused on my own path to healing.

For some reason, the thought brought to mind the memory of plunging through the woods in the dark at Ranger School: head down, eyes focused on the compass—who knew if I was aiming right. I hadn't been looking up at my surroundings, and the experience had ended up temporarily blinding me. I'd piled on more injuries rather than successfully and expediently getting to my destination. *Failure.*

Well—what if I lifted my head up? What if, in the midst of feeling my way toward whatever purpose God might have in store for me, I paid attention to the people around me? I didn't really know where I was going, and everything was taking longer than I wanted it to.

But even so—what if I tried acting like a leader again?

If I can't lead my guys in Afghanistan, I thought, *I could still try to lead by example to some of the guys around here.*

I began paying closer attention to everyone around me. Every day, it seemed, there were opportunities to check in with someone, share a bit about my recovery, encourage someone else along their own journey. It wasn't just the patients who needed encouragement either, I realized. Plenty of the staff looked discouraged and tired. I started memorizing their names and tried to remember the snippets they shared with me.

"Hey, Sheila! How'd your son do at the track meet?"

"Mateo. How do you think the Aggies will do this weekend against Texas?"

Initiating those interactions took some effort at first, because I was so used to being inside my own pain and recovery. But once I got started, it was easy to continue. It felt *good* seeing others be encouraged. Eventually, it became easy. Checking in with others became something I looked forward to. They made me feel invigorated with new purpose.

About a week after my interaction with Captain Ortiz, I saw him in the hallway with a Physical Therapist. When Auntie Bet came by my room later, I asked her how he was doing. "Is he still holed up in his room?"

"No!" she said, cheerfully. "He got motivated after you talked to him. He's doing all his therapy now. He even said 'Thank you' to me today. Whatever you said to him must have kicked him in the ass." She smiled. "Another model patient! Like you!"

I grinned. "Well, that's awesome. Do you know if his wife is visiting him again?"

"I wasn't aware that she'd stopped, but she was by this morning."

I nodded, satisfied. *Good.*

The interactions made me want to work harder at my *own* recovery, so that I had more milestones to report. I wasn't necessarily aiming for breakthroughs anymore; I was more content to track the small, incremental gains—mostly because I knew that's what everyone else was tracking also. If I could cheer on Paul's engagement with therapy—couldn't I register my own progress too?

The long-term goal was still to get back to Afghanistan: that was the mission. In the meantime, I wasn't about to waste this moment. I could redeem this time.

* * *

Mother and I started venturing outside of the hospital campus for meals out. The first time was for another celebration: Kevin Jensen, Mike Debolt, and Philip Kopfensteiner had all finished up their treatment at BAMC. In fact, they'd all been a stage ahead of me. While I was still unconscious or on the ketamine, they'd moved to the step-down unit. Once I was on the step-down unit, they'd graduated to outpatient. I hadn't seen them much around the hospital. But once I was discharged, Mother put together a celebratory dinner at a nearby

Tex-Mex. She'd even invited my grandparents and my childhood pastor.

I felt a little self-conscious, to be honest. I hadn't been off the hospital campus since the accident, and now I was being ushered into a crowded restaurant like a debutante. I had tried dressing up in a collared shirt, but I couldn't button the sleeves because of my bandages. I had bandages around my neck as well, so the shirt wouldn't button as high as I would have normally worn it. My face was completely exposed, in all its red, shiny, scabby glory. Mother had gotten me a ball cap that said "Purple Heart" on it, to satisfy people's unspoken questions; in theory, it was also supposed to offer my face a little extra cover. It didn't. I stuck out.

I tried to remind myself, *Everyone here loves me. They're all here to encourage me. They're celebrating the fact that I graduated to outpatient treatment.*

It helped that the guys from my platoon didn't hold back from ribbing me—that made things feel more normal. Philip grinned as I slowly took a tiny bite. "Last time I saw you, LT, you couldn't eat that Canadian MRE fast enough."

Mike snorted with laughter. "Yeah, you were stuffing your blueberry cobbler down and yelling into the radio with your mouth full." He imitated me. "Wuhn-fix, dis is free-fix. Do you need affifftance?"

I laughed. "Now, look at me," I said. "I can't even eat half of my dinner in an hour."

"I'll finish your enchiladas for you, LT," Kevin offered.

"So selfless, Jensen."

"Yes, Sir! Anything for the Lieutenant, Sir!"

Some of the other restaurant patrons glanced over me. Children stared. I decided I wasn't going to let it bother me. Their response was natural. If I had been a kid seeing a burn victim for the first time, I probably would have stared too.

I was just going to focus on the people in front of me.

Kevin filled me in on their recovery. They had all but finished up their treatment and PT. Soon, Kevin explained, they were going to join the US-based portion of our unit and finish out their enlistment there at Fort Hood—just a few hours north of San Antonio.

"So, none of you are redeploying?" I asked.

He shook his head. "No, Sir."

"Don't you want to?" I asked.

He grinned. "It's okay, LT. I don't think any of us mind staying on US soil."

That was a surprise to me.

We had to wrap up dinner by 7:00 to ensure I had enough time to do my shower and bandage routine. The guys hugged me goodbye, patting me carefully on the back. I felt sad, watching them take off. It had been good to see them.

After the Tex-Mex dinner, Mother and I decided we were ready to start venturing beyond the hospital more often. One Sunday, we tried out a local church. One week, we went to the grocery store and picked out some food for home-cooked meals. We tried doing "normal life" again.

It didn't exactly feel normal though. Every time we were out anywhere, there were people: looking. Staring.

There was no mistaking that I'd been through something terrible that had left me horribly wounded. I didn't have the benefit of being able to hide my scars. But strangely, I began to feel a weird freedom in that. For most of my life, I'd tried to hide any areas of weakness I discovered in myself. But that option wasn't available to me anymore. Rather than feeling sorry for myself, I found myself feeling sad for people who still felt compelled to cover up their pain.

"Thank you for your service," a man said to me in church, looking at my "Purple Heart" hat.

"You're welcome," I said. "It was an honor to serve. How are you doing?"

"How am I doing? I should ask how *you're* doing," he said nervously.

I nodded. "I'm actually feeling a lot of joy right now. It feels like I'm learning what life is supposed to be all about. God spared my life, and things aren't easy, but I'm taking it one step at a time."

He looked taken aback. "The fact that you could express joy when you're..." He trailed off awkwardly. "Well...it's inspiring. Good reminder for me to push through my own stuff."

I remembered Cliff saying at the end of my birthday dinner that people might be inspired by my story. I hadn't believed him at the time. Surely, the sight of my disfigurement would cause people to feel shocked or even disgusted. How could it ever be a source of inspiration?

But, as it turned out, it was that unmistakable evidence of pain that some people seemed drawn to. Especially when I focused on showing up the way Cliff did—interested in others, curious, encouraging, full of joy—the effect was surprising. I didn't fully understand it, but people said seeing me and talking to me made them feel hope.

Sometimes. Not all the time.

A lot of the time, people responded with pity. At least, that's how I interpreted it. After yet another stranger anonymously paid for Mother's and my dinner out, I told her I was going to stop wearing the Purple Heart hat.

"Why? It helps people understand what happened to you. It shows that you were serving your country."

"It makes people feel *sorry* for me," I said. "I don't want to be a charity case. If people want to know what happened to me, they can come talk to me."

One night, Mother and I got dinner at the Cracker Barrel. The place was packed. We squeezed into a narrow booth on one side of a walkway that had tables closely set on the other side. I could feel Mother staring at my face. Before we'd left the hotel, I'd noticed that several scabs were oozing pus. I hadn't thought much of it; I knew they'd deal with it the next day in the burn unit. But Mother looked concerned.

"Does it look that bad?" I asked.

She shrugged. "It's pretty rough. I'm just trying to think of whether or not I should scrub them in your debridement shower or leave them alone."

A server passed close beside us in the aisle, brushing my sleeve. "Excuse me," I heard him say. He walked farther down the walkway and set waters on a table where a family was seated. "You know, there are arcade games for kids at the front," he said.

"Can we?" one of the children at the table asked. The mom handed them some change, and the kids eagerly jumped up from their seats. "Come on!"

They hurried down the walkway toward my table. The older boy in front glanced at me.

"Woah—" he said. His eyes grew wide.

"What?" his sister behind him asked.

"Shh!" the boy said, and glanced at me again. The girl followed his gaze. When she saw me, she gasped.

"What?" the youngest brother asked, tucked behind his sister. "What are you guys talking about?"

"Joey, be quiet. Hurry up." The three scurried past.

Mother and I exchanged looks. I looked down at my menu.

We forgot about the kids for a bit. Our conversation turned to news from home. Father was finally out of his casts and moving normally again. Daniel was getting ready for deployment. One of my younger brothers seemed to be having a harder time lately. Mother suddenly broke off, mid update.

"Don't look at him," a child's voice hissed behind me.

Reflexively and regrettably, I looked over my shoulder. It was the three children again. Both the older boy and girl dropped their eyes. The youngest boy gaped at me. "Look at that guy!" he said, loudly.

"Come *on* Joey," his sister said and tugged his hand, pulling him past me.

He craned his head over his shoulder. "Did you see that guy?!" he said again. "Mommy, is that Two-Face, from Batman? Is that a bad guy?"

Mother and I locked eyes again. There was an awkward pause. "Samuel." She spoke hesitantly. "Don't think about that. Children are just…they're just little."

"I feel bad. I don't want to scare anybody."

"Don't feel bad," she said. "It's not your fault."

We didn't talk much through dinner. I kept my gaze down and focused on eating. Mother attempted to engage me in conversation several times, but I didn't feel like chatting.

Toward the end of the meal, I heard the kids run by me again—saw their shoes flash past as I stared down at the carpet. "Excuse me," Mother said. I looked up at her, then realized she wasn't talking to me. "Excuse me," she repeated. "Could I talk to you for a moment?"

The kids' parents paused near our table. "Hello?"

"This is my son, Samuel," Mother said. "I think your kids were walking by and they saw him. He got wounded over in the war. We just wanted to explain because he does not want them to be scared of him."

The woman smiled sympathetically at me. "I hope they weren't rude. We're so sorry you got hurt."

"Thank you for your service," the husband cut in.

Mother continued. "I don't want to keep you, but could you just explain to your children about what they saw? That he was burned—that's why he looks like this. We don't want them to have nightmares."

"Of course," the wife said. "We appreciate you explaining. God bless you." They left.

I stared down at my plate, still piled with food.

Inspiration, pity, and nightmares. Somehow, I generated all three.

* * *

That night, Mother and I went through our regular ordeal. After the unwrapping and the painful debridement shower, she wrapped me in towels and blankets. I was always so cold after the shower—my body temperature still wasn't regulating the way it should. Holding the blankets and towels around me, I climbed under the covers in the bed for another layer of warmth.

"I feel almost drunk, I'm so tired," Mother remarked. She went to the CD player to turn on her worship music.

"Me too."

"We still got all the rewrapping to do."

"I know."

Once I was finally warm enough, I uncovered one arm. Mother started the slow, gentle process of wrapping the bandages around my fragile skin. We'd learned that each arm took about five songs. The legs each took seven. The CD played twice through before we were all done.

"Samuel," Mother sighed, looking tired. "I forget what to do next."

"You can start on the other leg now, Mother." I moved it out from under the blankets.

She hummed along in a weary way with the music, murmuring Scripture to herself. "I can do all things through Christ who strengthens me."

Finally, the bandaging was finished. Both of us were worn out. She pulled a chair up next to my bed and set herself down heavily. "Alright, Son," she said, opening her Bible. "Let's read Romans 5 tonight." She read a few phrases and then her voice shifted. She spoke with more intensity. *"We can rejoice, too, when we run into problems and trials, for we know that they help us develop endurance. And endurance develops strength of character, and character strengthens our confident hope of salvation. And this hope will not lead to disappointment. For we know how dearly God loves us, because he has given us the Holy Spirit to fill our hearts with his love."*

She paused and stared at the words. "Oh, Son, this is a good Word to us," she said, and read it again. *"Problems and trials…help us develop endurance. And this hope will not lead to disappointment."*

"That's all true," I said quietly.

"It *is* true. We can be *thankful* for this trial. Because it is making you stronger on the inside. It is helping you develop endurance, and strengthens your character. And leads to deeper hope."

I believed those words. So then, I simply needed to accept them. *Maybe I don't need to know what the end point is,* I thought. *Or even how to get there. Maybe I just…keep moving forward. Hope that one day I see the good things that the scripture promises.*

I swallowed. "Mother, I was remembering… When I was standing there, on fire, I was thinking about everything that I'd done. Everything that had gotten me success. You know, getting into West Point, and being the stroke on Varsity, and moving toward my goal to be a Special Forces Officer… But when I was standing there on fire, I knew everything I'd done in my life so far couldn't get me out of that situation. It couldn't save me. And that's when I threw up my arms and cried out, 'Jesus, save me.'"

Mother nodded. "I remember you said a little about that when you were talking to Cliff." She stared at me, her expression soft. "You know, we've been teaching you about Jesus since you were a little boy. But I'm not sure I've ever heard you talk about God like this before—the way you have since your accident." She paused. "You surrendered to Him."

"I guess I did."

"Do you think it took being on fire for you to be able to give up your will to the Lord?"

I thought about that. Feeling so tired, under those blankets—my thoughts moved slowly. "Maybe. I'm not sure."

"Well, I admit, I've wondered about that." She looked at me; I could see her eyes evaluating the skin on my face. "Before you got burned, Samuel, you were so handsome." I rolled my eyes. "You were, you were so handsome. And there were so many sweet, pretty girls at your high school, wanting you to be their boyfriend. You thought you were too good for all of them."

"No," I protested. "I just had to stay focused if I wanted to get into West Point."

"You had your own vision of what you wanted to do," she paraphrased. "You were competent. And you were self-reliant. And you were very arrogant and prideful."

I didn't protest this time. I knew she was right. "Should have gotten myself a girlfriend when I had the chance," I tried to joke. "Doubt anyone's going to take me now. I'd give our kids nightmares."

She didn't like my joke. Her expression was sad. "I know it must have been hard with those little children tonight at the restaurant. I suppose there's going to be a lot more of that. Maybe you'll just have to get used to it. But...God can bring good out of this still."

God can bring good. That was another thought I didn't want to wrestle with—I was too tired to wrestle with it. I just wanted to accept that it was true. I wanted to hope that, even if I felt lost, I wasn't failing. I wanted to hope that somehow, this was all part of what God had intended.

"Mother...I think if God didn't have a purpose for me, I would have just died there on the battlefield. If my mission was already complete and I'd done everything He wanted me to do, I would have just died."

"But you lived. He's got a call on your life."

"I think so."

She nodded silently. "Even though it hurts me to my bones to see you hurt the way you are—if getting burned is what it took for the Lord to draw you to Himself...so be it."

"So be it," I repeated.

CHAPTER 9

HOPE AND MIRACLES

From L to R: me—getting ready to graduate West Point with my father and Daniel. Daniel enlisted and is wearing his Navy uniform. May 2006.

Teddy and I jostled each other good naturedly as we walked into Chemistry, the first Tuesday of the new school year. We'd become friends during basketball season the previous winter, but hadn't hung out much since then. "How was your summer?" I asked.

He nodded. "Good! I mostly hung out with my brother and his friends. You know—Chris Hess, Jake Barrett."

Jake Barrett. I knew him—or, knew *of* him. He'd gotten accepted to the Air Force Academy the year before which automatically made him a big deal in my mind. "How's Jake doing? Does he like the Academy so far?"

Teddy shrugged. "He's doing okay, I guess, but he's not at the Air Force Academy."

"What are you talking about?"

"Well, he was dating Michelle and he was planning to ship off to the Air Force Academy in a couple of weeks, but then she made a big deal about it. She begged him not to go and said he should come to the University of Arkansas with her."

I was shocked. "What kind of girlfriend would ask him to do that?"

Teddy shrugged again. "Well, she must have made a pretty good case because he dropped out of the Academy and switched his enrollment."

My jaw dropped. "He switched his enrollment? He felt *that* much pressure from his girlfriend, that he walked away from the *Air Force Academy*?" The thought of Jake turning down the kind of opportunity that I literally dreamed about at night made me feel almost nauseous. I felt shocked and upset. "Well…hopefully that works out well for him, then."

"I don't think it is," Teddy replied. "Because she started dating someone else once she got there. She broke up with Jake three weeks after they moved into the dorms."

Our teacher called the class to attention before I could respond. I felt physically ill to think of the *waste* Teddy had just described. To give up an opportunity like the Academy…for a girl who didn't even have the decency to respect his dreams…and then she broke up with him after all that?! I stared down at my chemistry notebook, ignoring whatever the teacher was talking about.

I picked up my pencil and in all caps, I wrote, *I'M NOT GOING TO ALLOW A RELATIONSHIP TO EVEN HAVE AN OPPORTUNITY TO ALTER MY COURSE.*

In just a few more months, I'd be starting my own applications to the military academies. I made up my mind to avoid dating entirely until I was there: enrolled. Arrived. A cadet. I wasn't about to let any relationship mess that up.

As the months went on though, that was easier said than done. There were plenty of opportunities to get involved with girls from high school or youth group during my last two years of high school. Some of my buddies egged me on—calling attention to my crushes, urging me to ask a girl for her number, complaining that my resolution was stupid and pointless. At times, I wondered if that was because they wanted me to stay in Conway, like they planned. Maybe they didn't want me to head off to a military academy.

But I held firm: no girls.

Not even Dani.

Dani was a friend from high school—*just* a friend, I told myself, countless times. I was admittedly attracted to her. And there was definite chemistry. But I was determined not to date, and besides, she usually had a boyfriend. That helped keep the friendship platonic.

I still thought about her often though—even after enrolling in West Point. She was one of the only people from high school I stayed in touch with. I remember one phone call when she teased me: "You're going to forget about me soon, I know it. You'll fall in love with one of those West Point girls."

"What West Point girls?" I joked. "Eighty-five percent of my class is dudes."

"And I bet all fifteen percent of the girls have a crush on *you*."

We flirted—that was part of the friendship, I told myself. Just playful banter—we joked around and teased each other.

Once, during my senior year, Dani took a trip to New York. She was checking out med schools in the city and offered to take the train out to West Point for the day. I eagerly agreed, remembering that Dani had told me in one of our recent conversations that she was single again.

I picked her up from the train station in the late afternoon. She was surprised at how chilly the wind was, and I gave her my jacket to wear. I took her to the Firsty Club for dinner—the West Point Seniors' imitation of an Officer's Club—and we stayed late, enjoying drinks. Dani sat next to me in a booth, cuddled up against me.

Should I say something? I wondered. Her warmth against me felt good.

"How many years have we been friends now, Sam Brown?" she asked sleepily, playing with my fingers.

"Not sure. Eight?" I asked. I felt distracted. *She's clearly interested,* I thought. *I should just go for it. Maybe it's finally time for us to try this. And if it is—I should take the lead and say something.*

I hesitated, trying to make up my mind. *We could do long distance until I graduate, then get a little time together before I leave for Fort Benning. There might be time for a visit between Benning and Texas, and then we could stay in touch while I'm on deployment.* Thinking through the logistics of what a relationship would mean instantly dampened my romantic instincts. Was long distance, followed by deployment, really fair to ask of her? Was it the best thing for me?

No, I concluded. The resolution was familiar and instantly brought a sense of peace. Right now—I *knew*—I needed to stay focused on the mission of preparing to be the best leader I could possibly be for my soldiers. That meant no distractions. No girls. I couldn't let anything compromise my ability to stay the course.

When I put Dani back on the train that night, she blew me a kiss. "So long for now, Sam Brown."

I nodded. "So long for now." The train pulled away. I felt satisfied that I'd made the right decision. She was on her own mission, and so was I.

There would be other opportunities to date and have a family later on, I reminded myself. I wanted that—I'd always wanted that. *Later*, I told myself. *It's only a matter of time.*

* * *

Mother and me, excited to get dinner off the hospital campus. November 2008.

BROOKE ARMY MEDICAL CENTER, NOVEMBER 2008.

The day after Halloween, Mother and I noticed a harvest decal sticker in the nurses' office window. This seemed to cause her equal parts pleasure and anxiety. "Oh my goodness, it's almost Thanksgiving," she fretted. "And then Christmas." Mother had always loved decorating for the holidays—but in our sterile little hotel room, there wasn't much we could do.

"Do you think they'd let you go home for the holidays?" she asked. Then she seemed to make up her mind. "Let's make it a goal."

The medical staff deliberated over my status for a while, and finally determined I had stabilized enough to travel away from the burn unit right after Thanksgiving through Christmas—so long as I agreed to meet a number of conditions.

First, we established a contingency plan with the hospital local to my parents' house, in case I needed medical care. Second, I had to continue doing physical therapy at a local clinic. The BAMC physical therapists spent several hours on the phone, briefing the hometown therapist about what was needed for my PT.

Third, I had to stay on top of my nutrition. I'd lost a lot of weight after the intubation, and even more as a result of my terrible eating. I'd also lost a lot of my lean muscle mass, a common result among burn patients. The BAMC dietitians had put me on a regimen of high-calorie protein drinks to supplement my caloric intake. Ahead of going home, they wanted to up the ante. A different kind of protein shake was known for helping to restore lean muscle mass, but it had some adverse side effects.

A few days before my scheduled departure, Mother and I waited in the seating area just outside the elevator on the seventh floor, where we'd agreed to meet with a dietitian. When the elevator doors opened, a young woman in scrubs stepped out. She held herself confidently, I noticed. And she was extremely pretty.

"Lieutenant Brown?" she asked, smiling brightly. "I'm Lieutenant Larsen, one of the burn unit dietitians."

"You're a Lieutenant too?" That was interesting.

"That's right. And I understand we're preparing you for convalescent leave? So we need to make sure you're set with these nutritional supplements."

She asked a number of questions—how many supplements was I already taking? (Ten a day.) Was this my primary source of nutrition at this point? (Yes.) "What do you know about these new supplements?" she asked.

"They're going to make me ripped again," I joked.

She looked at me, startled, then laughed. She was extra pretty when she laughed. "Okay, well—sort of. They will help restore your lean muscle, yes. But they can also be hard on your liver, so we're going to do some tests to ensure your liver function is healthy. Are you okay with that?"

"I'll follow any order you give me, Lieutenant." Her eyes sparkled. And her hair was a simple but sporty bob cut. She just seemed so *bright*.

She blushed. "Well—okay. We wouldn't recommend this supplement regimen for a lot of burn patients, but I've been told you've been working really hard and have made great progress. So, I think you're a good candidate for them."

"I think you're a good dietitian." I liked the way she talked to me. She spoke to me like a person, not just a patient. Many of the other nurses or therapists acted like I was just part of their job. But this dietitian seemed warm and open, like she actually cared about me as an individual.

"Thank you." She smiled. "Assuming your liver function looks good, we'll ship the supplements to you."

Mother spoke up. "When will they arrive? He can't go without these supplements for even a day. These drinks are how he's getting most of his calories right now. I'd prefer it if we could just take some with us before we leave."

The dietitian's eyes widened nervously, looking at Mother. "We don't currently have a month's supply of them on hand, but I will make sure they arrive on time." Mother looked at her critically. "In fact," the dietitian continued, "I'll call you to confirm you've received them. And if you haven't, I'll follow up with the shipping company and… raise hell. Or do whatever's necessary to get them to you on time."

Mother nodded, satisfied. "That's what I like to hear."

* * *

It was good to be home for Christmas—even if "home" didn't totally feel like home. Mother and Father had bought a new house in Virginia shortly before my deployment and I'd only been there once before. Still, it was a huge improvement from the hospital hotel. My family was there: Father, still hobbling around from his motorcycle accident. My three younger siblings were running around, rushing off to get together with their friends, finishing end-of-semester projects, heading out for various Christmas church activities. Even Daniel managed to get home for a few days from his training at Fort Bragg.

The day after we arrived, Mother led us all in putting up Christmas decorations. We kept the fire going in the living room, and there were cozy leather chairs to lounge in next to the Christmas tree. Best of all, I didn't have to be at the hospital, going through my relentless lineup of appointments every day. The daily visit to the local physical therapy clinic was nothing compared to what I'd been doing over the past month. It felt like a true vacation.

I was happy to get time with Daniel, although my injuries were understandably troubling to him—so much so that, when he deployed, he was intent on avenging me. Christmas 2008.

True to the dietitian's word, the special nutritional supplements had arrived the day Mother and I returned home. She called the next day on my parents' home phone. "Samuel!" Mother called. "It's for you! It's that Lieutenant Larsen from the hospital."

Lieutenant Larsen? I looked for a private place to take the call. I didn't want to take the phone outside—it was too cold. I hurried up the stairs to a small office just off the landing and shut the door.

"Hello?"

A young female voice spoke. "Hi, Lieutenant Brown? It's Lieutenant Larsen, the burn unit dietitian you met with."

She sounded bright and warm, even over the phone. "Yes, I remember you," I said. "How are you?"

"Oh—fine. I'm just calling to make sure you received the supplements?"

"Yes! Thank you. They arrived."

"Perfect! That's all I needed to know. Okay, well, enjoy the holid—"

"Wait!" I said. I wasn't ready for the conversation to end. I searched for a question. "Are you going to be able to take some vacation time over the holidays?"

She paused. "Actually, yes, I'm home right now."

"You're calling me from *home?* When you're on vacation? You're such a committed dietitian!" She laughed. It felt good to make her laugh. "Where is home for you?"

She cleared her throat. "South Dakota. Okay, well, I hope your vacation is great, and—"

"South Dakota! I've never been there. What's it like?"

I asked question after question, trying to keep her on the phone. We talked about food for a while—I figured that was a topic she'd like, since she was a dietitian. At one point, I tried teasing her. "You kind of stick out on the burn unit, you know."

"Excuse me?" she said, in mock offense. "*You're* telling *me* that *I* stick out?"

"You do," I insisted. "You're one of the only Lieutenants, first of all. Most of the other military people there are either the enlisted guys that got wounded, or the doctors who are Lieutenant Colonels or even higher ranks. And even though there are a lot of female medical staffers, most of them are older than you—like, ten or twenty years. How old are you?"

"Twenty-four."

I was delighted. "We're the same age! You're like the female version of me."

"Or...maybe not? I think I can spot a few differences."

I managed to keep her on the phone for about ten minutes, but finally, in a very professional manner and with some finality, she excused herself. I had to let her go.

We talked once more during the vacation. She called a second time to confirm the arrival of the next shipment of supplements. I retreated to the same office and once again, tried to keep her on the phone as long as possible, looking to build on the little bit of connectivity we'd established before. I asked her about how her work was going. I asked her what she liked to do. I made a joke about donuts—surely dietitians would think junk food jokes were funny?

I wanted to ask if she had a boyfriend, but I didn't. I sensed it would cross a line. I also had no illusions about how she might see me. Attracting a woman, I knew, was now fully out of the realm of the possible for me. But I was willing to settle for being her friend.

Each time after the phone calls ended, I sat in the office for a few extra minutes, feeling low. The energy I felt during the calls was replaced with a sinking disappointment.

Talking with her made me realize how lonely I was.

* * *

After the holidays, in January of 2009, Mother and I returned to San Antonio: back to the gray, sterile hotel room. Our arrival felt depressing. In Virginia, I'd been doing the bare minimum of maintaining my therapy routine, with no gauntlet of daily splint fittings, or surgical prep. Plus, I'd been in the warmth and familiarity of home, in the company of my family.

Now, we were back. I knew I'd have to pick up the intense therapy regimen again, and restart all the surgical procedures. I'd have to go to all the administrative meetings, and talk with the case manager, and do the occupational therapy. It sounded like a drag. And this hotel room only made it worse.

Mother stared critically at the space. "I don't believe there's anything we could possibly do to make this hotel room cozy." That was one of the most critical things Tanya Brown could say about a space. "I think my New Year's resolution is to find us an apartment." She looked over at me. "What about you, Son? Do you have any New Year's resolutions?"

I looked at her as though it were obvious. "Get back to the guys in Afghanistan."

My window to make that happen was growing smaller, I knew. There were only six months left on the deployment. My physical therapy progress had plateaued and—despite my high hopes for the "muscle-building nutrition shakes"—I was still extremely weak. I'd started running again, which ironically was easier than eating. Given that my lower legs hadn't been burned and the running motion didn't require huge flexibility or movements, it was doable to run two or three miles. But my overall mobility with all the contracting scar tissue remained limited. I still needed help bathing and bandaging myself. Most of the activities of daily living continued to feel like a challenge. And my skin was still a red, oozing, plasticky, scabby mess.

I was fully aware of the physical demands of being an Infantry Officer. To lead effectively, I would need to carry a huge amount of weight. I'd need to be able to respond quickly and flexibly in a crisis. I'd need a full range of movement. I would need to be able to eat an MRE, for crying out loud.

I still didn't have the strength or mobility to care for myself very well, let alone anyone else. Deep down, in a place I refused to acknowledge, I could see the writing on the wall.

I didn't have enough time.

The doctors and therapists had told me for months that my

recovery process was going to be longer and more intensive than I imagined—or even wanted to recognize. "You can set goals and plan," one therapist had told me. "And you might see a lot of success as a result of those goals and plans. But at the end of the day, real life is going to play out differently. You may have to recalibrate."

I didn't want to recalibrate.

One day, a few weeks after Mother and I had gotten back, I heard that Sergeant Adam Clark had checked back into the burn unit. Sergeant Clark had been the patient I'd looked to as the example in my early days on the step-down unit: the one everyone praised as the model of how to keep a good attitude and engage with therapy. It surprised me to learn he was back.

"Is he getting another surgery?" I asked James, the Physician's Assistant who ran the burn unit. "I thought he had completed all of his treatment."

"He *had* completed his treatment," James told me.

"So, why's he here?"

James shook his head. "Confidential patient information."

I walked down the hallway and saw a woman I recognized as his wife. She looked tearful. "Ma'am?" I said. "I'm Sam Brown, I got to know your husband when he was finishing up his treatment. I hope everything's okay?"

She shook her head. "No. It's really not. But I'm hoping, now that we're here, things will start getting better." Through tears, she explained that Adam had become so dependent on his narcotic pain meds that he'd needed to be brought back to BAMC for a medication detox. He'd been put into a medically induced coma so that he could be weaned off the opioids.

I was shocked, but tried not to show it. She was already distraught. Instead, I asked if I could pray for them, and she agreed. I could feel her shoulders shake under my hand as I prayed there in the hallway.

Later, in between appointments, I couldn't stop thinking about Sergeant Clark. I did the math. He had gotten injured about eighteen months earlier—that meant he was way ahead of me on the timeline.

But he was still in the midst of his recovery. He wasn't ready to go out and lead troops. Even if he *wasn't* dealing with the narcotic dependence, it was obvious that he still needed to regain a lot of strength.

So—what did that mean for me?

It was also heavy to consider how addictive these painkillers were—painkillers I was popping multiple times a day. If I didn't take seriously how dangerous they were, I'd end up in Sergeant Clark's same position. There had been days when, in an effort to push a little harder and make a little more progress, I'd taken an extra dose.

I resolved to stop that, immediately.

As soon as I did, I realized my New Year's resolution to get back to my guys in Afghanistan wasn't going to happen. Recovery was going to be slow and intense. There was no way to hurry it up, even for the best of patients. Even for me.

I wasn't ever going to be able to redeploy.

It was a bleak realization. I sat on a chair in a waiting area by the elevator, staring at the fake succulent plant on the glass table. If I couldn't look forward to redeployment—what *did* I have to look forward to?

My mind cast around, leafing through the variations of my life plans I'd always maintained. I had wanted to advance my career and move to the Special Forces. That didn't seem likely now. I had always thought, once I was done with the military, I'd start a family. But that seemed impossible now too. What woman would ever fall in love with me?

I looked down at my frame, trying to picture how others viewed me. I was covered in pressure garments—knit tubing which wrapped tightly around my arms, hands, legs, and neck to put compression on the scar tissue. Anywhere that wasn't covered looked raw and red. One of my lower eyelids had contracted so much from scarring that it pulled away from my eyeball. My ears looked like cooked, shriveled bacon fat. When I moved, the movements were stiff, like Frankenstein's monster. The basketball shorts and T-shirt I wore hung loosely on my emaciated frame.

Hollowed out, I thought. Some years later, another veteran named David Rose wrote about his life experience in a memoir named *Spent Shell Casings*. That perfectly described how I felt.

A spent shell casing: that's what I was. A biological expenditure of war.

I looked down the hallway. One man lay on a gurney. Another glassy eyed soldier moved his arm back and forth in a repetitive motion, probably a PT exercise. My eyes landed on the door to Sergeant Clark's room where I imagined him lying there, comatose. It was impossible to move through the hospital without seeing the bloody and mangled impact of war on human beings.

All of us: spent shell casings.

And I wasn't going back.

* * *

In the weeks that followed, I searched for some sort of new motivation to sustain my efforts. It was too painful to have nothing to work toward, so I finally landed on a middle ground: if I couldn't get back to my platoon, I could still work to build back enough function to serve as an Infantry Officer. I had missed the rest of this deployment, but maybe I could still heal enough to be deployed further down the road.

It was a strategy built on die-hard denial, but it gave me a goal again. Before and after each next surgery, I did everything they told me to do, to heal as fast as possible. I drank my protein shakes. I shoved bites of solid food into the tiny hole of my mouth. Mother and I kept up the wound debridement and the bandaging and the lathering of pharmaceutical creams. I upped my runs from three miles to four. I kept working at it.

Mother was also motivated to see my continued healing—but her ideas of progress were more dramatic.

Or, maybe a better word is "supernatural."

That January, Mother came up with a plan. "I've been reading up about a church in Northern California," she informed me one day.

"They believe in miraculous healing. I think we should fly out there and have them pray for you."

I was quiet. I wasn't opposed to the idea—but I also didn't have a sense that being miraculously healed was God's trajectory for me.

"You've got so many people praying for you, Samuel," Mother said. "Think of all the people here in San Antonio praying for us. Plus the folks from our church in Virginia, and our old church in Arkansas, and my friends, they're *all* praying for you. And people keep telling me they believe you're going to experience miraculous healing: your skin will be fully restored to its normal appearance and functionality. I believe that! God can do it."

I believed that too. Miracles, in my mind, were fully possible. I also knew that the people Mother had mentioned wholeheartedly loved me and cared for me. Their faith was genuine—they really believed a miracle was imminent.

Part of me hoped they were right, but another part of me held back. I didn't have the same conviction the rest of them did, that my face and body should be fully restored to normalcy. But I didn't feel like I could voice that doubt to Mother. So many people—and her, especially—believed so passionately in my full restoration, I didn't want to cause them to stumble in their faith.

It was a weird pressure to carry: for my mottled face and scarred body to be at the center of so many people's fervent expectations of God.

But—why not? I accepted their prayers and their hopes. Maybe God *would* heal me.

Mother booked our tickets to San Jose. When we arrived on a Saturday morning, we rented a car and drove straight to the church.

I had never heard of this church, their pastor, or his reputation for miraculous healing, but Mother seemed well-informed. "Saturday afternoon is when they do their time of healing prayers. It's okay to just show up. That's what people do."

The church volunteers must have known immediately what we were there for when we walked in. I was in my typical get-up: a collared shirt which couldn't mask the pressure bandage around my neck; the sleeves unbuttoned to accommodate the bandages around my hands. And my face: thickly swollen from the hypertrophic scarring, a shiny, plasticky mask of reddish purple. My lower left eyelid had been essentially pulled inside out from the contracting tissue. The ball cap I wore couldn't mask the gnarled, shriveled stumps of my ears.

The smiling greeter at the door opened her eyes wide as we approached. Her smile faltered before returning with unnatural intensity. It was a reaction I'd gotten used to.

We were quickly shepherded to a small meeting room where there were a dozen or so people. The prayer volunteers introduced themselves, and a woman around my mother's age opened the meeting.

"We believe our God can do miraculous healings. Do you believe that?"

"Yes," we all answered. My answer was sincere. I did believe that.

Her voice raised passionately. "We know that when we pray, God *hears* us, and that when He hears us, He *answers*. Do you believe that?"

"Yes," we all said again. But inwardly I thought, *That doesn't necessarily mean He always grants miraculous healing, just because we ask.*

"But we must come to Him in *faith*. As the Apostle James states, '*The prayer of a righteous person is powerful and effective.*' And Christ said, '*If you have faith the size of a mustard seed, you will say to this mountain,* "*Move from here to there,*" *and it will move.*' That is what faith can do!"

"Amen!" Mother chorused.

I felt a stab of guilt. Would my doubts prevent God from healing me? Was my faith insufficient?

The woman leading the meeting prayed fervently to open the time, then invited people to request healing prayer. One young woman spoke up and explained her ailment: she'd been experiencing severe stomach aches for the better part of a year.

Several of the prayer volunteers launched into a prayer for this young woman. They prayed powerfully and authoritatively, as though they were confident in God's willingness to do what they asked. After they had concluded prayer for her, another man explained that his knee surgery had failed. Immediately, they began prayer for him, in the same zealous and confident manner.

Once those prayers came to a lull, Mother began to speak up about me. She was interrupted by the woman leading the meeting. "Yes, I can see that this dear brother is in need of healing," the woman said. "We are going to pray for him in a special way."

I felt seized by a bizarre desire to laugh at the position we were all in. Surely, I was a taller order than they were used to—literally and figuratively. I had shown up before this earnest team of prayer warriors as a massively disfigured burn victim, one who'd flown halfway across the country with his mother, asking them to pray for complete healing and restoration of a body's worth of burned flesh. Talk about moving a mountain. God's healing of me wasn't going to be subtle, like disappearing stomach pains or a healed knee. If this prayer for a miracle "failed"—everyone would know it.

When the other people had all been prayed for, a smaller group of volunteers invited me and Mother into a private room. I sensed their nervousness. Were they scared that their healing prayers might not "work"? And if they didn't, what would they conclude about their faith? Once again, I felt a burden of pressure. I began to hope the miracle *would* happen—not for my sake, but for theirs, and especially for Mother's.

After separating me from the others, the prayer volunteers conferred quietly together in a corner, out of earshot where Mother and I waited. Finally, they came over. "Brother, we'd like to invite you to lie down," an older man said.

One by one, they prayed for me. But this time, the tone of their prayers was noticeably different. With all the others, they had almost *demanded* God's healing. But in my case, their prayers were more tentative. It seemed as though they were weakly pleading with God, making their requests, but with an air of uncertainty. "Dear Lord, if you want to heal our brother Samuel, please do so."

Is this prayer for God? I thought, my mind wandering. *Or are they trying to curb our expectations and prepare us for nothing happening?*

Mother prayed last. Her prayer was the only one that matched the confidence and fervor of the healing prayers from the other room. I listened to her repeat my name and prayed my own prayer. *Lord, You could heal my face for her sake,* I prayed silently. *She wants it so badly.*

Within me, I felt Him pressing back something full of love— something that felt like the kindest, most gentle *No.*

The amens came, one by one. We opened our eyes. Mother looked at me. She smiled, her eyes wet with disappointment. There was an awkward silence.

"Thank you," I said.

The older man looked at me with a conciliatory expression. "God answers prayers for healing in all sorts of ways. And we will continue to pray for you." He paused. "You know, Brother, I don't even see your scars when I look at your face. All I see are your eyes."

"Yes, I don't even notice the scars when I talk to you," another woman repeated softly.

There was a pause.

"Thank you," I said again.

Mother gently took my bandaged hand, and we began walking out of the church. We didn't speak. I could sense her disappointment, and I didn't want to make things worse by talking about what had just happened. But inside, my thoughts bubbled up.

I've already *experienced a miracle,* I wanted to tell her.

I'm alive.

* * *

Mother's preoccupation with my face was understandable. I couldn't blame her for hoping for a miracle. In the past several months, my facial disfigurement had grown significantly worse.

A month after the accident, I had looked at my face in the mirror and concluded it wasn't *that* bad. I could still recognize myself.

But I couldn't recognize myself anymore.

Due to my hypertrophic scarring condition—the physical response where the body essentially doesn't know when to stop piling on scar tissue—my face had started to transform in a way that neither I nor the doctors could control. Instead of the tissue calming down over time, the scar tissue on my face had seemed to grow angrier and more reactive. The tissue itself was becoming more and more red, thickening every day and becoming less pliable.

When I saw my reflection in the mirror now, it looked like I had a permanently contorted mask melted onto my face: immovable, frozen in its distortion. Every glance at a reflective surface confronted me with the reality that my image was now unalterably and severely disfigured.

There was no cream I could use to calm the skin down. There was no medication I could take that would shut off my body's scarring response. The only way to address such facial disfigurement was to replace each part of my face with a skin graft, harvested from somewhere else on my body.

Further complicating that option was the fact that I experienced hypertrophic scarring anywhere the doctors cut away healthy skin for the grafts. Those donor sites would begin scarring, and eventually become angry and red just like my face. So—I could put healthy skin on my face and hope it grafted in successfully, but it essentially meant sacrificing another healthy part of my body to do so.

Those were my choices: either accept the facial scarring and remain disfigured, or pursue highly invasive and permanent facial reconstruction.

It was hard to know what to do with the man in the mirror. My physical identity had been grotesquely altered. My professional identity was now seriously at risk. With the exception of my spiritual identity—which was the *only* part of my life that seemed to be growing rather than contracting—every aspect of who I was and had hoped to be was in major transition and beyond my control. None of it was moving in a direction that I had wanted or planned.

The loss seemed to encompass every hope I'd had for the future. I'd always hoped to have a family eventually, but had subordinated that dream behind serving my country first. But now, my "service to country" had brought me to a place where having a family of my own seemed impossible.

What woman could look at me with love? What child could see me as anything but monstrous?

* * *

One afternoon in early February, I was lying face down on a padded table in the physical therapy room. The physical therapy assistant, Dawn, was working on stretching out the scar tissue between my back and arm. It was a painful series of exercises that required breaking the scar tissue apart. I had closed my eyes and gone to that quiet, dark place in my mind where it felt easier to endure the pain.

Suddenly, I heard the door open, and an unfamiliar voice greeted some of the other therapists in the room. They responded enthusiastically—apparently, this was a guy they all knew and recognized. I listened, interested.

The newcomer's voice was chipper and upbeat. I started to glean snippets from his conversation with the therapists: he had also been burned; he was also a military guy. He'd come back to BAMC to check in on the people who had taken care of him and let them know he was doing well. He kept expressing his gratitude: "You guys did so much to help me out. I'm so thankful for all of you."

I heard fast little footsteps and then a child's voice breaking into the sound of the adult conversations. It sounded like a toddler—possibly two or three, I guessed. The little voice lisped out, "Who are you talking to, Daddy?"

"This is Dr. Scott, bud. He helped your daddy get all better after his accident."

I heard the little running footsteps again—they were coming right over to me. I opened my eyes. The toddler was standing right next to the padded table where I lay, looking at me at eye level. His face broke into a delighted smile. "Daddy, look!" he crowed. "It's another daddy!"

I craned my head around as best I could to get a glimpse at the guy who'd come into the room. Like me, he had significant facial burns.

I felt a huge surge of hope well up. If I ever *could* get married—if any woman would have me—maybe my own child would simply see me as "dad." That toddler, in his innocence, had never known his dad to look any other way. When he saw me, he didn't feel fear; he didn't feel judgment. All he saw was another dad.

My thoughts seized on a longing. *If I ever became a dad, maybe my own children wouldn't be afraid of me.*

But as soon as I acknowledged that desire and hope, a sense of intensified loss followed. Love, marriage, and a family all seemed completely out of my reach.

After the appointment, I went to the hospital cafeteria and ate a silent lunch, my thoughts turning over, arguing with themselves. I took the elevator back to the burn unit and walked aimlessly around. There was no one to talk to and I still had an hour before my last appointment.

I decided to go find one of the hospital chaplains, Warren Haggray. He'd checked on me often in the past, but I'd usually waved him on. I'd never felt the need for any sort of in-depth conversation with the chaplains because, spiritually, I was doing fine and my recovery was going about as well as I could control.

Today though, I decided I needed an in-depth conversation.

Warren's office was down in the basement of the hospital. The door was open. When I entered, I felt surprised at the shabbiness of the space. It was small—probably only about a ten-by-ten foot room. There was no window, only a fluorescent light. But Warren had tried to make it more homey by adding a lamp. There were bookshelves piled high with books behind his desk.

Warren looked up from his book. He seemed surprised that it was me.

"Sam! Please, sit down."

I sat down.

I didn't know how to begin.

After a pause, he prompted me. "Why don't you tell me a little bit about why you're here?"

I cast around for a starting place. "My mom and I traveled to California recently. We were hoping I'd be miraculously healed at this charismatic church."

He nodded, his eyebrows furrowed. "Tell me about that."

"Well—I'm not sure *I* was hoping for it. I know my mother was hoping for it. She especially wanted my face to be healed."

"But *you* weren't hoping for that?"

"I don't know," I said. "It's not that I don't believe in miracles... I just didn't sense that a miraculous transformation of my face was God's will for me." I tried to explain myself. "If we believe that God is good, and that He has a plan and purpose for all things, then we're supposed to trust God and be subordinate to Him as our leader—right?"

He smiled. "So far, we're on the same page."

"Well, so—here's a situation that's beyond my control, but it's not beyond God's control. He's the one that allowed this reality for me. So, who am I to beg for something different and say, 'This isn't good enough'?"

Warren studied me. "So why did you go on the trip?"

"I went because...I thought God might intervene for the benefit of others. If I'm extremely disfigured and God heals me, maybe that's how He demonstrates His healing power to others, as a way of confirming His existence. Maybe a miraculous healing would be a way to inspire faith in someone with an otherwise hard heart. I don't know. I could see God doing something like that. And who am I to not be willing to be a tool for that? But I also don't know what God's plans are for me."

"So..." Warren paused. "What happened in California? Did God heal you?"

I gave a sharp laugh. "*Look* at me." Warren raised his eyebrows.

I backtracked. "I mean—yes, God healed me. In the most important ways, God healed me. But externally, I'm clearly still very disfigured. Obviously."

"And how do you feel about your disfigurement?"

"I'm afraid..." I hesitated. "Well—I'm afraid that my scars will prevent me from ever having a meaningful relationship."

He nodded—a big up-and-down motion of dawning comprehension, as though we had finally arrived at the crux of the matter.

"I came here to talk to you because I'm trying to get some objective perspective," I said. "My mother says the right woman will see past all my scars, but...she's biased. I want to know if you think I should just accept that I'm probably not going to have a family. I mean—who would marry me now?" I waited. He didn't speak. "I can let that hope go if it's not going to happen. I just need someone to tell me clearly, so that I can accept it."

He looked at me with compassion. "You'd like to get married and have a family one day."

"Yes," I nodded sharply. I felt like I might cry. "But I don't see how that's possible. I get it—honestly. I can't judge anyone for being disturbed by my appearance, so much so that she would have a hard time being in a personal, intimate relationship with me. I'm just struggling to accept it." I gestured to him. "You're someone I consider to be an objective person. I'm hoping you can set the right expectation for me."

Warren continued to study me. He didn't reply. I looked back at him, impatient for his response and steeling myself against it. "So, is this something that I should realistically hold out hope for? Or should I just remove that hope from my mind, so that it doesn't torment me?"

Warren smiled. "Sam. You're a strong man, with a strong faith. And you have a beautiful heart. Do I think you could eventually get married and have a family one day? Absolutely. You *should not* give up on finding someone that you can love, who will love you back."

I began crying.

I don't think I stopped crying for the next ten minutes.

Anything that Warren said would have been tough to hear, but his denial would have been easier to believe. If he'd told me I should resign myself to never having a family, I would have agreed. That made logical sense: it was easier to accept that I could never have a wife or children.

Choosing to believe what he said—that I shouldn't lose hope—meant not walling off that desire. It meant not separating myself from it. It meant that I had to stay vulnerable and open to that hope.

Through my own eyes, I just didn't see how that desire could ever be fulfilled.

But Warren had told me to hope.

So, maybe it wasn't the most dangerous, foolish, reckless thing to hope.

I finally managed to stop crying. Warren prayed for me. He gave me a hug.

Then, I left.

I took the elevator back up to the fourth floor. I had one final appointment with James, the Physician's Assistant who ran the burn unit. He was going to talk me through the logistics for my upcoming surgery: an eyelid release operation, to allow my lower left lid to properly rest against my eyeball again.

Still thinking about my conversation with Warren, I only half listened as James explained the details: it wasn't a major procedure; it would probably only require one night in the hospital. "And before you check out, we'll have you meet with the dietitian to discuss your nutritional care, post-surgery."

That got my attention. "The dietitian?" I asked.

He nodded. "Lieutenant Larsen. Do you remember her? She set you up with your protein drinks before your convalescent leave."

I nodded. Yes.

I remembered her.

Thinking about Lieutenant Larsen made me equal parts elated and depressed. She was exactly the kind of woman I would have pursued before my accident, and exactly the kind—I was sure—who would now never be interested in me.

I left the hospital thinking about her bright smile. Her sparkly eyes. Her laugh. The way she talked to me like a person, not a patient. *But maybe that's an act,* I wondered. *Maybe she just pretends to see me that way out of compassion.*

I could still try to be her friend. Even if that was all I could hope for, a friendship would be better than nothing. Maybe I could stifle the desire for anything more.

If only, I thought.

* * *

But speaking of Lieutenant Larsen, it's best that I introduce you to her directly.

She tells this next part of the story better than I do.

CHAPTER 10

AMY'S CHAPTER

WRITTEN BY AMY BROWN

Lieutenants Larsen and Brown, at the rodeo. February 2009.

The burn unit did not make a great first impression.

When I first toured the burn unit at Brooke Army Medical Center during my Master's program, it was a struggle to hold back my horror and disgust. I heard screams coming from the shower room. There were strange smells. The patients' physical condition was stomach-turning. And on top of that, the ICU rooms were kept between ninety and ninety-five degrees, because burn patients can't thermal-regulate. Keeping the rooms at body temperature meant the metabolically stressed patients burned significantly less calories—but the heat, combined with the sights and smells that hit me as soon as I entered the burn unit, literally caused black circles to start closing in on my vision. I had to sit down until my dizziness passed.

I remember thinking, *I will NEVER work in a burn unit.*

But then, somehow, I did. One of my favorite instructors, a Lieutenant Colonel, called me to her office one day. "Lieutenant Larsen, you might want to consider doing your master's research in the burn unit," she suggested.

I laughed and told her, essentially, *no thanks.* "Besides," I explained, "I'm slated to go to Africa and study the effects of zinc on diarrhea. I'm really excited about that assignment."

She made the tiniest eye roll. "Well, I can understand why you're excited about the prospect of working with kids in Africa. But that diarrhea research is simple and straightforward. Frankly, I think you'd get bored with it. Someone with your level of proficiency in clinical nutrition would be better utilized in more complex work."

I attempted to protest, but she pressed her case. "Amy, the burn unit is *fascinating* for a strong clinical nutritionist. Each burn unit patient is a big puzzle to put back together. You need to understand all the disease processes, all the patient's habits and goals, and everything that's going on in the body to know how to treat them appropriately. You're working with intubated patients, IV-feeding patients—*you* know how complex that is."

I did—and I also knew how much those puzzles and challenges

excited me. The Lieutenant Colonel continued. "And a burn unit dietitian is an *invaluable* part of the team. We're able to see things the doctors miss. Like, for instance—why is it a big deal that burns affect bone metabolism?"

I couldn't help rattling off the answer. "Burns tend to increase bone metabolism, and when calcium and phosphorus are taken out of your bones, they can get into the blood. The blood can transport them all through your body and they may settle in places like your joints, causing heterotopic ossification."

She nodded, pleased. "Exactly. But do you think the doctors are focused on a lab noting calcium and phosphorus levels? No. They're focused on healing the wound and getting the patient through therapy. But *we* know that if a patient's joints freeze up because his bones aren't getting adequate nutrients, that PT isn't going to go well. And now the patient is discouraged, and their quality of life is affected, and so on. Strong nutritional care can be a game changer that impacts the patient's life for the *rest* of their life."

I was beginning to feel persuaded, in spite of myself. She explained that the burn unit was one of the few areas of clinical care in the hospital where dietitians were considered a crucial part of the recovery team. Even the surgeons agreed that proper patient nutrition was more important than their skin graft surgeries, because a graft won't heal if a patient's nutritional needs are not being met. "Good luck finding that level of respect in any other area of the hospital," she pointed out. "Most of the time, we're considered helpful, but not essential. In the burn unit, nutrition is anything *but* auxiliary. It's the foundation for all the other medical and therapeutic interventions. If you work on the burn unit, you'd be part of a team that actually *feels* like a team."

Huh, I thought. *That might be worth the weird smells and the high temperatures.*

"And," the Lieutenant Colonel went on, "there's the research element. You'd be able to teach cutting edge research and also *conduct* research."

"What about Barry?" I asked, finally getting a word in. "Isn't he slated for the burn unit? Would I be replacing him?"

The Lieutenant Colonel pursed her lips and touched her fingers together like a tent. "How can I put this tactfully? We're launching this Master's Program on the burn unit for the first time this year and it's going to be monitored. We need to be sure that it represents us well. Hence, why I'm talking to you." She smiled. "Besides, I think you'd not only excel on the burn unit, I think you'd enjoy it. Once you get over its little idiosyncrasies."

I paused, hesitating over what answer to give her. She stared at me. "I'm asking you to think of the needs of the Army, Lieutenant. Can I count on you?"

"Okay," I said, finally beaten by her persuasive arguments and intimidation. "Yes."

As it turned out, she was right. Over the weeks and months I spent on the floor conducting my research, I ended up falling in love with the place. I surprised myself several weeks in when I realized that I was thinking of the burn unit as a fun—yes, *fun*—environment.

It helped that I eventually got used to the heat and the smells. I also got used to the scars. Some of the other medical workers told me that eventually I would become immune to the patients' scarring, and they were right. After a few weeks, the patients began to seem as ordinary as someone I might run into at the grocery store, or in the park. The scarring and disfigurement became so familiar that patients distinguished themselves more via their attitudes, and their approach to healing. I began seeing the people behind the burns.

During the final week of my staff rotation, a new patient arrived— one Lieutenant Brown. His rank and age caught my attention. A Lieutenant on the burn unit was a rarity because the majority of patients we saw from the military were enlisted. It was the front line soldiers who most often got hit by enemy fire or an IED, whereas the officers usually kept themselves farther back. But here was this Lieutenant. And not only was he my same rank, we were the same age.

That's interesting, I thought. I remember seeing him through the window of his room. He was covered in gauze, head to foot, still in the ICU. I felt a strange desire to talk to him—which didn't make sense to me. I tried to rationalize the pull toward him. Maybe it was just the weird coincidence of our rank and age?

In any case though, he was intubated. No need to talk to him.

Several days later, I heard he'd been extubated. That meant he needed to speak with a dietitian! My desire to talk to him hadn't gone away. If anything, the pull felt bizarrely stronger. And now, I had an excuse to go see him. I hurried to his room, mentally assembling a few talking points: I could explain the approach to his nutritional care. I could discuss the importance of certain key supplements.

But when I entered, I was taken aback by *all* the people who filled the room. There was a crowd! At least two care providers, a couple physical therapists, his mother, and three or four friends—all of them were gathered around his bed. Apparently I wasn't the only one who'd seen the extubation as a good opportunity to visit Sam Brown.

I smiled and waved. I raised my voice. "I'll come back another day!" No one heard me.

It was only after I left the room that it occurred to me I *wouldn't* be able to come back another day. That day was Friday and it was the final week of my staff rotation. I wouldn't be coming back to the burn unit for another two months—not until I started my duty assignment.

I felt a twinge of disappointment. Someone else would have to discuss nutrition with Lieutenant Brown.

The next two weeks were full of test prep for the Registered Dietitian exam to wrap up the internship. After that came a couple weeks of personal leave, then I returned to the hospital for inprocessing and orientation to my new assignment. I finally returned to the burn unit the first week of November.

One day, I was discussing the various burn patients with a case manager to ensure good clinical care. She began raving about one patient in particular, talking about how exceptionally well he was doing. "His motivation is incredible," she enthused. "And it's beautiful to see his faith, it's the anchoring force in his life. I wonder if that's one of the reasons he's doing so well."

"Which patient is this?" I asked. I'd missed his name.

"Brown. Sam Brown. Tall and very thin." Her eyes brightened as she registered a connection. "He's a First Lieutenant, like you. Was he here already when you were last on the ward?"

I nodded and—weirdly, embarrassingly—felt my heart pounding.

"Well, watch him," she said. "You'll see. He's not angry. He's full of joy. It's amazing to witness. I'm sure you'll get to know him in our work together."

So, I watched him. I observed him walking around the hospital, moving in and out of the therapy rooms. Sometimes I saw him with his mother as she read to him out of her Bible. I sometimes spotted him waiting for his next appointment or chatting with another patient. And I had to agree with the case manager: this guy was *different*.

He was incredibly motivated, first of all. I found out he had started running nearly three miles within a month of his discharge—before his wounds were even healed. He did that several times a week. That level of discipline amazed me.

And he walked with such confidence. He wasn't slouched over; he wasn't hiding; he didn't try to avoid people's eyes by walking quickly—all patterns of behavior that were common in other burn patients. He walked with his head up, as though he was at ease. He also talked to many of the people he walked past, both patients and medical practitioners. "How are you doing?" he'd ask them in a tone that implied he actually cared to know. "How are you *doing*?"

And when he talked to those other people, you could see joy radiating from him. It was bizarre. Signs of joy on the burn unit floor were few and far between. Many patients were deeply depressed, plenty were angry, and even the ones with good family support who tended to do better had a wry, cynical attitude. From any one of them, I regularly heard them say things like, "This sucks. It's a terrible spot to be in. I want to get out of here as soon as I possibly can."

But not the tall Lieutenant. He was unmistakably, impossibly joyful. It was hard not to notice him and feel impressed.

To be clear, Sam Brown was not looking good at the time—not by any means. He was *so* skinny, even under his covering of bandages. His face was thickly scarred, and dramatically disfigured. His ears were gnarled. Where he'd already received grafts, the skin was shiny, oozy, and dimpled like chicken skin. Anywhere he hadn't received grafts—like his face—was bright red, thick, bumpy, and the texture of plastic.

Most people would have seen Sam Brown as a victim of war whose life had been destroyed by terrorism. That's not how I saw him. *This guy's got it going ON,* I thought. *He's got his life together.*

Not like me.

I was a mess.

On September 12, 2008—eight days after his Humvee was blown up by an IED—Lieutenant Sam Brown was at Brooke Army Medical Center, fighting nightmares in a ketamine-induced hallucination. It was on that day, September 12, 2008, that I blew up my life.

Three days after Sam had first arrived in the ICU, I'd had an abortion. I had grown up in a family that emphasized moral legalism—there were clear rules for right living, and if you broke one of them, watch out. I had been raised to believe that getting an abortion was the *one* thing you must never, ever, ever do. It was also something that, as an adolescent, I assumed I would never, ever, ever do. I was willing to extend understanding to anyone else who made that choice for themselves—but, in my self-righteousness, I believed *I* would never do such a thing.

Then I saw the positive pregnancy test.

I didn't believe it at first—we had been using protection. But the second test was positive too. I called my boyfriend in a panic and told him I was pregnant. I'm not sure what I expected from him—maybe sympathy, maybe assurance that he would help me, somehow.

"Well, you need to get an abortion," he said. His voice was firm, unequivocal.

"That's not something I ever, ever thought I would do," I said through tears.

"You need to get an abortion," he repeated.

I called up the Army Clinic, hoping that someone there could provide a neutral explanation of what my options might be. Instead, I got another cut-and-dry response. The nurse on the phone said matter-of-factly, "Just so you know, I had an abortion, and now I have three kids and I'm happily married. So, my life is better because of it."

Was this really the only option available to me? "I feel really confused and scared," I told her.

"Call Planned Parenthood and make an appointment," she said. "You'll feel better once it's over."

The woman at Planned Parenthood told me I needed to come in soon—time was running out. I learned later on, that wasn't true; I could have taken more time to make the decision. But I felt pressure on every side to *do it*, to *get it done*. Every bit of the situation made me feel trapped—the pregnancy, my relationship, my ambitions, the advice I received from all sides, which went against everything I'd been taught. On top of that, I felt bowled over with fear and shame. I felt like my back was against a wall, and the walls were closing in. Everything seemed to communicate that there was just one door out—so, I pursued that door.

I took the medicine on a Friday morning. Then I went to work, feeling like a shred of myself. After work, I went home to my empty house, alone.

I remained alone all weekend, as my body processed the abortion. It felt impossible to process the emotions that went with it.

I thought I had chosen freedom, but I did not feel free. I reeled at the eternal consequences that seemed to be pressing in on me. *I just did an unredeemable sin,* I thought bleakly. *So, I guess I'm going to hell now. That's what I've chosen.*

I had always considered myself to be a good person. I did the right things, I obeyed the laws, I was contributing to society. If God let good people into heaven, I had always assumed I'd be welcomed in.

But on September 12, I realized the truth. I felt utterly wretched. I finally realized what a sinner I was. I had no righteousness of my own—no hope.

My next conclusion was born out of despair. *I may as well live it up here now, because this life is all I've got. If I'm going to hell anyway, I may as well sin big.*

The next Monday, I went back to work. It was the first official day of my master's program on the burn unit. One of the first patients I encountered on my rounds was Lieutenant Sam Brown. He was still intubated and wrapped in gauze, fighting to live.

As Sam began his process of healing, I began actively dying. Sam woke up from the fog of his hallucinations, as I was dulling my consciousness through alcohol and partying. Sam began receiving wound care as I piled new wounds of self-loathing, on top of despair, on top of my boyfriend's harsh treatment. While nurses were scrubbing Sam's dead tissue off in the debriding showers, I was deadening my values and my moral compass.

By the time I returned to the burn unit in November, I was in one of the darkest places of my life.

Yet there was Sam Brown, walking through the hallways. The tall, skinny burn patient who radiated confidence and joy. It took me aback. I'd see him making jokes with other patients, checking in on his care providers—the *patient*, checking on his *providers*—and I just couldn't make sense of him.

The evening after the case manager had told me about Sam's faith, I lay in bed in my dark bedroom. I pressed my eyes shut. What was wrong with me? I was partying like crazy. I was trying to "live my best life" before the hellfire and brimstone caught up with me. So, why did I feel so depressed?

Sam's radiant joy looked and felt *so different* from the darkness that seemed to swarm inside me. My sin felt overwhelming. On top of the abortion which felt unforgivable, I'd piled on so many others that made me feel deeply ashamed.

His scars are all on the outside, I thought with envy. They were unmistakable: there for everyone to see. And yet his inner spirit emanated from him as something arresting and beautiful.

My scars were all internal. Underneath my polished, professional, pretty exterior, I felt like a monster. How long would it be until my inner darkness emanated from me like a cloud and swallowed me entirely?

I knew I needed help. I doubted God cared about me or would listen to me. I didn't even know if I believed in His existence anymore. But maybe faith was worth a last-ditch attempt to get out of this hole.

God, help me, I prayed.

I waited. Nothing happened. No spiritual force welled up inside me to pull me out of my swamp.

I lay in my bed and cried.

The next day, I went back to work. I saw him again: walking through the hallways. Checking in on his providers. I still had never spoken to Sam. But watching him recover, I became captivated by who he was—by who he seemed to be.

(Yes, this is something most people have a hard time believing at first, but I noticed Sam Brown way before Sam noticed me.)

Who *was* he anyway? I tried to shake myself out of my weird fascination by doing what any twenty-something would have done in 2008: I looked him up on Facebook. Maybe more data would cure my curiosity. Maybe he'd have obnoxious pictures or stupid quotes.

Instead, my research had the opposite effect. I saw pictures of him from before he was burned. I read his bio. I concluded that he was still pretty interesting.

He was very, very interesting.

I'd never spoken to him. He was burnt to a crisp. I had a boyfriend. Yet I was developing a major crush on Sam Brown.

It was embarrassing.

Right before Thanksgiving, I was bantering with James, the Physician's Assistant I shared an office with. We'd become friends, and James had heard me share plenty about my toxic relationship. He'd also heard me make a number of impressed observations about Sam

Brown. That day, I actually had an appointment with Sam—and his mother.

"You're pretty new here, Amy," he said, "So I'm going to help you out and give you some advice."

I spun toward him in my office chair and smiled. "Okay," I said. "Let's hear it."

"Burn unit mamas are next-level protective. And there are two moms in particular you don't want to mess with." He named a patient whose name washed past me. The second name didn't. "...And Sam Brown's mom. She will *lay the hammer down* on you if you mess up her son's care in any way."

I swallowed nervously. "I'm supposed to talk to Sam Brown and his mom this afternoon," I told him. "To discuss his nutrition while he goes home for the holidays."

He nodded and raised his eyebrows. "I know. *Be nice.* Don't mess up."

When the elevator doors opened, there was Sam and his mother. She was wearing a jacket with a military badge. With a jolt, I realized it said *Colonel.*

My heart began pounding. I was already nervous as a result of my weird crush, which felt awkward and inappropriate; then, my PA had put the fear of Tanya Brown in me; and now, she was wearing the badge of a Colonel? *You'd better nail this, Amy,* I thought. *Otherwise, you could end your career right here.*

I forced a smile. Gave a professional greeting. Started talking about nutritional supplements with Sam. Then we started talking about ensuring the nutritional supplements actually arrived on time—and suddenly, the possibility of them *not* arriving seemed like doomsday. *I will FOR SURE lose my job if they don't arrive right when they should,* I thought.

"Why don't I get your phone number so that I can make sure they arrive on time?" I suggested.

"You want my *phone number?*" Sam asked, delighted. "Sure, you can have my phone number."

He was being flirty. Why was he being flirty?? I forced myself to engage as a consummate professional. Even so, I could feel my heart pounding. I touched my face with one hand and put the other on my hip, which immediately felt awkward, so then I held both hands out in front of me, but what was that?? I tucked them into the pocket of my scrubs. *There.* I smiled brightly again. "So, I'll call you." *Professional.*

Over the holidays, I called him twice from my parents' house in South Dakota. My reason for calling was, again, purely professional: I just needed to confirm that he'd received the supplements he needed. Regardless of the fact that my stomach did somersaults before I dialed each time, and regardless of the fact that he was *so flirty* over the phone, I forced myself to act the way I believed a highly professional dietitian would.

Then we'd hang up.

And I would keep thinking about him.

I came back to work in late January, but didn't cross paths with Sam. In between appointments and consultations, James and I caught up about the holidays in our shared office. I spent more time than necessary telling him about the conversations with Sam. "I swear, he was flirting with me," I confided.

James hooted in scandalized delight over this. He was less enthusiastic when I described my interactions with my boyfriend.

"The word 'trainwreck' comes to mind," he remarked.

I looked over at him. "It's not as bad as I make it sound," I said. Inwardly, I thought, *It's actually worse.*

One morning, I showed up to work after having been at a nutrition conference for a few days. When I arrived at my office, James said, "Hey, I kept Lieutenant Brown an extra day for you."

"What?" I asked, confused.

"He had his eyelid release surgery. He expected to go home yesterday, but I kept him an extra day for you."

I stared at James. "Why?"

He gave me a patronizing look, as though he needed to break things down for my slow comprehension. "So that you can check his labs and have conversations with him about his medications and do your blah blah blah dietitian work. And also because I know you have a huge crush on him."

"James!" I protested. "I have a *boyfriend.*"

"Oh yes, I forgot. Incidentally, Sam asked me if you had a boyfriend."

I was stunned. "He did? What did he say?"

"He just asked me if I happened to know whether or not Lieutenant Larsen was dating anyone."

My stomach did a jumpy little dance. "And what did you tell him?"

"I told him you weren't."

"*James!*" I was aghast. He shrugged, unapologetically, and grinned.

"Well—well, I *do* need to talk to Lieutenant Brown about some medication. As a matter of fact," I said coolly. "So, thanks." James nodded crisply and turned back to his computer with a satisfied little smile.

Sam and I talked. We discussed medication and his return to therapy and how it was going with the nutritional supplements. I was firmly boundaried and wholly professional.

But even professionals can laugh at a patient's jokes, right? And the heart-pounding response was involuntary, so I don't know how I could have helped that.

Later that afternoon, Sam knocked on my office door. James opened it and gestured to his desk chair. "Come on in, Sam. Sit down!" he said. "I've got to go check on a patient!" James flashed a grin at me and then bolted out into the hallway.

Sam looked at me. "Hey, Lieutenant Larsen. What are you working on?"

I glanced at my computer. "I'm calculating the caloric requirements for a patient."

"Calories or kilocalories?"

I sat up straighter in my chair. "You know about kilocalories?" My heart began pounding again. Was it possible Sam actually knew the difference between a calorie and kilocalorie?

He rattled off the definition of a calorie—like, the *textbook* definition. Then he grinned, sheepishly. "I learned that in high school Chemistry. I can't remember anything else I learned that year, but for some reason that stuck with me."

Hearing a man rattle off the correct definition of a calorie was undeniably attractive. *Wow,* I thought. *This guy gets me!* I gulped. "Well. I am impressed that you know that."

Apparently assured of his welcome, Sam sat down in James' chair. "So…Lieutenant Larsen. There aren't really a lot of other officers around here. And there's really no one my age I can hang out with." He was speaking slowly and hesitantly. It was endearing. "So, I was just wondering…would you ever want some Lieutenant time?"

Lieutenant time? I thought. I laughed. "Um…I don't know if I'm allowed to do that, but I can check into it and see if I can hang out with you."

He nodded rapidly. "Great. We can just be…friendly Lieutenants."

I stifled another laugh and nodded. Sam stood up and grinned. Then he nodded awkwardly again and walked out. After a minute, James poked his head back in the office. "*So?*" he demanded.

"Sam asked me if I might want 'Lieutenant time,'" I said.

James grimaced. "Is that supposed to be soldier lingo for a date?"

"I'm not sure what kind of lingo it is." I laughed. "But he knew the correct definition of a calorie. So, that was cool."

James nodded thoughtfully. "Thank God he had something to redeem 'Lieutenant time.'"

The next morning, I checked in with the ICU Burn Dietitian who ran our team. I explained Sam's invitation. "Is that appropriate…?" I asked.

She looked at me thoughtfully. "I'm sure it's fine," she said. "It's not uncommon for burn patients to hang out with providers outside of work, given how long we end up working with them. There are lots of friendships that form. I suppose the only reason you'd want to practice caution is if there's any chance of a romantic interest on either side. In that case, we'd probably want to assign him another dietitian."

I nodded in understanding. My cheeks burned. "I think…it's probably a good idea to assign him another dietitian."

Her eyebrows raised and she smiled. "Really?"

"Better safe than sorry," I said lamely.

Sam's suggestion for "Lieutenant time" ended up being the San Antonio rodeo. Apparently, someone had given him tickets. I was game—except the rodeo was on February 14, Valentine's Day.

I called my boyfriend. "Hey. Did you have any plans for us, for Valentine's Day?"

"Not really," he answered.

That's what I'd guessed. "I got invited to go to the rodeo by one of the burn unit patients, Sam Brown," I said. "Do you mind?"

He laughed. "One of the crispy critters invited you to the rodeo? Sure. Have fun."

That took care of that.

The rodeo was a blast. Outside of the hospital, it felt easier to relax and be myself with Sam. I was surprised by how easy it was to fall into conversation. Every so often, I'd see someone look at him with alarm, but he never seemed to register people's reactions to him—or maybe they just didn't bother him. The only time he seemed self-conscious was when we were eating. I'd gotten a big, juicy burger. Sam had ordered a hot dog.

"It's the only thing that will fit in my mouth," he said sheepishly. He pulled the dog out of the bun and set it in the small cardboard container. Using a plastic knife and fork, he cut the hot dog into very thin slices. Carefully, he placed one thin slice on top of his fork and slid it sideways into the small opening of his mouth.

I looked at him apologetically, then took a massive bite out of my burger. Mayonnaise and ketchup squirted out the side.

He watched me wistfully. Then his eyes took on the glint of a wiseass. "Don't eat too many of those, they'll go to your hips."

That *cracked me up.* "Maybe we should work some of these into *your* diet, Sam," I teased.

He looked down at his emaciated legs. "Are you implying I'm not at the peak of physical perfection?" I grinned and shrugged.

Toward the end of the rodeo, Sam leaned over toward me. "I'm supposed to go to a wedding next weekend," he said. "It's in Houston. Want to go with me? It would be great to have some company on the drive."

I felt a thrill. Another date? Was *this* a date? "Is it an overnight thing?" I asked.

He nodded. "But it's a family event. My parents will be there. Everything will be fully chaperoned."

I nodded slowly, registering both his flirtatious implications and the fact that his "fully chaperoned" comment was a sign he probably thought I lived with a whole lot more propriety than I actually did. What would this Bible-reading, joy-emanating man think of my wild partying lifestyle? I didn't want to know.

I called up my boyfriend and filled him in on my plans. Once again, he didn't care.

The following weekend, Sam climbed into the passenger seat of my car and we began the long drive to Houston. He shared more about his childhood, and his time at West Point, and stories from his military training. I kept peppering him with questions. I didn't want to talk about myself. Anything to keep him from finding out who I really was behind my professional exterior. Anything to keep him from recognizing the rot inside.

At the wedding, I saw his mother again and warmly greeted her, trying not to let my nervousness show. I also met his father for the first time.

"Colonel Brown? Ah, so *you're* the Colonel. I remember seeing your badge on a coat Mrs. Brown had been wearing. Pleasure to meet you, Sir."

The ceremony was short. Everyone seemed eager to get through the "serious stuff" and start the party. Sitting at one of the reception tables, I remarked to Sam, "I can remember the first wedding I went to, as a little girl. It seemed *magical* to me. I thought it was proof fairy tales were real."

"Happily ever after?" he supplied.

I gave a short laugh. "That was the impression of a very *young* girl. Obviously, I know now that relationships and marriage are a lot more complicated than that. Not sure anyone gets a fairy-tale ending."

He studied me. "So what do you think marriage is about now?"

I thought about that. "I envision marriage being a lifelong, faithful commitment."

"Me too."

He glanced at me sideways. "I always hoped I'd end up being married to my best friend."

"Same. Like, that we'd do everything together. And I hope that my marriage feels like a partnership," I said. "I want us to feel like a team." Even while I was speaking, it occurred to me that my current boyfriend fit none of these descriptions.

"And that we'd have similar values," Sam suggested.

I nodded again. "I always hoped that my future husband would have a strong love of God."

"*Really?*" Sam said. He turned to face me directly. "Well, that is *very* interesting. Are you a Christian?"

I nearly spat out my drink. *Actually, I'm going to hell in a handbasket.* "Not exactly. I mean—I was raised religious, but...that hasn't really been my thing for a while." I was thankful the lights were low so Sam couldn't see me turn red. That was one advantage of his scarring, I thought, wryly: he never gave away a blush.

He stared at me thoughtfully, which made me inwardly cringe. Had I given too much away? Would he guess what a sinner I actually was?

"But you want a husband who loves God?" he asked.

I couldn't explain why I felt that way. But I knew, even as I surprised myself with the words I'd spoken, they were true. Regardless of how I was living, I wanted God to be a fixture in my life. That seemed like too much to ask of God, given how miserably I'd let Him down. But maybe I could have that "God fixture" vicariously if I married a guy who was closer to holiness.

I shrugged. "I've just always felt like God is an important part of a marriage, for some reason."

Our conversation was interrupted by Tanya, who leaned across the table toward us. "Samuel," she said, speaking loudly over the chatter of the other wedding guests. "I've decided I'm going to be moving back to Virginia in a few weeks."

"What? Why?" he asked.

"Well, Samuel, it's been almost six months and your younger siblings need their mother back home. You're stable enough that you can start caring for yourself. Besides—" She gestured to me and smiled. "I think it's best your mother gets herself out of the way so things can develop here."

I dropped my eyes into my lap. *Were* things developing here? I pushed away the thought of my boyfriend, then immediately wondered what Sam would think of me if he knew I had a boyfriend… or if he knew about the partying…or the abortion. *I'm such a mess,* I thought.

A noisy guest sitting near Tanya drunkenly gestured with his drink, then guffawed loudly. "That's what I'm talking 'bout!" he called to a couple grinding on the dance floor. Tanya looked at him distastefully.

"Well, I've had enough of chit-chat," she announced abruptly. "Samuel. Will you please share your testimony with our table? I think it's time for something edifying."

Sam didn't skip a beat. He sat up straight—the posture of a soldier. "I grew up in the church. I was always taught about Jesus and God, but I didn't truly put my trust in Him then, even though I thought I did. My trust was in my own mind and abilities."

The drunken wedding guest had swiveled his head toward Sam and was studying him. "Is this the story of what happened to your face? Because I've been wondering what the hell happened to you all night."

"Hush," Tanya said. "Let him tell it."

Sam nodded. "I experienced a lot of success—West Point, then Ranger School, then I was assigned to the First Infantry Division to lead a platoon on deployment. But then during my deployment in

Afghanistan, my vehicle hit an IED," he said. "I was sitting right in front of the diesel tank and got covered in the gas and the flammable material from the explosive device. And all of that caught on fire."

"Holy shit," the guy breathed out, staring slack-mouthed at Sam. "How'd you get put out?"

I stared at Sam, curious. I'd never heard him tell the story of his accident, although I knew a few of the details from his medical history. I'd wanted to ask, but hadn't worked up the nerve.

Sam continued. "First off, I somehow found myself standing out-side the vehicle, on my feet, without any memory of how I got there. I think that was a miracle. And then, I threw my arms into the air and yelled out, 'Jesus, save me!'"

"That's my favorite part," Tanya breathed. She leaned toward me and tapped my hand. "He was also calling out for his mother."

The guy shook his head in drunken amazement. "And he saved you." He snapped. "Just like that?"

"No, not exactly," Sam smiled. "I tried 'stop, drop, and roll,' which didn't work. So then I got up and ran, which made the flames worse. And then I had three final thoughts: first, 'How long does it take to burn to death?'"

"Holy shit," the guy repeated.

"Second: what is the transition between this life and the next going to be? And a follow-up realization, which was…that I had no idea where I was going."

I felt a weight on my chest. I'd been thinking those same thoughts a lot recently. But I hadn't called out for Jesus—I'd concluded that I was going to hell.

Sam finished. "And then my last thought was just…giving up the will to live." Across the table, Tanya nodded soberly. She had tears in her eyes.

I stared at Sam. "So, then what happened?" I prompted.

"I heard the voice of one of my guys, Kevin Jensen, yell out, 'Sir, I've got you!' And he jumped down next to me, and started putting out the flames." At the mention of his other soldier's name, Sam's voice got thick and choked up. After a pause, he said, "I believe that God saved me for a purpose, and that the life I live now is not my own."

"Praise God," Tanya said quietly.

The wedding guest sighed. "That's heavy." He tossed the rest of his drink back. "You're a real badass, man. I hope you have a great life now. We're all pulling for you." He got up from the table and went out to the dance floor.

"Thanks," Sam said. He glanced over at me. I didn't make eye contact with him.

How does that *happen?* I wondered. *How do you get to a place where you're literally burning alive and your response is to call out for JESUS, rather than shout out curse words?*

I don't remember what else we talked about that night. After the wedding, we went back to Sam's relative's house and went to bed in our separate rooms. I lay in bed awake and stared at the ceiling. My thoughts were stuck on one certain conclusion.

Whatever he has, I need.

The next morning, Sam and I got back in my car and began the long drive back to San Antonio. I didn't have an arsenal of questions prepared this time; I had too much on my mind. As a result, Sam managed to ask *me* a question.

"So… You heard me tell my testimony yesterday. My story about why I follow Jesus. What did you think of it?"

I sucked in my breath. "Well…" I hesitated. Then, I decided I may as well be candid. "If *I* was on fire in the desert, that would not have been my response: 'Jesus, save me.'"

"What would have been your response?" he asked.

"Probably a four-letter word." I tried to laugh, although I knew that neither of us found it funny.

Sam looked over at me. "I'm concerned about your salvation."

My jaw dropped. I looked back at him. I couldn't believe the audacity of what he'd said, but I also felt gratified to hear *someone* say aloud the thought that had been haunting me for the past four months. After a stunned silence, I said, "Well—that's great, because I am too!"

The words hung between us for a moment. It was the truest thing I'd said to him. In fact, it was the truest thing I'd said to anyone in months.

After a beat, Sam nodded. "All right. Well, can I tell you about Jesus?"

For the next fifteen minutes, Sam explained who Jesus was. He explained that we were created to live in harmony with God and one another, but humans rebelled against God, leading to all the brokenness and pain in the world. He told me that Jesus was God in human form—that Jesus had come to earth to live a perfect life and show us a way back to wholeness and peace. "Jesus allowed Himself to be killed like a criminal on the cross to atone for all of our sins," Sam said. "He died on the cross for me and you. And then He rose from the dead, which showed His power over sin and death. That's why Jesus is such a big deal—He frees us from our guilt and shame and brokenness and pride. He did all of that because He loves you, Amy."

"Interesting," I said. In my mind I was thinking, *That's cool that you say that. But you don't know what I've done.*

I didn't say that out loud though. I didn't want my scars to scare him off.

Finally, I got as close as possible by saying, "Maybe Jesus isn't enough for everyone's sins. Maybe some sins are just too bad."

Sam didn't manage to convert me during that car ride. But by the time we arrived back in San Antonio, I had agreed to go to church with him.

We had a number of loaded conversations over the next few weeks. Every time God came up, Sam kept emphasizing the same truth: Jesus *was* enough for my sin. He found me scriptures to prove his points. I wasn't convinced. I still believed I was too far gone.

One night, we were finishing up dinner on the patio at the Alamo Heights Panera. Sam was trying to explain the power of God's grace, and that Jesus' death on the cross was enough for whatever sins I'd committed. I interrupted him. "Sam, you don't get it. You don't know what I've *done*."

He stared at me. "I don't need to know what you've done."

"Yes, you *do*. Christians are good people. Look at you—you're, like, on this pedestal. I'm not a good person. I thought I was, but I'm not." I started to cry. I looked around me, self-conscious.

"Do you want to go to the car?" he asked. I nodded.

Sitting in my car, in that Panera parking lot, I confessed everything. I told him about the abortion. I told him about all the partying. I told him about my awful boyfriend. "See?" I said through tears. "That's why I can't believe Jesus is enough for me."

Sam seemed sobered by my confession, but undeterred. He began flipping through his Bible. "Listen to this, from Acts 22," he said. "This is the Apostle Paul talking—he wrote most of the New Testament and was one of the most important leaders of the early church. But before he became a Christian, he actually hunted down Christians and arrested them. He even helped kill the first martyr, Stephen. In these verses, he's protesting to God about how sinful he is."

Like me, I thought.

"'*Lord… I took Christians out of every Jewish place of worship. I had them beaten and put in prison,*'" Sam read, "'*Also when Stephen was killed, I stood there and watched them throw stones at him. Those who threw the stones had me watch their coats.*'" He looked up from the Bible. "Amy—*this* is the guy that God inspired to write the New Testament! But before he believed in Jesus, he stood by and clapped while another Christian was being killed. If Jesus is enough for him, don't you think it's possible that Jesus is enough for you?"

I stared at Sam through tears. *Could* it be possible?

He moved toward me and took my hand in his bandaged one. "Everything you've done, Amy—that's not who you are. You are loved by God. And you're forgiven. So… You just don't need to worry about that anymore."

I sobbed out a laugh. "That feels really good to hear."

"It's true," he said gently.

My face crumpled again. "I can't believe you're not rejecting me right now," I said. "I thought you'd hear all that and be like, 'That's a bit much for me. Thanks for sharing that, but now we're done.' But you're not." He squeezed my hand. "And it feels really good to not be rejected."

"It sort of blows my mind that you thought that *I* would reject *you*," he said quietly. "Most people look at me and think…" His voice trailed off.

I looked at him. "Sam. You are *such* an exceptional, kind person. You inspire me."

He stared down at our clasped hands and spoke my own words back to me. "That feels really good to hear."

We prayed together. My own words felt clumsy—I still wondered if God even wanted to hear from me. But when Sam prayed, the words were full of grace and love and faith. It felt like I had been suffocating in a small, dark space and then someone threw open the door and filled it with oxygen. By the time we said "Amen," I felt lighter. The experience was draining—both physically and emotionally. But the shame had also drained out too.

A few days later, Sam and I went on a run together. This was something else that astounded me: he could keep pace with me in a 5K, despite all those gnarly burns. "I've been thinking about something," he said, staring ahead at the path.

"What's that?" I panted.

"The other night, you mentioned that you had a boyfriend."

I felt a stab of guilt. *Sort of.* We jogged a few yards before I answered. "It's not a good relationship."

"Can you help me understand… What's going on in *this* relationship?" he asked. "I mean, we've just been hanging out a lot. I was mainly hoping for a friendship to start with. I didn't think I should expect anything more. But… I'm wondering…" *Slap, slap, slap.* The sound of our shoes hitting the pavement collided with the blood pounding in my ears. "Well—*should* I hope for anything more?"

"Yes," I said simply.

He looked sharply at me. "Yes?"

I nodded. "Yes."

It was hard to get out any more than that word—especially at the pace we were going. I knew how different this relationship with Sam was from anything else I'd experienced. This wasn't just a fun dating thing, or a crush based on physical attractiveness. This was something much, much deeper. For the first time in my life, I was profoundly emotionally invested with a man I respected more than anyone I'd ever met—one who also respected *me*.

I looked over at him. "I'm committed."

"Well—me too!" He stopped running and grinned. "So—are we doing this?"

I stopped and laughed. "We're doing this."

He cocked his face. "Hang on though—I don't want to just date for fun," he said. "I only want to date you long enough to figure out if there are any red flags. If we date, I'm thinking it's with the intention of getting married."

"Well, that's a pretty huge paradigm shift for me," I admitted. "I've always dated 'to see where things go,' not to look for red flags. But frankly, I'm kind of over dating for entertainment. It feels like a waste."

He studied me. "You're not freaked out by me bringing up marriage?"

"Surprisingly...no." I shook my head. "I don't want something casual with you."

I broke up with the boyfriend—ex-boyfriend—that afternoon.

Sam and I spent the next month dating with the kind of over-achieving zeal both of us tended to practice in every other area of our lives. Knowing that we were dating with the intention of getting married, we focused our conversations on the big stuff: what we wanted out of life, our hopes and goals, our expectations of a marriage partner, and so on. In conversations with Sam and through my new church attendance, I kept learning about God and Jesus.

In mid-April, Sam and I were nearing a month of being "officially" together. "Hey, Amy," he said to me. "I like round numbers."

I looked over at him and grinned. Where was *this* going? "Cool. I like round numbers too."

"I was discharged from the hospital almost exactly one month after being admitted. My mother was here for almost exactly six months. And now we've been dating for almost a month—"

"You want to get engaged by April 19, when we've dated exactly a month?" I asked.

He opened his mouth and then closed it. Then he cracked a little smile and didn't say anything. I didn't know it then, but he had already bought the ring.

It was fast—it was crazy fast. But we had discussed that no one could ever truly know another person until you were married to them. Until you're actually living together, doing life side by side, it's too easy to put your best foot forward. We decided that marriage meant the commitment to work through it, regardless of what challenges came up. With God at the center of our relationship, we'd find a way to navigate our challenges and stay together.

Conveniently, we were going to be traveling to New York together on April 19 because Sam had been invited to speak at a West Point military event. On the 18th, we were walking together in Central Park and found ourselves in a beautiful spot. The sun was shining; we saw blossoming trees perfectly reflected in a nearby pond. Everything was perfect.

This is it, I urged him, mentally. *Propose right here.*

"Do you have anything on your mind?" I prompted.

He sighed, happily. "Doesn't the sunshine feel good?"

He moved us forward on the path, and we left the perfect spot. Our conversation turned toward the West Point event from the day before, and I realized he wasn't going to propose. I felt annoyed.

He didn't propose that night at dinner, or back in the hotel room that night. The next morning, we had brunch plans. Sam needed to take a shower and get ready.

This was a new realization for me: burn patients take *so long to get ready.* The unwrapping, the wound care, the re-wrapping…I started feeling impatient. "Sam, we've got stuff we need to do. Can you please hurry up?"

He had climbed back into bed after getting out of the shower and called me over to him.

I hurried over. "You ready? Let's go!"

He looked at me and smiled. He didn't say anything.

"Sam—*what?* What's going on?"

He pulled a velvet box out from underneath the pillow. "I just wanted to know if you would marry me."

I laughed—relieved that the wait was over. "Yes!"

So then, we were engaged! It hadn't happened in the perfect spot. Sam hadn't been in the perfect kneeling position. And it had all occurred in the midst of delayed plans and wound care.

It wasn't the proposal of my dreams, but in retrospect, it was perfectly fitting for the years of marriage ahead of us.

We planned for a six-month engagement, but both of our parents had scheduling conflicts. When we went back to the calendar to look at other options, we realized that—between Sam's surgery schedule and my work—our only other option was Memorial Day weekend: five weeks away.

We threw the wedding together. All we needed was a dress, a photographer, and a place—right? I got a dress. We booked a photographer. And one of Sam's friends agreed to host us at their beautiful home in Hill Country north of San Antonio, Texas. Our immediate families came—that was the first day my parents met Sam. It was all a little crazy.

Sam asked his friend, Warren Haggray, the hospital chaplain, to marry us. As he boomed out a prayer in his strong voice, he said what both Sam and I were feeling:

"Lord, we praise You for bringing these two beloved souls together. Thank You that Amy is able to see Sam for the amazing person he is. Thank You that Sam is able to see Amy as a beautifully redeemed soul. Thank You for their commitment to each other and their commitment to You as their Lord and Savior. Bless them as they learn to live together and help them to navigate the challenges ahead. In Jesus' name, Amen."

It was a good prayer. And we needed every bit of that blessing. Those first years of marriage were some of the most beautiful, wonderful, and challenging years of our lives.

CHAPTER 11

SCARFACE

The young face of a boy going into high school with a goal of being accepted to a military academy. Spring 1998.

On the Monday before spring break, all the students at Conway High School filed into the auditorium for a mandatory assembly. They did the same one every year: some variation of an anti-drinking, anti-drug campaign meant to scare students from getting drunk or high over the break.

My buddies and I were distracted and loopy being this close to a week's worth of freedom. As far as we were concerned, this assembly was just one more hour to kill until Friday afternoon when we could race out the big, brick building into the sunshine. I think most students were like that—everyone kept talking and laughing, even after the teachers turned out the lights and angrily shushed us.

A video was projected onto the large screen at the front of the auditorium. Slowly, a narrative unfolded. A girl's voice began describing her spring break trip to Florida with her friends while a series of pictures appeared on the screen. First, a picture of three girls next to a car packed up with gear. Then, a picture of them on the beach in their bikinis. A picture of them at a restaurant, sipping cokes through straws, looking sunburned. My friends and I were only half paying attention—less focused on the story than the cute girls in the bikinis.

"We got invited to a party by some guys we met on the beach..." The girl's voice continued narrating. New pictures appeared: the girls dressed in tube tops and tight jeans, holding drinks in a crowd of party-goers, looking drunk. Someone in the audience whooped and called out, "Hell, yeah!"

"We were having such a great time, but then we had to get back to our hotel... My friend thought she was okay to drive..."

We knew the end of the story: we'd heard it every year. They drove drunk and got in an accident, and someone probably got hurt—blah, blah, blah.

Suddenly, the video switched from the pictures of the cute girls in their party attire to the narrator talking on camera. The entire audience gasped. The distracted chattering was replaced with a stunned silence.

The girl was completely mutilated. The car had caught on fire in the accident, she explained. She'd been badly burned. Her face was horribly disfigured and grotesque.

"*Damn!*" one of my friends hissed.

"She looks like a monster," I heard a freshman whisper. A guy near me muttered a crass joke; a girl beside him hissed a rebuke. The girl looked like she was near tears.

After the video, the principal got on stage and lamely repeated the main message: don't be stupid. Don't drink and drive. Don't do drugs or party over spring break. As soon as the bell rang, we all bolted out of the auditorium, eager to get out of there and put distance between ourselves and that awful face.

But it followed me. Every time I went into the bathroom for the rest of that week, I saw that girl's face on the posters that had been hung up by the school staff. The posters were simple: they featured a portrait of the severely disfigured girl next to the stark warning: *Don't drink and drive.*

My stomach turned every time I looked at her. The permanence of her injuries was horrifying, especially considering how cute and normal she'd looked before. *How terrible to lose your identity like that,* I thought. *Not just to be changed, but to look monstrous.* I washed my hands at the sink and tore my eyes from the poster in the reflected mirror, focusing instead on my own face. *I'd rather die than go through life, looking like that,* I concluded. *If I were in her shoes, I think I'd kill myself.*

It wasn't something I dwelled on for days or hours at a time; it was just a passing contemplation whenever I spotted the poster, easy enough to walk away from.

I was glad it hadn't happened to me.

I assumed it never would.

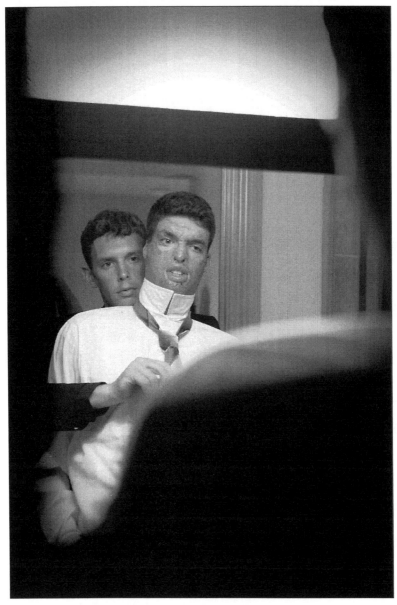

With Daniel, my best man, the afternoon of my wedding with Amy. May 2009.

On the morning of the wedding, I stood in the bathroom of my friend's house where the ceremony would take place. Daniel was with me, ready to serve as my best man. I held out my tie to him. I was still having trouble manipulating things with my hands.

Wordlessly, Daniel accepted the tie and gestured for me to turn toward the mirror and squat down a bit. Standing behind me and peering into the mirror, he wrapped his arms around my shoulders and tied the tie. His motions were deft. His face, appearing next to mine, was handsome and smooth.

I stared in the mirror at myself: the groom. My facial scarring had been trending in a bad direction. After my first date with Amy, I'd had the hope that my face would start to go through its own little healing process—that the scar tissue might become harder to see, and more pliable. It worked that way for some guys. Instead, every day it seemed like the scarring was getting worse.

"There," Daniel said, giving the tie a final tug. "Ready for the bride."

At the moment, I was thinking more about the rest of the Larsens. "Did you know that was the first time I met Amy's parents?" I said to Daniel.

"You mean this morning? At breakfast?"

I nodded. "Yeah."

Daniel shook his head in disbelief. "You think you made a good first impression?"

I tried to smile. "Well. I don't think I look anything like her other boyfriends."

Daniel chuckled. Only because I knew him so well, I could hear the trace of bitterness in it. I don't think he'd gotten used to my scars yet. "Seriously though—you think her parents liked you?"

I considered my interactions with Amy's family over breakfast. "They played along well. Amy says I should be thankful they're midwesterners, because they don't know how to be anything other than polite." Daniel laughed again. "But in private, her mom asked her if she was pregnant."

He locked eyes with me. "Is she?"

"No. I think her mom thought that was the only reason Amy would marry someone like me." I paused. "I don't think they expect us to stay married."

"Oh," Daniel said. "Well. You just gotta prove them wrong."

I looked back in the mirror at myself. "Beauty and the Beast."

Daniel stood beside me and put his arm around my shoulders, staring at my reflection in the mirror. "Hey. Don't knock the Beast. Remember? He's a prince underneath." He patted my chest. "Amy's getting the best guy there is."

The ceremony went off without a hitch. Both of us felt relaxed—we had only a small number of guests, and Warren's presence put us both at ease. During the meal afterwards, Mother pulled her Bible out of her purse and cleared her throat.

Daniel tapped his fork on his glass. "Listen up! Mother of the groom has something to say."

"This is from Genesis chapter two," Mother announced. She adjusted her glasses. *The Lord God made a woman from the rib, and he brought her to the man. Then, 'At last!' the man exclaimed. 'This one is bone from my bone and flesh from my flesh. She will be called "woman" because she was taken from "man."' This explains why a man leaves his father and mother and is joined to his wife, and the two are united into one."*

Mother looked up from the Bible and made eye contact with Amy. "Amy. I'm so thankful you've been able to see Samuel for the man that he is. I want to welcome you to the family. You and Samuel are united as one now." I squeezed Amy's hand under the table. "May our good Lord bless you both."

*Our wedding—an answer to prayer and the end of my fear that I'd never
have a family. Warren Haggray is in the background. May 2009.*

In our wedding pictures from that day, Amy is radiant in her white dress. Her smooth, dark hair frames her face underneath her white veil. She looks at me with her bright smile and sparkling eyes—the man of her dreams. How? Her love for me must have been impossible for anyone to understand who only saw our picture. My face looks like somebody took a blowtorch to a wax figure and got it all distorted, then let it solidify in place. My lips and mouth are so swollen that it's hard to tell if I'm even smiling. (I was—or trying to.) The only normal part of my face is the peach-colored crescent moon underneath my left eye where a skin graft had successfully taken.

But thank God, Amy saw past that. She saw me for who I was— the man I was trying to be.

Neither of us had any idea what my face would end up looking like. It might get much worse. Or—over a long series of facial surgeries—it might eventually look something closer to normal, a Frankenstein's monster assemblage of skin patches.

We knew we were committing to a life together, for better or worse. But Amy had elected to marry someone who needed intense care, right from the start—and "worse" was coming at us, hot.

* * *

Some aspects of newlywed life looked perfectly normal. We moved into Amy's house, which she'd bought just a year earlier, fifteen minutes east of Brooke Army Medical Center. We went for morning runs together. After establishing that we were both dog people during our brief dating period, we adopted a Belgian Malinois for me to befriend Amy's dog. We did dinner once a week with our good friends, George and Sharon. We ate out a lot and went to church on Sundays.

Other parts of newlywed life looked completely bizarre. Like— Hannibal Lecter, bizarre. With my facial disfigurement growing steadily worse, the doctors and therapists decided I should wear a clear plastic mask to put pressure on the scar tissue. They scanned my face then made a specialized mold for the mask, but even so, it was horribly uncomfortable. And it was just *weird*. I already looked completely disfigured, and then I had to wear a freakish mask for twelve hours a day? Forget about scaring small children; this mask would give *me* nightmares.

One Saturday afternoon, about a month into being married, Amy hurried to the door after someone rang the doorbell. "Get excited, Sam," she said. "We've got visitors!"

"What? Who? Should I take off my mask?" It was too late. She'd already opened the door.

Anthony Roszko and two other guys from our platoon waited on the stoop. Their deployment had ended. They were back.

I called out his name and hurried to the door as they entered in. I leaned over and gave him a hug, patting his back. Anthony limply patted mine. When I pulled away, he looked stunned.

That stupid mask. "Here, let me take this off," I said. "It's creepy." I pulled the mask off. "That's better. Way more comfortable too. It's so good to see you!"

Anthony's eyes darted away but he smiled tightly. "Good to see you, man."

Amy—either oblivious to Anthony's reaction or all too aware of it—ran interference. "Sit down, you guys! Let me grab some drinks."

Anthony sat down awkwardly on the couch, avoiding my eyes. He looked around the small living room. "This is a great place you have."

"Yeah, Amy bought this place. It's everything we need." We bantered about the house, the yard, the neighborhood—small talk. I asked them about the rest of their deployment; that kept us going for a while.

At one point, Anthony excused himself, holding up his phone. "It's my brother, gotta take this." I hadn't heard the phone ring.

I watched him pace in our front yard, in front of the large living room window. He talked rapidly into the phone and seemed agitated. After about thirty minutes, he came back into the house. He still avoided looking at me, other than quick glances.

"I'm sorry it never worked out for me to return to you guys," I said. "That was my goal for the first few months in the hospital. I was so determined to get well fast enough that I could redeploy with our platoon."

He nodded stiffly. "Yeah, I remember you saying that on the phone. You told us how well you were doing."

"I'm still hoping to go back as an Infantry Officer. That's my goal for healing now."

Anthony nodded again, silently. "Your will has always been really strong, Sam. I'm proud of you for having the will to keep going."

"Thanks, man."

He glanced at my face. "Do they…you mentioned something about facial reconstruction? How much recovery and surgery is left?"

"A little bit—" I began.

Amy interrupted me. "Quite a lot. But we'll take the surgeries one at a time. It will be a while before it's done. Maybe another year or two."

"Not that long," I amended. "I'm a quick healer." I tried to smile.

"Yeah." He glanced at me then looked away again. "You always told us on the phone how well you were doing." It was a point he seemed fixated on.

They left after an hour. Amy studied me. "You don't seem as excited as I expected you'd be, after seeing those guys."

I stared out the window at Anthony's retreating car. In Afghanistan, we'd joked around like brothers. He'd known my mind almost better than anyone besides Steven. Why had he been so weird? And why had he taken that thirty-minute phone call when they only had an hour to visit?

And why didn't he look at me? I thought, knowing the answer. I stared down at the mask in my hand. This mask was supposed to help me, but my scar tissue was too much—it didn't seem to be doing any good. I looked back out the window. Anthony's car was gone.

That afternoon, I shoved the mask in the back of the bathroom cupboard where we kept other first aid supplies. I didn't plan to wear it again. What was the point?

I banked on the surgeries instead. A new surgery was scheduled for every four weeks, and life became oriented around the surgeries' imposed rhythms. The week leading up to the surgery involved several prep appointments. Amy chose to come to them all, lining up her work lunch break with whatever time the appointment was scheduled, then heading back to work as soon as it ended. While she worked, I continued my full-time routine of physical and occupational therapy appointments.

On the day of surgery, I went in at 5:00 a.m. Amy drove in with me to keep me company until they took me back to the operating room, then she'd head to work until she got news I was done. I usually had to stay at the hospital for a few days afterwards, which meant Amy visited me early, went to work, raced home after work to let the dogs out, came back to the hospital, and stayed with me until 9:00 p.m. when visiting hours were over. At that point, she'd head home, crash into bed, and wake up at 5:00 a.m. the next morning to start her routine all over again.

Amy's work demands were exacerbated by the fact that the ICU dietitian she worked with had taken a long stretch of leave. Her work hours weren't just longer; they were also more demanding as Amy had to help carry the load of her absent colleague in addition to her own full schedule—bouncing back and forth between the ICU, the step-down unit, and outpatient rehab. When Amy first asked her supervisor for time off during one of my surgeries, she was given a hard no.

She told me about the conversation later, at home. "There was just *no* flexibility or understanding from her. Her attitude was like, 'Well, you knew what you were getting into when you married him. This is your life now, so good luck. You've still got to get all your work done.'"

I swallowed hard and tried not to let those words sink in: *This is your life now, so good luck.* "What did you say?"

"What *could* I say?" She sighed hard. "I just have to get all my work done."

In retrospect, I should have been more sensitive to Amy's burnout. I had gotten so used to the life and routine of an Infantry Officer, I didn't often stop to consider how exhausting Amy's schedule was.

Since I'd enrolled at West Point, life had consisted of getting up at 5:00 a.m. and working hard all day. There *was* no life outside of military duties and the mission at hand. The mission at hand in this season was to grind through this series of surgeries and rehab and therapies. Amy was a Lieutenant; she knew the drill. As she said once to me, "It is what it is. We just have to trust the process."

That's right: we just had to trust the process and keep going—that was our shared mission.

It didn't occur to me that most new brides imagine married life will look different than boot camp.

To Amy's infinite credit, she never complained about the demands of my care. One night, we were in the bathroom, going through the lengthy wound care routine that defined the weeks, post-surgery. While it wasn't the hours-long process that Mother and I had endured together, it was still an ordeal.

"Do you ever get tired of this?" I asked one evening in the bathroom, while Amy carefully dabbed a special cream over the fresh grafts on my chin.

"Are you kidding me? The wound care is one of my favorite parts." She pulled back and looked at me, giving me one of her bright smiles.

"What?" I asked, incredulous. "Why?"

She shrugged and went back to her dabbing. "It just feels like a sweet moment between you and me. I like being able to take care of you in a way that no one else can. Our friends can have us over for conversation, and we can always go out for a meal. But this is something you legitimately need help with, and I like being the one to meet that need."

But even if Amy refused to complain about being my full-time caregiver, the strain on her began to show itself in other ways. One night, we were eating sushi rolls together from our normal sushi joint. As usual, they'd obliged with our request to cut my rolls into very, very thin pieces that I could fit into my mouth.

"I almost lost it on that visiting professor today," she said, her mouth full of Spicy Tuna roll.

"The infection control doctor? Why? I thought he was a big deal."

"He *is* a big deal, and he knows it," she vented. "After his lecture this morning, he came to the burn unit to do rounds with us and kept stopping to teach. We were doing rounds for close to *three* hours, standing the whole time…" I winced. I knew how hard Amy had been working to complete her rounds efficiently to get all her work done. Three hours was twice as long as it would have normally taken her. "And so I was drinking *water*. Imagine that—I'm standing on my feet in the hot burn unit for three hours and I have the audacity to drink water."

"That was audacious?"

"Apparently, yes! Because he made some snide comment about me drinking an open water container and how inappropriate that was because it could 'release spores.' I almost lost it on him."

That surprised me. Amy knew how to handle difficult people. She was a pro at navigating all sorts of difficult moods among the patients and stressed-out providers on the burn unit. Something like this wouldn't normally rattle her.

"I mean, I didn't *actually* lose it. I just looked at him with eye daggers. Then Dr. Renz made a joke that diffused the situation and we moved on. That was probably a good thing, because otherwise, I might have gone over and slapped that guy."

She lapsed into sudden silence. I took another careful bite of sushi, and studied my wife. What did her expression mean? I hadn't learned the nuances of her moods yet.

Amy pushed her hands through her hair and laughed. "My fuse is so short right now. I'm so stressed out."

I nodded. I didn't know what to say.

There wasn't a lot of downtime for us that summer. It was just work, rehab, recovery, surgery, repeat. But we had an end goal: in September, we'd go on the honeymoon.

We'd delayed the honeymoon on purpose. When we got married in May, I wasn't "travel ready." Doing a month of convalescent leave at my parents' home in Virginia had been hard enough, and that was with Mother helping me as a trained caregiver, doing physical therapy every day, and relying on specialized shipments of supplements. (Thanks, Amy.) A honeymoon cruise was a serious step up, and we both knew I wasn't ready to go off my hospital leash—even with a skilled medical provider as my wife. We decided to do the honeymoon when we'd originally planned to do the wedding: in September, when I'd hopefully be in stronger shape after a summer's worth of intense surgeries and rehab.

But then those plans changed too.

One evening post-surgery, Amy and I sat in my hospital room. She was catching me up on her day. I was still loopy on pain meds but doing my best to pay attention.

"So, I heard something kind of weird today. Well—I don't know if it's 'weird.' Interesting, maybe. I mean, more *concerning* than anything else."

"What?" I asked.

"Another dietitian I once took a class with has been on deployment in Iraq. But apparently, she expressed some suicidal ideation and they're taking it very seriously. They packed her up and sent her back stateside. She's done with the deployment."

I wasn't sure why Amy found this so especially weird or interesting. Mental health issues were not unusual during deployments. My thoughts struggled to make connections through the fog of the pain meds. "Did you know her well?"

"No. Barely at all. But Sam—there aren't many dietitians in the Army."

I nodded and waited. "You're very special?" I suggested, still looking for the thread.

"*Sam.*" She laughed impatiently, then became serious. "The Army can't plan for such a sudden vacancy. They're going to need to pull a replacement dietitian from one of the big medical centers, and it could only be this one, or Walter Reed."

Slowly, I began to realize what Amy was communicating. "You think it will be you?"

"I'm the lowest ranking and the most expendable, at either facility. So, yes." She sighed. "We might need to prepare…for me to deploy."

A deployment? I had been so obsessed with getting myself re-deployed, I hadn't thought about the Army calling upon my very capable wife. I felt a mixture of excitement for her, jealousy, fear, and dread. Could I manage without Amy?

She must have been thinking the same thing. "I could try to fight it, if it comes down like that," she said without much conviction. "I could explain that I'm needed here, as your caregiver."

I didn't like the sound of that. I wasn't *completely* helpless. Far be it from me to hold Amy back from the call of duty—even if I really, really didn't want her to go. "I could manage," I said, not fully convinced. "I've been leaning on you as a crutch, a little bit. This would force me to be more independent."

Amy nodded, ready to agree. "In some ways, this might be better in the long run," she suggested. "I'd be joining the deployment halfway into its duration, so I'd be gone for less time than if it was a full one."

I nodded, thinking about what her absence would mean for me. *No honeymoon. No surgeries until she got back. No Amy.*

I shrugged. "It hasn't happened yet. Let's just wait and see what they do."

"Good call," she agreed. She looked at her watch. "It's nearly nine. I should go."

* * *

Within two weeks, Amy was called into her OIC's office (officer in charge). They gave her the news she was expecting: in a matter of days, she'd deploy to Iraq.

She told me the news during her lunch break. Her voice was energized; her eyes sparkled. "I know this is a huge change of plans," she acknowledged, "but it's also a big opportunity for me."

It didn't occur to me that an Iraq deployment might seem like less work and more fun than the grind Amy had been currently experiencing. All I could think about was months on end without her. But I tried to shove that disappointment under pragmatic considerations and a focus on duty.

That night over dinner, I tried to rally myself for the prospect, going over the same rationale Amy had already provided. "I don't even know if we *have* a veto power. But I'm not sure it's worth trying to exercise it, even if we do. You're probably going to have to deploy at some point. If you can do it now, it will be shorter than later."

She nodded. "We'll reschedule the honeymoon. And I spoke with your doctors today. They said we'll have to pause the facial reconstruction surgeries, but you'll still be able to do surgeries on your arms and hands."

Pause the facial reconstruction surgeries. I tried not to think about what that might mean for my appearance. Would the hypertrophic scarring continue to build up tissue while Amy was gone? Would I look even worse by the time she got home?

"Six months," she said. "Mid-September to late March. It sounds like a long time, but it will go fast." She looked at me apologetically. "I'll miss you."

I'll miss you too, I wanted to say, but the obviousness of this fact was too painful to say aloud. Amy had been the best thing to happen to me—not just since the accident, but ever. She had quickly become my best friend, and her companionship was the best part of every day. Beyond the emotional ties, Amy and I both knew my healing couldn't move forward without a carepartner. Mother couldn't sub in. She had put in her dues already—and besides, she was needed at home in Virginia.

It was time for me to start functioning independently, even if that meant dealing with the current version of my face for another six months.

"I love you," I said. "And I'll be fine. I'll focus on rehab. This will be really good for your military career. And who knows, you might even have a good time."

She nodded, her eyes shining. "I hope so."

***

With Amy gone, my healing progress entered into a holding pattern. The therapy and rehab continued, but the surgeries essentially stopped. I might have had one minor one on my hand. That was as much as could be managed without someone at home helping me with wound care, post-surgery.

I hung out with the dogs. I visited with friends. I went running. I headed to Virginia to spend the holidays with my family again.

Finally, in February—a month early—she was back. *Amy.*

Her eyes still sparkled, but her smile was a bit less bright, like someone had turned down the dimmer one notch. Just two weeks before Amy's deployment ended, a rocket landed fifteen feet away from her. Although it didn't detonate—if it had, she would have died—it still sent a shower of shrapnel flying through the vicinity which shredded two container housing units used as latrines. Amy happened to be in the bathroom at the time, and her stall was the single place in a wide radius that the shrapnel didn't penetrate. She was the only person there who walked away with no external wounds.

"I know it was God," she told me, clearly shaken with the memory. "The Lord put His hands around my little bathroom stall and just protected me. But I was so stunned by the whole incident. I felt like I was in a daze. The other women in there were all wounded. I was the first one to see them and try to treat them until others arrived."

The experience had shaken her up. I was so glad to have her home, even if she was a different person than the woman who'd left. We started getting to know each other again.

And we finally booked a honeymoon.

Hawaii in April, we'd decided. Hawaii was a popular honeymoon destination—surely, that meant we'd have a good time. We didn't fully think through what tropical sunshine would mean for my fragile, scarred skin, nor did we really have a sense of what we liked to do on vacations together.

But—we couldn't go wrong with Hawaii. Right?

Instead of Hawaiian shirts, I wore long sleeves and a goofy sunhat everywhere I went—even into the water. One of the first experiences we booked was snorkeling in Oahu's Hanauma Bay. The brochure had made it an easy sell—a *natural, protected area...stunning coral reefs... one of the top snorkeling destinations in the world.* We bought snorkels and masks and little fins.

Amy splashed off into the bay. She paused and turned around, waiting for me to join her. I waved her ahead. "You go!"

I stared at my snorkel. How was I going to get this thing in my tiny mouth? I tried shoving it past my swollen lips and put my face in the water. Instantly, my mouth filled with the salty ocean. I couldn't make a seal over the mouthpiece. I tried again, pushing the mouthpiece in farther and biting down with my teeth. I pushed off, willing my body to participate in this paradisal experience. Once again, my mouth filled with water.

I pulled away the tube, frustrated. I could see Amy floating peacefully around thirty yards away. *Fine,* I thought. *I'll just hold my breath and use the mask.* I stuck my head underwater. As soon as I needed to breathe, I had to kick my legs to pop my head up fully to get a decent breath. There was no way to peacefully float and admire the coral or the fishes—I had to keep going vertical again to get my head out of the water. My pathetic floating was exacerbated by the fact that I had almost no body fat to help keep my six feet, four inches worth of bones buoyant. I kept sinking down, then spluttering back up. No cute little clown fish or striking sea stars were sticking around for *that.*

For months, I'd oriented my focus on what I *could* do: the new gains I'd made, the activities I'd reclaimed, the *progress.* But here, in this Hawaiian paradise, on my honeymoon, wearing this stupid snorkel gear, I felt hit with my limitations.

Amy was drifting farther away. I knew I wasn't going to be able to keep up. The frustration kept mounting. *This is just SNORKELING. It should be EASY.* I tried again, doing my best to take a deeper breath and plunging my mask into the water. Even as I did so, it occurred to me that my inhalation injuries most likely were inhibiting my lungs' capacity to hold a breath. I stretched my body out in the water, willing myself to float, willing myself to enjoy it. My tall, skinny body wasn't having it. My legs sank, my lungs gasped for air. I flailed and splashed.

Finally, I gave up. I swam back to the beach and sat in the sand. Eventually, Amy joined me. "What's wrong? Did you not like it?"

"I just can't participate," I explained, hating the negative way I sounded. "The tube won't fit in my mouth, and I can't float."

Amy was sympathetic. "Do you want me to sit here with you?"

"No, you should enjoy it."

She protested for a while, and I protested back until she finally waded back into the water, glancing guiltily back at me. On the bus ride back to the hotel, Amy didn't tell me about the fish or the turtles she'd seen. She didn't describe the coral.

We just sat in silence.

In Kauai, we decided to try the pool instead. That felt lame. Here I was: with my gorgeous wife, on a beautiful island, with great beaches at an incredible resort, but I needed to limit myself to the pool. From the shallow end, I could see the beach and the ocean, just a stone's throw away. While Amy sunbathed poolside, I waded around in my long-sleeve rashguard, with my wide-brimmed sun hat.

I felt ridiculous.

A little kid began to approach me. He had his head down in the water, goggles on, and was splashing his legs while holding onto a kickboard. He swam closer, obviously not registering the man that was standing in the shallow end close by. Finally, an arm's distance away, he must have seen my feet. He popped his head out of the water, tugged his goggles off, and looked up.

He stared at me, eyes wide, jaw dropped—an expression of shock and horror. I wasn't surprised. I'd gotten used to this. But I wanted to somehow make myself seem less scary. I decided to try a joke.

"Make sure you wear sunscreen, kid," I said. "Otherwise, you could end up looking like this."

His eyes grew even wider. He turned around and started kicking furiously back to the other side of the pool. "Mom!" he yelled out. "MOM! I need more sunscreen!!"

That made me chuckle. I looked over at Amy to see if she'd followed the interaction. Her face was covered by a magazine, her brow covered by her hat.

We spent most of our two weeks driving around the islands, looking at pretty things, assuming that's how most couples enjoyed their Hawaiian honeymoons, and not really enjoying ourselves. Finally, we hit on an inspiration.

"Want to try a hike?" Amy asked me. "This one on the Nā Pali Coast is supposed to be beautiful."

A hike wouldn't involve stupid equipment or call attention to my limitations with sun exposure. And—thanks to my running habit—the one impressive thing I could do physically at that point was put one foot in front of the other. *I could hike.* "YES," I said. "Let's do a hike."

When we pulled into the parking lot, we were surprised to find many vacant spaces. The sign at the head of the trail informed us that the Nā Pali Coast experienced its own climate, and that the rainy season lasted from November to April. As if on cue, we heard a distant roll of thunder above us. Rain began to fall.

"You still game for this?" Amy asked.

"We are going to do this hike if it kills me."

"Let's do it!"

The trail shouldn't have been difficult, but the rain turned the path into clay-like mud which was incredibly slippery. Amy slid her hiking sandals forward like an ice skater. "I'm clay skating," she said.

The path curved up out of the trees and began skirting a high cliff. The ocean swirled far below us—at least a couple hundred feet. "No skating here," I cautioned.

"I can't believe there's no fence or guardrail or anything," Amy said, peering over the edge.

We made our way carefully along the cliff's rim, then began moving back downhill. By the time we made it to the beach, we felt enormous satisfaction with ourselves.

"We survived!" Amy crowed. She turned to me. "It's two more miles to the waterfall. Do you want to keep going?"

I didn't, but I wasn't about to admit it. "I'm game if you are."

"Really? You're not too cold?"

"I'm not too cold if you're not too cold." We studied each other, each trying to discern what the other's actual feelings were. "If you want to do it, let's do it," I said.

"You want to do it?" she asked.

I concluded she must want to go. I nodded. "Let's do it."

We made our way across a creek at the far end of the beach, balancing on stepping stones to get across, then picked up the trail as it wound back into a forest. The rain began to pour. We followed the trail to another creek crossing and managed to leap across it. I studied the creek. "Amy, look at how fast the water's rising from the rain."

She studied it. "Dang!"

The trail crossed the creek two more times as we wound our way along it to the waterfall. Each time, the crossing was more intense, the current stronger. Finally, we found the waterfall.

"It's great!" she called to me, over the roar of the falls mixed with the sound of the rain.

"It's amazing!" I agreed, shivering.

"Want to go back?" she yelled. I nodded, violently.

We made it to the first creek crossing. The creek was now raging, the water risen thigh high. Amy was alarmed. "Sam, I don't think we should try to cross."

"Let's try staying on this side of it," I suggested. "Maybe we can just follow the creek back to the trailhead without trying to cross over." Amy accepted my suggestion. That was unfortunate.

We got lost.

After thirty minutes of trying to find our way back to the trail and failing, we found ourselves edging along a fifty-foot drop off, looking down at the creek roaring with white water. "Careful," Amy urged. The thick vegetation pushed us right up against the edge.

"You know, I don't think this is a real trail at all," I said, trying to ignore my trepidation. "I think we're following a pig trail or a goat tra—"

Suddenly, I had the horrible sensation of no longer being connected to the ground, of no longer having control over my shape in the universe. Amy let out a sharp gasp. I was falling.

I landed right at the cliff's edge. My right leg swung off of it, dangling fifty feet above the rushing water. My left leg and butt had landed on the slippery mud of the trail. I felt Amy's hand grab my arm as I stared down into the roaring creek. She tugged me back. I scrambled away from the edge.

"We have *got* to find our way out of here," she burst out. "Is anyone else on this trail?!" she yelled. "Where is the trail?!"

We heard distant voices. "Oh my gosh, thank God!" Amy said. "Where are you?"

"Are you guys on the trail?" I called out.

Following their voices, we made it back to the original crossing. Several people stood on the other side. By holding hands with them and making a kind of bridge, Amy and I were able to get across the creek.

"You look like you've seen some gnarly action," one of the men yelled to me over the roar of the waterfall. "You think we'll make it back alive?" I couldn't tell if he was referring to my wounds or our fatigued, drenched-to-the-bone look after emerging from the forest back onto the trail.

"We'd better!" I yelled back. "I didn't survive being blown up just to drown in a river!"

In the company of our new friends, we managed to navigate two more creek crossings by locking arms together. Amy kept remarking how amazing and terrifying and sketchy the whole thing is. "What were we *thinking?*" she asked me, her tone a mixture of exhilaration and fear.

We finally made our way back to the beach where there was the fourth and final creek crossing. But this crossing—where all the force of the tributaries converged and plunged into the ocean—was by far the highest and most furious. A group of people, all of us soaking wet and shivering, had gathered at its bank. One by one, we saw couples and individuals try to cross it. There was no safe way. The rocky part where we'd crossed the first time was now covered with water, and the rocks underneath made the water foam like rapids. *That* didn't look good. We watched several people try to cross there. They made it across, but barely, and we could see the force of the current as the water foamed furiously up to their midsection.

The other option was closer to the ocean, where the water widened across the softer banks of the beach and seemed to quiet down. Still, most people were opting for the higher crossing. Neither option looked good, but there was no other way to get around the creek; the beach was surrounded by cliffs on either side. The *only* way forward was through the water. Somehow, we had to get across to the trail if we hoped to make it back to the car.

We agreed to try the lower crossing, where the river widened and seemed to calm before meeting the ocean. Holding hands, we stepped in. Amy swore, and I immediately understood why: the combination of the ocean waves and the current from the river aggressively pulled the sand out from underneath our feet. We took another step, the water now up to our thighs, rain still pouring down. There was nothing firm to stand on. The ground we stood on was dissolving under our feet.

I took another step and suddenly was swept into the water. I heard Amy call my name and grip my hand. Frantically, I floundered, trying to get a purchase on something. My foot pushed against something— more shifting sand. I righted myself.

"Do NOT drown!" Amy yelled at me fiercely. "Let's get *out* of here!"

Hurriedly, we pushed across the rest of the river and made it to the other side. We breathed a sigh of relief.

Amy shook her head. "If there was any doubt that God has a purpose for us, He's answered that today. Because we both should have drowned and you should have plummeted to your death when you fell off that cliff. HOLY COW, Sam!"

"Let's wait to celebrate until we've made it back to the car," I said. "Two more miles to go."

She shook her head again in disbelief.

We began making our way up the slippery trail. Our sandals were caked with mud and traction felt impossible. Both of us fell several times.

We reached the stretch along the cliff and looked at each other. "Don't even think about cliff diving here, Sam," Amy warned. Slowly, we began edging along the trail. I glanced over the cliff. The water below looked dark gray and angry. Waves smashed against the rock face hundreds of feet down. As the trail finally curved away from the cliff and back into the forest, both of us exhaled.

Thank God, the rest of the hike was nothing more than wet and slippery. We both cheered when we saw our rental car in the parking lot. We climbed in, dripping, muddy, and shivering. As we drove back to our hotel, the clouds above us cleared. We saw blue sky. A rainbow stretched from the rainy coast behind us in a glimmering bridge toward the sunny beaches we were driving toward. It was like the morning's harrowing ordeal had never happened.

That night, at dinner—after hot showers, a long nap, and a fresh change of clothes—we recapped. Amy's takeaway conclusion surprised me.

"Don't think I'm crazy," she said.

"Always a good way to begin a conversation," I grinned.

"I think I might *love* hiking."

"*What?*"

"I know!" she said, delighted. "We nearly died several times, and it was dangerous. But also, it was *beautiful.* The waterfall was really fun. I loved getting away from the city. And Sam—don't you think it's amazing that our bodies did that? Like—*your* body did that! You made it through all that rainy nastiness, eight miles round trip. I'm just so proud of you for not giving up and being willing to do adventurous activities with me!"

"Huh." Amy was right. It *was* sort of incredible that we'd managed it. And when we'd been in the middle of it all, I wasn't thinking about being a burn victim or being disfigured. We were just taking in beauty, working as a team, trying to help each other get back to the trailhead. In fact—when I considered the snorkeling, the pool, and the shopping—I had to admit the hike was shaping up to be the trip highlight so far. Now that we'd survived it.

"Let's do more hikes when we get home," I suggested. She nodded, satisfied.

* * *

With Amy's deployment behind us and having successfully survived the honeymoon, the summer of 2010 found us settling back into life in San Antonio. It also became The Summer of My Face. "Time heals all wounds" was now officially a debunked cliché in my book. Time had not healed my wounds. Time had made my wounds much worse—big and red and bumpy and thick. I turned to the surgical approach instead.

Me, saluting the flag at a change of command ceremony, roughly sixteen months after the accident.

I knew facial reconstruction would be a massive undertaking—Amy and I both did. But the severity and disfiguration of my scars at that point seemed impossible to live with, long-term. The disfigurement wasn't just the kind of thing that made small children bolt for more sunscreen; it was impacting my ability to live and function productively in the world. It was a bizarre thing to commit to a process that would leave me, once again, unrecognizable, but facial reconstruction seemed like the only path forward. In that way, it wasn't unlike our Kauai hike: fording the river looked pretty unforgiving—but what else was there to do?

So, we plunged in.

The facial reconstruction involved cutting off the bumpy red scar tissue on my face and grafting on healthy skin over the top of my facial structure. That healthy skin was "harvested" from other parts of my body in one of two ways: a "partial thickness" graft involved skimming a thin layer of skin off the top of an unburned part of the body. In theory, that process would enable the graft site to scab and then heal with new healthy skin, enabling doctors to use that site multiple times.

"In theory." That didn't work on my body, unfortunately. By the time we began my facial reconstruction, we had learned that my body reacted with hypertrophic scarring to any partial thickness grafts. Any little "skim off the top" slice produced new angry red tissue which became worse than useless; it became another site of badly scarred disfiguration.

That left us with Option 2: full-thickness grafts. With a full-thickness graft, you take out a section of skin at its full thickness: a nice skin steak. Then, doctors take the edges of the surrounding skin, pull them together, and sew it closed. That approach had worked better with my hypertrophic scarring reaction, but it had its limitations. Each site of a full-thickness graft could only be used once. That skin wasn't growing back. My body's few remaining sites of healthy, unburned, unscarred skin became extremely precious real estate.

In order to maximize the potential of these precious areas of healthy skin—and also because skin grafts naturally shrink after being removed—part of my pre-op for each surgery involved stretching out the donor skin ahead of time. This involved balloons and saline, which sounds more fun than it actually was. During a preparatory surgery, the surgeon inserted a small rectangular bag underneath my skin at the donor site which was connected to a port. At weekly appointments, a doctor or PA would take a saline syringe and connect it to the port which they could feel through my skin. They pumped saline into the bag, gradually expanding the skin over time. This forced the skin to grow, making it easier to get a larger full-thickness graft with enough remaining stretch to stitch together the remaining skin.

During the surgery, the expanded skin was cut and harvested, then grafted onto my face in an area where they'd cut away the scar tissue. So long as the graft got proper blood flow and I got proper nutrition, the graft would take. If it didn't, the graft would eventually die: turning black and putting me in a position to have to start that graft process over.

The person leading this big facial adventure was Dr. Robert Spence. Dr. Spence normally worked at Johns Hopkins in Baltimore but traveled to San Antonio one week per month to do reconstructive surgeries on the burn patients at BAMC. In between the surgeries, he met with patients to consult about their upcoming surgeries and line up their surgical prep. That meant whenever Dr. Spence was in town, we were consulting about my next month's surgery—let's say, my upper lip—and then I'd go under the knife for whatever it was we'd discussed during the previous month's consult—let's say, my nose.

I felt lucky to be working with Dr. Spence. He was widely considered to be the best burn plastic surgeon in the world, and I was getting him toward the end of his career, when he had years of accumulated knowledge and skill. With him leading the charge, we'd end up replacing all of the skin from my eyes and ears, down to my neck.

We couldn't do it all in one surgery; we did it piece by piece, like assembling a puzzle. My upper lip was its own surgery. Then came my lower lip. My chin came next. Then my upper neck, below my jaw. Between each surgery, we were prepping the donor site: filling the little bags with saline, stretching the skin, praying it would take. The Summer of My Face turned into the Autumn of My Face and then on into winter. Every successful new graft was cause for celebration.

By the spring of 2011, we were gearing up for my cheeks. These presented a new challenge, due to their larger size. Dr. Spence broke down the approach in our pre-op consult.

"We're going to get more creative with this surgery," he said. "I'm concerned that there's a high risk of these larger grafts failing unless we maintain good blood flow. So, here's how I think we can accomplish that." He motioned toward my collarbone. "We're going to do the donor site here, at your clavicle. We'll really bloat and grow the skin there, but we're not going to sever all the veins. Instead, we're going to leave something called a pedicle attached—basically, a blood vessel that's still attached to its original site."

"How do we move the skin onto my cheek, then?" I asked.

"We're going to rotate it," he said.

"*What?*" Amy asked. "How will that work?"

He set his hand flat on my clavicle, with his thumb resting on my collarbone. "Imagine that my thumb is the pedicle and the rest of my hand is the graft. We take the skin—" Then he rotated his hand up toward my cheek, keeping his thumb connected to the bump of my collarbone. "But keep the pedicle connected to its blood source so the graft never loses good blood flow. After about a week, the graft will start to take to the site and begin producing its own blood, at which point we can sever the pedicle."

"How long will the prep take?" Amy asked.

"It will be a two-month process. And we'll try to do both cheeks at the same time."

The night before the surgery, Amy caught me studying my reflection in the mirror. We made eye contact. "You nervous about this one?" she asked.

I studied my face again. "A little. If it works, it would be huge." There were small portions of healthy pink on my face—the half-moon under my left eye; my nose; my lips and chin. Everything straight down the middle had now emerged as more recognizably human. But the sides of my face still looked like they'd been melted by a blowtorch. The surgery tomorrow had the chance to transform all that. "My whole face might be peachy pink soon." I looked down at Amy. "Wouldn't that be nice to look at?"

"You're already my favorite person to look at," she said. "No matter what facial version we're on."

Early the next morning, Amy said goodbye to me as they wheeled me into the operating room. "See you when you wake up!" she called.

Hours later, I blinked awake. Dr. Spence was sitting next to the bed. That was weird—usually, he only stopped by briefly. Amy was sitting on the other side. She looked concerned.

"What is it?" I asked thickly, still groggy from the pain meds.

"We've had a complication," Dr. Spence said, letting out a quick exhale, as though trying to stifle his frustration. "The pedicle blood vessel wasn't where we expected it to be, which meant we weren't able to do the rotational flap."

"You didn't do it?"

"We did the full-thickness graft on one side, but there's no active blood supply. We had already cut away the scar tissue so…" Dr. Spence pressed his eyes closed. "That was really our only option."

I tried to piece together conclusions through the fog of the medication. "So…what happened to the other side?"

"They didn't do the other side," Amy said quietly. "They're going to wait until there's a better plan in place."

"And there's no good blood flow to the graft you did?"

He shook his head tightly.

"What are the odds that it takes?" I asked.

He glanced over at Amy. "Eat everything she tells you to eat." He paused. "And get everyone you know to pray."

We followed his instructions. But even with Amy's nutritional regimen and an army of prayer warriors, the new graft on my cheek turned gray. Later, it turned black. Like—the black of your computer screen when it's shut off. Totally, horribly, black.

It had died.

One side of my face was still mottled and red. The other looked like charcoal. And adding insult to injury, my risk of infection with the dead skin sitting on the raw tissue beneath went way up.

We knew we had to start over. That was crushing. All the effort to make things better and reclaim some sort of redeemed facial identity had only ended up with a dead graft.

Death. When would it stop following me?

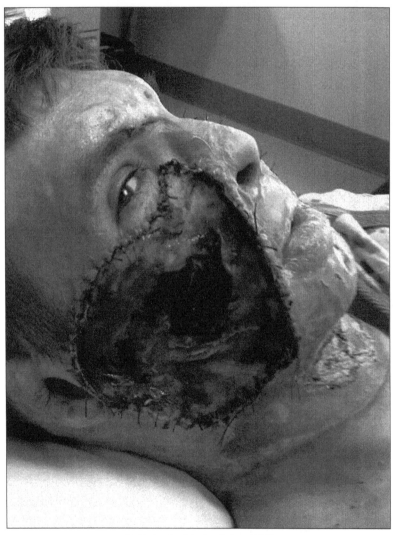

The blackened and dead graft. August 2010.

Regardless of whether I wanted to or not, the only option was to continue plunging forward, one step at a time.

The facial reconstruction dragged on. Each cheek was an ordeal. The graft for my neck was also a huge surgery, which thankfully was successful. Dr. Spence informed us proudly that it was the largest full-thickness reconstructive skin graft he'd ever done.

We wrapped things up with my ears—those gnarled little bits of scarred tissue that looked like cooked bacon which still clung to the sides of my head. After deliberating over a number of options, we decided to cut them off and opt for prosthetic ones instead.

"I remember when I had to decide whether or not to amputate my finger," I told Amy. "It felt like such a big deal. Now look at me. Cutting my ears off."

"You've come so far," she said with mock pride. She patted me on the back.

After three years of recovery and more than a year working on The Face, we were nearing a point that felt complete. I didn't necessarily love where I was at, but I knew that I was approaching the slippery slope of turning plastic surgery into a never-ending project. I still looked like a burn victim—but I looked a whole lot better than on my wedding day. Wasn't I always going to be able to find something to find fault with? I decided I could choose to accept it instead, and try to move on.

Besides, I was just *tired.* My motivation to do all the work of healing seemed to wane with each subsequent surgery. I wanted life to be about something other than making myself prettier.

One afternoon, I got a call from a guy I knew through a wounded veterans organization. He had gotten inspired after meeting me at an event and had started a non-profit to help burn survivors. He was very aggressive—in a positive way—about raising money and doing research about the latest medical advancements in burn survivor care. I'd grown to respect him and everything he was doing for guys like me.

I could hear his excitement over the phone. "Sam, I've gotten in contact with a plastic surgeon who just completed the world's first full face transplant in China. It was successful! And he's willing to do a full face transplant on you, at *no* cost. He would do it as part of his research."

"Really," I said, almost in disbelief.

"It would mean a scar-free face, Sam. A fresh start. There's a high likelihood you wouldn't even look like a burn survivor anymore."

I asked a few more questions. We agreed to talk again soon.

That night, Amy asked me how I was feeling about the conversation as we got ready for bed. I shrugged. "I don't know, babe. I was finally feeling kind of happy with where I'm at. I know *this* could be a better outcome—" I gestured at my face. "But there's also risk. It could be worse."

She nodded, looking serious.

"It's been a ton of time and work already...and I'm really okay with where I'm at. I've started feeling familiar with how I look now. There's almost a comfort in living in what's known."

"We've gone through *so* much to get to this point," she said. We climbed into bed and pulled up the covers. I looked at her next to me on the pillow.

"The guy said I might not even look like a burn survivor anymore. It would be a scar-free face."

Amy furrowed her eyebrows. "But your scars are such a huge part of your story. I fell in love with you because of who you were underneath the scars, but also *because* of the scars. It was the combination of seeing your joy despite the evidence of what you'd gone through that was so amazing to me. For goodness' sake, Sam, your scars are a huge reason I know Jesus."

The impact of what she was saying wasn't lost on me. "I think the guy means well. He's coming from a nice place," I said.

"I'm sure he is," she agreed.

"He's probably not going to believe it if I turn down a scar-free face, done by a world-class surgeon at no cost to me. But...I just don't feel like it's worth it."

Amy sighed, contentedly. "That's how I feel too. I'm glad we're on the same page." She kissed my nose. "You look good."

"I'm happy where we're at. Are you happy with where we're at?"

She turned off the light and snuggled down next to me. "I've always been happy."

I thought about Amy's words as her breathing grew deep and even next to me. It was true—my scars had become part of my story. They were part of my identity now. And it was a part of my identity I didn't want to lose.

CHAPTER 12

WOUNDED WARRIOR

Preparing to deploy and proudly sporting the "Big Red 1" patch of the First Infantry Division—though this patch was in combat gray. Around April 2008.

I knew where I was going.

Toward the end of my Infantry Officer training, I was assigned to the Second Brigade, First Cavalry Division, headed to Iraq. As soon as I wrapped up my training, I would head to Fort Hood, Texas, to prepare for the deployment. I'd spoken with the personnel there and had a plan to pick up all the gear being issued to me for that specific deployment. I knew I wouldn't have long in Fort Hood before I got on a plane and joined the unit in Iraq.

I knew all of that.

Less than two weeks before I was scheduled to leave Fort Benning, the plan changed. A group of around thirty of us got called out one morning at formation. "Wait for everyone else to clear out," we were ordered. We waited. Everyone else was dismissed.

An officer stepped forward. "The group of y'all thought that you knew what unit you were going to. Well, plans have changed. You've heard the phrase, 'needs of the Army.' The Army has just decided it needs to stand up a new Infantry brigade. They're going to pull one together from scratch, and y'all are gonna be part of that new brigade. So, congratulations on being the first soldiers to join—" He studied the piece of paper he held. "Third Brigade of the First Infantry Division. You will likely have one year to train up before you lead your troops in either Iraq or Afghanistan." He looked back up at us and nodded sharply. "That's your new unit assignment."

As soon as I heard him say "First Infantry Division," I was instantly taken back to a memory from childhood.

It was a family road trip. I was still a young kid, but I already knew I wanted to be in the military when I grew up. I had no plan, thought, or idea about doing anything else. I remember squinting out the window, watching fields go by through dusty clouds. While driving through Kansas, my father decided to have us stop at Fort Riley, home of the First Infantry Division.

We went to the gift shop. It was air-conditioned and cool, a respite from the hot sun outside. Mother and Father told me I could pick out a souvenir.

I wandered, looking at T-shirts, mugs, keychains. None of them captured my attention.

Then I found a basket of large brass coins. I picked one up. It felt heavy in my palm—a good kind of heft. I studied it. In the middle of the coin was a raised image of the First Infantry Division patch—a green patch with a big, red "1" in the center. Around the outer edge of the coin was inscribed a motto: *No mission too difficult, no sacrifice too great. Duty first.*

The clarity and call of the motto sent a thrill through me, even as a kid.

We bought the coin. I studied it in the car and held it tight in my hand until it became warm and sweaty. Back home in Arkansas, the coin became one of my most prized possessions. I cherished it throughout my childhood, carrying it everywhere. I knew that motto by heart. It became something sacred to me: a kind of commandment to live by.

When I arrived at Fort Hood to join up with the new brigade, I picked up my gear from the Central Issue Facility. Back in my apartment just outside post, I dug through my duffel bag and pulled out one of my uniforms. There it was: the green patch. The "Big Red 1." The motto flashed through my mind. Later, it was repeated over and over by our officers throughout the deployment preparation.

No mission too difficult, no sacrifice too great. Duty first.

I had been assigned to the First Infantry Division, and the motto I'd memorized as a kid was now *my* unit's motto. It felt like destiny, somehow. I'd arrived exactly where I was meant to be. I was going exactly where I was meant to go.

Plans had changed—but I still knew that.

A "Wounded Warrior." Spring 2011.

Way back on the hospital grounds, behind the barracks which housed recovering enlisted soldiers, there were a few small trailers. As I approached them, I thought of the "portables" my middle school used when the student population overwhelmed the main building: little, shabby, one-story structures. I scanned the small nameplates on the doors until I found the one I was looking for: "Wounded Warrior Battalion: Bravo Company."

I paused before climbing the stairs. I was in a bad mood.

My healing journey was drawing to a close—after three years, I was finally preparing to "graduate" from the endless therapy sessions and surgeries that had defined my life since the accident in September of 2008. I had looked forward to this threshold as the moment when the military would take me back. Once I was healed, I could return to service. I could start up my career as an Infantry Officer again—ideally, contributing all the new knowledge and experiences I'd gained over the past few years to lead with greater wisdom and efficacy. This goal had kept me going.

Instead, the military was kicking me out.

"You don't have to take it personally," Amy had urged me. "A medical retirement is honorable. It means you served and sacrificed for your country. They *appreciate* you."

But that's not how it felt. I'd dreamed about a career in the military for my entire life. I didn't *want* to be medically retired—I wanted to serve my country. Without that service to look forward to, I wasn't sure what was left. I couldn't even lean on my temporary mission of encouraging the soldiers and staff in the burn unit anymore, since I was moving on from the hospital.

I'd been in such a great place for much of my healing journey, but now the last vestiges of my former identity were being pulled out of my grasp. Empty-handed, I felt anxious, frustrated, and unanchored.

Who was I supposed to be, if not a leader? What was I supposed to do now, if not serve?

The worst part was, the military was trying to make me feel good about it. First, they'd promoted me to Captain—a promotion that I accepted as a matter of course, one which Amy had also received in due time. And now, they wanted to give me an award.

I sighed as I climbed the creaking steps of the trailer. When I opened the door, I was greeted with a blast of frigid air-conditioning. Inside, there were posters up all over the beige walls, arranged haphazardly. Some were motivational—or at least, that seemed to be the intent. Others were sterile bureaucratic government disclaimers and announcements. Behind a desk, there was a bulletin board covered messily with information about various events, resume workshops, suicide prevention classes, and so on. The desk in front of it was likewise piled with messy stacks of paper.

"Close the door behind you to keep the air in."

The man sitting behind the desk waved me in without looking up. With his beige shirt, pale skin, and ashy blond hair, he nearly disappeared into the stacks of papers around him.

I shut the door and stepped toward the desk. The structure groaned as I moved.

The man glanced up. "Captain Brown?"

"Yes, Sir."

He began rifling through some of the papers on his desk. "Hang on. I just saw your paperwork this morning..."

I waited. His fumbling with the papers seemed to exaggerate his large hands and thick fingers. "Looks like they keep you pretty busy in here," I remarked.

He sighed and shook his head. "Tons of paperwork goes into retiring people out of the military."

I nodded, trying not to let "retiring out of the military" feel like a personal insult. I looked at the motivational poster on the wall behind him. It was the silhouette of a soldier aiming a machine gun, backed by a yellow sky. A giant word at the bottom said, "BELIEVE." Underneath, in much smaller letters, I read, "*If we are strong, our strength will speak for itself.*"

Annoyed, I looked back down at the stout man at the desk. He looked like the type of guy who might have played sports in college—maybe wrestling or D2 football. He looked tired now. Worn out. Another casualty of the machine.

"There we go! Captain Samuel Brown." With a heavy sigh, he pulled a stapled packet of paper from the pile and looked up at me, seeming to register my face for the first time. He smiled blandly. "Congratulations. The Army intends to issue you a Meritorious Service Medal."

"No," I said, feeling a flash of anger.

"No?" His forehead wrinkled. "Why 'no'?"

"For the last three years, all I've done is endure therapy, surgeries, and convert oxygen to carbon dioxide. Meanwhile, there are young men and women literally putting their lives on the line right now, and in some cases dying. And most of the time, they get little or no recognition for that. I do not deserve a 'Meritorious' award, so please don't write me up for one."

The man blinked and looked down at the paperwork, then back up at me. "Well—but, this is customary. This is about your service as a whole. This is what we *do* for people who are retiring." He shook the paper. "You served honorably," he protested.

I bristled at the man's attempted affirmation. "Yes, I served honorably. But I still feel like accepting this award would be an insult to the people fighting in combat overseas."

This—whether or not I deserved it—felt like a consolation prize, written all over with pity. "Do not write me up for a Meritorious Service Medal. I will refuse to take it."

The man seemed on the verge of protesting again, then apparently decided it wasn't worth the effort. "All right. Well, in that case, your retirement date is September 27. Two months from now. You'll need to make an appointment to come back next week to fill out some paperwork. There'll be a lot of paperwork." He let out a sigh that wasn't quite a wheeze. "That's all for today then, Captain Brown."

It was a relief to get out of there.

As I walked back through the campus, my phone buzzed. I looked at the caller ID: *Anthony Roszko*. I picked it up. "Hey, man."

"LT!" Anthony's deep, familiar voice made me smile, despite my mood. I was thankful we'd stayed in touch, even after our awkward first meeting following his return from deployment. The old dynamic had been easy to find again after he got used to the shock of my burns and we'd maintained a strong friendship. "How are you doing?" he asked.

I didn't want to say much on that. "Doing fine. How about you?"

Anthony sighed. "Well, looks like my military career is over."

"Wait—what?" I asked. Was it possible Anthony was in the same boat I was in? I knew he'd sustained a number of injuries during his deployments. Was he being medically retired too?

"I mean—not *actually*," he said. "But I don't get to do the fun stuff anymore. They're parking me stateside. I've got an assignment at Fort Jackson, South Carolina, as a Staff NCO. No more deployments."

"A hard-charging guy like you, working a desk job?"

He sighed again. "Yeah, man. It sucks, right?"

I felt myself shifting back into the mode that had become second nature over the past two years—that of encourager. It was a relief to have a reason to shift out of my grim mental state into something more positive. "You've served honorably. You've been on multiple deployments. This is a good thing. Your body needs a break from the field. Hasn't your back been all messed up?"

"Yeah. And I'm still having issues with the shrapnel wounds."

"You should take advantage of this time to start addressing some of your medical stuff. Don't squander the opportunity to start doing PT on some of your physical injuries. Trust me, I know what I'm talking about."

He laughed. "I guess you do, LT. You're right, I know. Everything works out the way it's supposed to."

Everything works out the way it's supposed to. The phrase was characteristic of Anthony's stoicism. In fact, it was the kind of thing I would say too. I tried to apply the encouragement to the sting of my medical retirement. Is this really how things were supposed to work out?

"Besides," Anthony continued, "it's good for me to be there for my family. Bailey's going to use the GI bill to get her degree, and I'm going to be able to be with the kids more. Be more engaged as a dad."

"That's awesome, Roszko."

"You too right? You and Amy can get more family time, now that you're retiring." I swallowed hard. I didn't answer.

He tried again. "Any idea what you're going to do, LT?" he asked.

I paused, wishing I could answer Anthony with the confidence I used to feel as his platoon leader. "No, man. Not yet. And you've got to stop calling me LT. I won't be in the military much longer. It's just Sam now."

* * *

It was increasingly urgent that I figure out my next step.

For the last three years, my mission had been to heal. Now I had to find a new mission. Specifically, I needed to discover who I wanted to be professionally outside of the military. Amy was pregnant with our first child, and he would arrive before the end of the summer.

The fact that we were on the cusp of parenthood together felt like another miracle. When we'd first dated, Amy had told me she never intended to have children. Despite my own desire to be a dad, I'd accepted that. But a visit to Steven Smith and his family had changed her mind. He and his wife had made us the godparents of their daughter, and I'd watched Amy soften throughout the visit as she cuddled their baby. On the way home, she'd told me, "I've changed my mind about having kids. I *do* want that for us."

During her pregnancy, she'd also made the decision that she'd like to stay home with our children. I wanted to support her desire to be a stay-at-home mom, whether it was temporary or long term. I viewed it as my responsibility and duty to support her—especially given how much she had nurtured and supported me in the midst of my three-year recovery process.

Our relationship so far had been nothing like a traditional marriage where the husband has an identity related to his profession and takes responsibility for a large part of the financial burden. From the beginning of our relationship, I hadn't been able to do that. I had *no* professional identity. In fact, once I realized that military retirement was soon to be my reality, I confronted an identity crisis. I now felt like a shell of a man. I'd focused so entirely on my external physical recovery, clinging to the dream of returning to military service for so long, that—without it—I wasn't sure who to be at this point, or even who I was.

Amy had shouldered nearly every burden in our marriage: our finances, my care, the professional identity. We had chosen to come together during a time when we each struggled to see how anyone else could ever love us. That bond had forged a trust and commitment that had helped weld us together during our first couple years. But I hadn't been able to offer much to her beyond that.

And I *wanted* to. After all the encouragement and support she'd given me, she deserved it.

A lifeline seemed to present itself through one of the connections I'd made doing volunteer work in veterans communities. A wealthy businessman and military veteran in Dallas had decided to create a service-based startup to help veterans and wanted to hire me.

I told Amy about it one evening as we went for a walk. Once she'd entered her third trimester, we'd had to stop running together, but the dogs still gave us an excuse to go walking. We'd waited to go until dusk to try to beat the heat, but the muggy San Antonio air was still oppressive.

I was excited, telling Amy about the job. "He wants me to come on and help define the mission of the organization," I told her. "It would mean I'm in a position to serve people again—other veterans. If I can't be in the service myself anymore, I like that I could at least help other veterans."

"That sounds amazing!" she said. "When do you start?"

"I can start as soon as I'm ready. But Amy—there's kind of a small thing." I had been dreading telling her this next part. "He wants to base the startup in Dallas. I'm going to have to commute."

She looked at me with a shocked expression. The drone of cicadas filled up the pause before she spoke again. "You're going to commute to *Dallas*? That's a plane flight away, Sam."

I nodded. "Yeah. It will probably mean I'm gone for four days, then three days back. Or maybe five days gone, and I'll come home on the weekends."

She stared down at the cracked sidewalk. "We're about to have a *baby*, Sam."

"I know," I said quickly. "That's why I feel like I have to take this. This can help me provide for us. It's a great opportunity to do something I love—serving others in need, and I'll get to know people in a great network of successful professionals."

She nodded. Her eyes were shiny like she might cry. The dog lunged toward one of the big leafy trees, barking up into the branches at some unseen squirrel. Amy yanked the dog leash back. "Are you upset?" I asked.

She shrugged and shook her head. "I'm excited for you. But a commute to Dallas is not my favorite piece of news at the end of a crappy day."

"You've had a crappy day?" I asked. "What happened?"

Her voice got extra teary. "Work is really bad right now."

"What? *Why?*" The last I'd heard, Amy was killing it at work. She had recently earned a Certified Nutrition Support Clinician certification and was one of only a few dietitians in the Army to have it. In recognition of her particular expertise, she'd been moved from the burn unit to the medical intensive care unit and had been told to develop new protocols and research for all the other dietitians to follow. In the world of BAMC dietitians, she was a top performer.

"I got moved to patient tray duty today," she said. She burst into tears.

"*What?*" I demanded. A simple task like patient tray duty made no sense for someone with Amy's credentials and experience.

"They just pulled me out of the ICU. They gave me no warning—it was just like, 'You're leaving. This is no longer your job. You're going down to the basement to do patient tray service.' Sam, *everyone* thinks this is the worst job!"

"But why would they do that? Don't they know what an asset you are?"

"Because I'm *pregnant*," she said angrily. "No—not because I'm pregnant. Because I want to stay home with our kids. Because I'm planning to get out of the Army once I finish my term. And now the Army has decided that everything they've invested in me becoming a critical care dietitian was wasted. It's a *punishment*." She sobbed.

I looked for something to offer her by way of a tissue. There was nothing. I held out the bottom of my T-shirt, feeling useless. She shook her head and gestured ahead. We were coming up on our house.

"The worst thing is *how* they're going about it," she vented. "My Commanding Officer has actually been telling people, 'Oh, that Captain Brown, she thinks she's so special.' Like she didn't think it wouldn't get around to me. And then today, she calls me in—'I'm moving you to patient tray service.'" She let out another furious sob as she climbed the steps of our porch and began unleashing the dogs.

I shook my head in disbelief. The woman I loved more than anything was upset. Somehow, I needed to fix it.

"I'm going to go confront her about this," I said.

She looked over at me, alarmed. "Sam. Don't do that."

I felt a surge of righteous anger. "I'm going to."

The next day, I did. I sat down with Amy's OIC and lectured her about leadership. I don't remember exactly what I said or how this Lieutenant Colonel responded. I might have ultimately made things worse. But at least I had gone to battle for my wife. At least I had *tried*.

That seemed to be Amy's impression too. "I'm kind of scared about what might happen now," she told me that evening. "But it makes me feel really loved that you went to bat for me."

I was glad that was her impression. The experience had left me feeling mostly impotent.

We resigned ourselves to my Dallas commute. As Amy and our firstborn son were figuring out their new life and bonding together, I began regularly getting on flights to Dallas for my new professional life.

I tried to settle into a new groove—one in which the focus was no longer on me and my progress, but on others—one in which I no longer got the attention as a wounded warrior, but sought to *help* other wounded warriors. In many ways, the job was exactly what I'd been hoping for ever since the accident. I'd always wanted to live a life of service. A three-year long mission of healing had felt self-indulgent, regardless of how necessary it had been. Now, I was finally *well* enough to contribute. I was ready to forget the wounded warrior status and provide real value.

But ironically, it was my "wounded warrior" status that everyone seemed most interested in.

At event after event, I got the sense that I was viewed more as a novelty or a symbol of the suffering a generation of veterans endured in the global war on terror. I started getting invited to events for other groups—everything from private parties, to corporate retreats, and even fundraising events for nonprofits. Whoever had invited me seemed to take pride in my very visible war wounds. "Have you met Captain Sam Brown?" they'd say, holding my elbow as they addressed a group of well-dressed attendees. "He was burned alive when his vehicle hit an IED." This line would be said with a dramatic undertone and always seemed to have its desired effect on the wide-eyed guests: checks would be signed and handed over to the fundraiser with a sympathetic word about my wounds.

Other times, I seemed to give people a vicarious sense of patriotism. I would often hear things like, "Man, I almost joined the military, but I went to college instead. I thought about it though. I sure appreciate what you do so that all of us can be free. Here—let me buy you a beer." Acknowledging what I or others had been through seemed to satisfy their own sense of patriotic duty.

My hosts were happy. But I didn't feel like I was doing much.

I didn't *always* feel like a prop to be used for someone else's gain. I did forge some friendships with people during this time who genuinely appreciated me and never sought to do anything but be a friend. The gentleman who initially hired me for his non-profit was on that list of true friends. He and others like him provided genuine support for me in my own journey of transitioning from a life in the military to life as a civilian. But others seemed to view me simply as a wounded warrior who was useful for helping them achieve their own purposes.

On top of that, Amy was struggling. Roman was born in September of 2011, just before I was officially retired from the Army. We'd named him as a nod to Romans 5:3–5, the Bible verse that had been such an encouragement to me in the wake of the explosion: *"We can rejoice, too, when we run into problems and trials, for we know that they help us develop endurance. And endurance develops strength of character, and character strengthens our confident hope of salvation. And this hope will not lead to disappointment. For we know how dearly God loves us, because he has given us the Holy Spirit to fill our hearts with his love."* His birth felt symbolic of all the good that had come out of the hardest time of my life—especially given that he helped knit Amy and I together even more closely.

But my connection to Roman and Amy was more of a fact and less of an emotional reality. Amy spent most of Roman's infancy by herself, while I was away in Dallas. She handled those long nights of newborn crying alone and had to figure out parenthood by herself during the day. Even when I was home on the weekends, it didn't feel like a joyful reunion. I was clumsy with Roman, and Amy was clearly frustrated with my lack of presence, empathy, and understanding of Roman's needs—and hers.

I sensed things were going badly, but I also felt the need to make this job work. How else could I provide for my family? What other job would make use of my training in leadership and my experience as a veteran, but relative lack of industry experience? Until I gained more experience, knowledge, and connections in the "real world," I didn't think I'd have an easy time finding anything else.

I think we both felt trapped. I forged ahead, in the spirit of the First Infantry Division motto: *No mission too difficult, no sacrifice too great. Duty first.*

Amy wasn't having it though. One Sunday night, we stood on either side of the bed. She was folding laundry while I packed my suitcase for the next day's flight. "Sam," she said, her voice sharp. "This Dallas commute sucks." She folded a onesie and threw it in a pile on the comforter.

Guiltily, I placed a pair of slacks in the suitcase. "I know it's been hard. I'm sorry."

"I just feel like I invested all this time and energy into taking care of you. And then—once you're better, you just *move on*. There's a job for you in Dallas, so you take it, and it's like—'Cool, bye.'" She threw down another onesie. "*I* need help, Sam! I'm exhausted. I'm supposed to start work again soon to finish out my term, and you're not around."

I didn't know what to say. I didn't know how to fix it. "I'm sorry," I said again.

She looked up from the pile of tiny newborn clothes and stared at me. Her expression was hard with anger and disappointment. "It's just not very much fun being married to you right now."

I nodded.

Somehow—in trying to serve my wife and my son and provide a valuable service to others—I was failing at all of it.

I probably should have never gotten on a plane back to Dallas, but I did. Grimly, I attended meetings with the other two people who worked for my same startup. We were gradually identifying our service niche: to help veterans transition out of the military and try to figure out what they could do professionally. I had been vocal about this being a real need—probably because it was *my* need.

Not long after the conversation with Amy, I found myself at the ranch of a wealthy Dallas businessman. He was considering opening his ranch as a retreat space for veterans, and I'd been invited along with a few others. The guy who'd made the connection was one of my Dallas friends—or, as Amy would have said, one of my Dallas "*friends*," with air quotes. She had pointed out that several of these wealthy guys only seemed to return my calls when they needed something from me, or wanted me to show up to an event with them. "They never seem to follow up on your requests to be mentored by them in business," she noted. "You're such a relational person, Sam. But you're emotionally connecting with people who don't care about connecting with you the same way."

I hadn't wanted to believe her take on it, but it was hard not to consider her perspective at this ranch. My friend—"*friend*"—stayed close with me as we made the rounds. It was obvious that the company assembled was divided into roughly two groups: veterans with visible wounds, and businessmen who seemed to want to show us off. I was introduced as "Captain Sam Brown, War Hero." I was asked repeatedly to tell my story of getting wounded. At one point, I made eye contact with another veteran across the room—a fit-looking amputee wearing a prosthetic leg. He motioned his head toward the room of wealthy businessmen in their cowboy duds, then rolled his eyes. I knew exactly what he meant.

That night, I called Amy. "I think I'm going to be done," I told her.

"What? Really? You're coming home?"

"I just don't think I'm ever going to be seen as anything other than a "Wounded Warrior" in this veteran nonprofit space. And I don't want to just be known as that."

"Yeah." Amy sighed.

"Our nonprofit doesn't produce value—not yet, really, of any kind. We're still building out the processes and mentorship relationships which means we aren't providing much of a service yet. I get my salary through the generous donation of our benefactor. But it feels like when people used to buy Mother and me dinner because of my Purple Heart hat. I hate feeling like a charity case. I want to actually *add* value to a business."

"Come home," she said decidedly. "Add value by being here with your family."

I came home. I stayed home. We agreed that I would be a full-time dad while Amy went back to work and finished her term in the Army. This shift didn't look very impressive on my resume, but it did lead to a big improvement in my marriage. In between changing diapers and giving Roman bottles, I tried to figure out what might be next. Maybe business?

Amy wrapped up her term of service—six years of honorable service with a deployment to Iraq—and signaled for the exit ramp. For the first time since we'd known each other, neither of us had a reason to stay attached to BAMC. We made the decision to move permanently to Dallas, where I could try to leverage some of the connections I'd made there for a career shift.

But even then, I struggled. The Army had always surrounded me with mentors and provided a clear structure for advancement. In the void of that, I was trying to create new structure on my own—which was challenging. It seemed like every door I knocked on and every avenue I looked down was one more dead end.

With the arrival of our second child—a perfect little girl we named Esther—the matter once again started keeping me up at night. I'd rehearsed my entire life to be just one thing: A soldier. A military leader. A trained warrior for the United States Army.

With that off the table, I was lost. Who was I supposed to be?

In 2013, some acquaintances seemed to present an answer. I'd met these guys through my nonprofit work, and we'd run into each other several times at community events where Amy and I sometimes volunteered as a way to be civically engaged. They called me and asked if I could join them at a coffee shop one afternoon.

"Captain Brown," Aaron began with a large smile. "You knew us as corporate marketers, but we also do political consulting."

"That's right," Marty said. "We know you care about your community and about service. We've seen you doing civic engagement. And we also know you have a really compelling bio."

"West Point graduate, wounded warrior, worked for a veteran non-profit," Aaron supplied. He lowered his voice. "Burn victim."

"We think you'd make a great political candidate," Marty said.

I was taken aback. "I just like volunteering as a way to contribute to my community. I have no idea how campaigns work or even how to get engaged in the political process," I said.

Aaron waved his hand as though that were inconsequential. "That's not important. We can help you flesh that out. What people want is a responsible leader. A person of integrity!"

"And that's *you*," Marty said. "You know the importance of serving your country. You value service and duty."

They were speaking my language. Despite the weird vibe I was getting from them, I started to listen to their ideas. Eventually, I agreed to run for a State Assembly office in Texas.

My job, the political consultants explained, was to raise money. *Their* job was to market me and get the word out. They threw around political jargon and told me when to show up to events. They handed me new versions of speeches I'd written, making the original nearly unrecognizable.

It was a terrible campaign. Other than the fundraising—which, surprisingly, I was good at—the campaign was a joke. It didn't last long, and I didn't make it past the primary.

Aaron and Marty didn't seem perturbed by this. They focused on the fundraising haul. "Your story really resonates with people!" they enthused. "You brought in a *ton* of money, especially when considering this was only your first race. And, you came in a close third place—almost made the runoff." What they *didn't* say was that the fundraising dollars had more than covered their invoices.

The night after the failed primary, Amy and I slumped on the couch after getting the kids down. I reached for the remote to turn on the TV, but she batted it away. She gave me a nudge. "We should do an After Action Review."

Amy knew I liked doing these postmortems to analyze how and why a thing had unfolded the way it had. But it didn't feel good starting this one. "I feel like an idiot," I told her. "Those guys were using me the whole time."

She shook her head disapprovingly. "I never liked those guys." It was true. Amy had felt misgivings about Aaron and Marty from the start. I was starting to learn how reliable her gut instincts were.

"Why didn't I stop to think about *why* they wanted me to run in the first place?" I vented. "I actually thought they cared about the community. I thought they genuinely believed I would be good for the state." I shook my head. "No. They're political consultants, and the way they get paid is by finding people to run for office and fundraise their consulting fee. I was just their meal ticket. Their token *wounded warrior*."

Amy nodded. "Aaron and Marty suck. And we were suckers."

"Big time."

"But let's think of the bright side." She angled her body toward mine and snuggled into me. "You were a good fundraiser, relative to the others. There's something about your bio that connects with donors and voters."

"Yeah, but you can't win with just that. You have to actually have a message that makes voters want to vote for you. I didn't even know what my message *was*. I don't even know who *I* am right now, Amy."

Amy didn't rush to answer. My words hung there in our living room, like the lingering smell of a stale cigarette. "So...are we ever going to do this again?" she asked.

"Never," I said adamantly.

* * *

Over the next year, I made myself a political "consultant"—with air quotes. I didn't take anyone's money, but I did try to warn other people getting involved in politics about what had happened to me. I was pissed with the whole industry. The political process felt like one more dysfunctional machine—one more societal system that chewed people up, then spit them out, in the spirit of some greater "cause" which, at its root, seemed mainly driven by money. I felt disenfranchised with the whole thing.

When I'd been an outpatient in the burn ward, I had made it my mission to encourage and advise other burn patients along their recovery journey. I took on a similar mission now: I had an experience to share with others that might shed light on their own path ahead.

Occasionally, someone would reach out to me—oftentimes another veteran—who, like me, wanted to serve their community or state or country via a run for political office. If I got a call from them asking me to share my own experience, I downloaded *everything*. I shared all the lessons I'd learned to try to help them avoid the mistakes I'd made, such as blindly trusting the people who were getting paid out of a fundraising haul.

I never made a dollar with my "consulting." But I was free with my advice to anyone who asked. Ironically, that ended up keeping us more engaged with politics than we had intended to be after the disastrous campaign.

In the meantime, I kept hunting for the right job. I did commission work for a title company. I sometimes did a paid motivational speech. I did some sales work. None of it felt very permanent or fulfilling.

One afternoon in the fall of 2014, Amy and I loaded Esther and Roman into hiking backpacks and set out on a trail. Amy and I were always at our best on a hike, it seemed. Starting with that hike along the Nā Pali Coast on Kauai—which was either a spectacular disaster, or a catastrophic success, depending on your spin—we'd found that the experience of being outside together on a trail seemed to be our natural habitat. On a hiking trail, Amy didn't have to answer any questions about choosing to be a stay-at-home mom who had opted to leave a promising career. I didn't have to navigate anyone's expectations as a wounded warrior. We were just there: together, with our babies, taking in the beauty of nature and the reminder of all the big things we often forgot about.

I started processing my career path. "I'm starting to realize something, I think," I said to Amy.

"What's that?" she asked. She'd opted to wear Roman, and it made me happy to see his little head bobbing over the rim of the pack.

"Well—I'm good at leadership. I have good instincts and intuition for leading teams. But a big reason for that is because I was *trained* in leadership at West Point and Ranger School. I haven't really been trained in anything else. I don't have a certain business skill set or experience to fall back on."

"Could you look for a job that would use your leadership skills?"

"That's what I've been doing, but people don't tend to see me as a leader when I show up at an interview. They see me as a wounded—"

"A wounded warrior." Amy's voice synchronized with mine. She knew. "Well, *I* see you as a loving husband. And I believe in who you can become. You have so much to give, Sam."

Roman's chubby hand reached up and brushed a pine branch overhead. I smiled at his tiny ambition. "Thank you for saying that. It's just been hard to find anyone else who believes in me beyond the scars."

"Those people are missing so much."

"Be that as it may...I think I'm realizing I either need to enter business as an individual contributor...or maybe go get a new kind of training."

She turned around to look at me, swinging Roman to the side. I could see her pregnant abdomen just starting to reveal our third child, due in early 2015. Roman shot a smile at me, delighted to discover his daddy and baby sister were so close. I grinned and waved at him. "You mean, like go to grad school?" Amy asked.

"Yeah. Get an MBA. What do you think about that?"

"I think that's an *awesome* idea. Have you looked at any programs?"

I nodded. "A couple. I was just thinking...given how West Point prepared me for leadership, it might make sense to go back to school if I want tools to be successful in business."

Amy swung back around to forge ahead on the trail. "Do it. I'm a fan of this plan."

The whole crew hiking in Texas: me with Amy, Roman, Esther, and Ezra. March 2016.

The new goal was invigorating. It seemed as effective at getting me unstuck as Mother's goals had been in getting me out of the ICU. I got another boost on Christmas day when I got a phone call from Anthony Roszko. I stepped outside to take it, the lights from our tree casting a dim glow into our snowy backyard.

"Merry Christmas, Roszko!" I greeted him. "Man, talking to you is its own Christmas present. I love that you called!"

"I've got another present for you, LT," he said. "Bailey and I welcomed our second child three days ago. A son."

"*What?* Did you know Amy and I are expecting a son in February too? Aw, congrats man. That *is* a gift."

"That's not what I meant," Anthony said. "He's your namesake. We named him Samuel, after you."

I was stunned. "Anthony—that's better than any military award I could ever get. Of all the soldiers I led, I respect you and Steven the most. Steven asked me to be the godfather of his children, and now you—" I struggled for words. "You've named your son 'Samuel.'"

"After you," Anthony repeated.

I shook my head, struggling to wrap my head around it. "That's the greatest reward. The greatest honor. Thank you."

"You've been through so much, Sam." Anthony's gravelly voice was earnest. "And you just kept going. You stayed positive and kept working at your healing. It's been an encouragement to me, with my own healing. And if our son grows up to be anything like you, Bailey and I would be so proud."

"Thank you," I said again. The words couldn't fully express how honored I felt. We talked a bit longer. When we hung up, I looked back through the window at Amy and the kids. I smiled, seeing her big baby bump, seeing Roman and Esther playing with their new toys. I felt overwhelmed by what Anthony had just shared.

You just kept going, Anthony had said. *You stayed positive and kept working.* What a gift—another gift—to have a friend who could remind me of who I was. *And he's not the only one,* I thought. The same God who had helped me persevere before had never left. He was still with me.

In the summer of 2015, I enrolled in the MBA program at Southern Methodist University in Dallas. I attended classes all day Friday and Saturday, then worked at the title company the rest of the week. Amy held down the fort at home with Roman, now four; Esther, two;

and our newest member of the family—Ezra—now just a couple months old.

Being back in school felt like the ultimate reset. Every class gave me a new mission to get behind—a new skill to learn. I discovered that I had skills in business I'd never realized. My cohort was a bright, talented group of people, but even in their company, I tended to perform at the higher end of the class. That was a surprise to me, frankly. It had been so long since I'd been in a competitive performance environment, I'd almost forgotten what it felt like. For the past seven years, my identity had been "the wounded guy," and I'd almost gotten used to thinking of myself as damaged goods. But in the MBA environment—I was a serious competitor. I was a shrewd negotiator. I was *smart*.

It was a profound revelation. *I still had something to offer.* I still had ways to contribute real value, apart from my impressive scars. My identity was no longer confined to "Sam the wounded veteran." Now, I could try out being "Sam the businessman." That inspired confidence I hadn't felt in years. I wasn't an empty shell any longer; I could market myself with confidence that I had something to offer on Day One.

By the time graduation approached, I had a game plan all locked up. Brad, an executive at a large private equity management company, had taken me under his wing and promised me a job as the Director of Procurement. While many of the other people in my program began a lengthy series of interviews or dove into the startup process for a new company, I gave myself permission to just focus on finishing my classes well. I didn't need to seek out interviews or pursue a startup with some of my classmates. I felt great about my next step.

Three weeks before my scheduled start date, I started feeling concerned when Brad stopped responding to my calls and texts. I finally got a text from him: *Sorry to be MIA. I've been at the hospital. Had a bad pancreatitis attack. Jury is still out on my prognosis. Could be fatal?? Let's hope not. We may have to revisit your start date.*

I was shocked—and worried. I was worried about my friend, but also worried about my future. I'd put *all* my eggs in this basket. I had no back-up plan.

A few days after receiving his text, I went and visited him in the hospital. He had to pull away an oxygen mask to talk to me. "Sam," he wheezed. "Even if I manage to recover, I'm not sure I'm going to be able to continue working at all. The company is already restructuring to get someone new in my place."

What does this mean for me? I wanted to ask. I couldn't say something so insensitive out loud—not to a man who might be dying. But I was grateful when he answered my question anyway.

"The Director of Procurement job was a position I'd created for you. Sam, I'm not sure they'll be interested in hiring you if I'm not there. You may need to look into a fallback plan."

I nodded, thinking, *There is no fallback plan.* "I appreciate your honesty, Brad. I'm so sorry this has happened to you."

A month later—May of 2017—I received my Master of Business Administration diploma. That entire month, Brad had been in and out of the hospital. Amy and I resigned ourselves to the fact that my "perfect plan," once again, was not going to happen.

So, what did we do?

We headed for the mountains.

CHAPTER 13

CLIMBING
MOUNTAINS

Goofing off at Lake Tahoe, with Kristina. November 2010.

None of us could believe it had actually worked out. Amy's four-day reprieve from her grueling work schedule was the first big break. The General Officer commanding the hospital had just returned from deployment and felt four-day passes were an important part of keeping morale high. He'd mandated a four-day hospital-wide pass. Amy called me, elated, eager to book a getaway before anyone at the hospital could change their mind.

The flights to Reno were another gift: cheap and direct. Both of us had heard great things about hiking in Lake Tahoe, and this weekend seemed like the perfect opportunity to try it out.

The final blessing was that Kristina, Daniel's wife, was going to be able to fly in from Southern California last minute to meet up with us. Amy and Kristina were close friends, and Kristina had been lonely during Daniel's deployment. A weekend getaway in Tahoe felt like the ideal break for all of us.

No one felt particularly concerned that we were novice hikers. We didn't consider the fact that the paved footpaths of San Antonio might feel different than the snowy mountain trails in Tahoe. Amy and I didn't even bother to discuss the near-death experience on the Nā Pali Coast hike. We wanted to take in natural beauty and fresh air. We had no plan, but who really needed one? This was *happening*.

The change in scenery when we arrived in Nevada was instant. We'd gotten used to living in concrete cities in Texas—full of asphalt, humidity, and hazy skies, but with very little to look at on the horizon. Reno was different. The air was fresh and crisp as soon as we left the airport. Views of the Sierra Nevadas swept along the western horizon. And as we drove to Lake Tahoe in our rental car—with our dog, Leonidas, panting over our seats—the trees got taller and the views got more and more beautiful.

We planned to hike the Spooner Lake trail on Sunday morning, and took Saturday to drive around Lake Tahoe, pausing often to wander through the small mountain towns on its banks. We found a boutique pet store and got Leonidas some high-end dog treats. "Enjoy these," Amy told him. "They're the most bougie snacks you're ever going to get."

Sunday morning was bright and sunny. We arrived at the trailhead around nine and hit the bathroom. When Amy came out, she looked a little concerned. "Did the men's side have *bear* warning signs?"

I nodded. "They had a little calendar posted too, in a plastic sheet. Like, noting when bears are most likely to be active."

Amy stared at me. "And?"

"We should be fine. November is 'pre-hibernation,' apparently. Most bear sightings occur during the summer."

Kristina walked out of the bathroom, and Amy looked over at her. "Hey Kristina, what should we do if we come across a *bear*?"

Kristina laughed. "Oh. Well—I mean, whatever you do, don't run."

Amy gave me an ironic grin and nodded. "Okay. Cool."

The trail was just visible under the freshly fallen snow, which made everything smooth and sparkling white. I was amazed at how *good* it felt, being outside. In Texas, I'd always struggled with the heat and humidity which limited when and how I could enjoy being outdoors. Here, I didn't feel limited. The crispness of the cool air felt good to breathe in.

Our conversation on the trail often lapsed into stretches of contented silence. The hike was *quiet*. The snow and our distance from any city seemed to swallow up the sound. "I can smell the pine trees," Amy said happily.

I breathed in. "I don't smell pine trees," I said. "But I do smell *something*. What is that?"

"I smell something too," Kristina said. "Kind of a bad something. Sam—I think it's coming from the backpack."

We stopped and unzipped the pack. The strong odor hit us with force. Amy snatched something out of the backpack, sniffed it, and made a face. "It's Leonidas' beef liver dog treats. Gross."

Leonidas whimpered and pawed at the ground. I pulled out a treat and gave it to him. "He thinks they are extremely delicious," I said.

Kristina gagged. "That's not what I think," she responded. I threw them back in the bag and zipped it up.

Around three miles in, we reached a vista that looked out over the crystalline lake. There was a fallen tree there, and we sat down to take in the view. "It's *so* pretty," Kristina remarked.

"Imagine swimming here in the summertime," Amy mused.

"I like it even in the cold," I said. "I love the snow." Something about the place felt spacious and expansive—it felt easier to dream here.

The trail kept going, but we decided to turn around. We weren't sure how long it went or where it would end up, so we opted to make the vista our end point and begin trekking back. After a few minutes, Kristina stopped abruptly. She faced the trail behind us. "Did you guys just hear something?"

Amy and I stopped and listened. "What did you hear?" Amy asked.

Kristina waited, listening. "I thought I heard a twig or a branch break. Maybe not."

We kept on, relaxing back into silence. The only sounds were our boots crunching quietly in the snow. But suddenly, a bird began cawing loudly in the background.

That's weird, I thought. We hadn't heard anything like that for the entire hike. *I wonder if that's some kind of warning? Maybe it sees a predator?*

Amy and Kristina both stopped at the bird's caws and looked at each other nervously. Leonidas began to whine, then let out a few sharp barks.

"This is fun," I quipped.

Pushing on, we approached a creek crossing with thick vegetation on either side. As we eyed the creek, looking for the best spot to cross, we suddenly heard a loud growl behind us.

It confused me at first—it was so unlike anything else we'd heard. "Is that someone calling for help?" I asked.

The growl came again, louder. "No, that's a *bear!*" Amy cried.

"RUN!" Kristina yelled.

We leaped across the stream and began sprinting down the trail, trying not to slip in the snow. "Sam—it's probably after those dog treats!" Amy called. I whipped my backpack around to my front, still running, pulled out the stinky bag of beef livers and dumped it over my shoulder.

We ran the entire two miles back to the parking lot, never stopping until we'd collapsed into the car, slammed the doors shut, and locked it. "We're so stupid," Amy panted.

"Pathetic!" I agreed. "We set ourselves up for that. We were totally unprepared, and brought the smelliest dog treats known to man."

"I bet it was stalking us the whole time," Kristina said. "That was crazy."

Over dinner that night, the three of us began laughing as we recapped the ridiculous hike. "We're two for two, Sam," Amy pointed out. "Near-death experiences in both Hawaii *and* Lake Tahoe."

"Yeah, but I still enjoyed the hike," I said. "I *love* this place. I'd hike it again in a heartbeat. Just without the stupid dog treats."

"Me too," Kristina said. "Honestly, if we were better prepared, it would have been a totally different experience. It was *so* beautiful. Kind of makes me want to do more. Go farther. Maybe with a can of bear spray."

Amy nodded enthusiastically. The two of them began talking about what backpacking would look like—hiking farther in, loaded up with overnight gear. I listened to their planning, amused, and let my mind wander back to that view from the vista point.

I could live here, I thought—the place where limits were lifted, and new dreams rose to the surface. *I could do this every day.*

Amy, Esther, me, Roman, and Ezra. Thanksgiving 2018.

What now? I had my MBA, but my career plans had fallen through. It was tempting to think I was back at square one, but I knew that wasn't the case. I could envision a life beyond the military now and was confident about the value that I could contribute.

I just still needed to figure out *where* to contribute.

Dallas was feeling less and less appealing as a home base. Our season here had been a hard one, particularly for Amy. During the years I'd been completing my MBA program, she had struggled. The explosion at the end of her deployment hadn't left any visible marks on her, but it had created internal wounds. In the last two years, those had finally manifested. She'd become afraid of leaving our house, but was also afraid to stay home—nowhere felt safe. When ISIS led a series of attacks in 2016, she'd become overwhelmed with fear, convinced that the terrorist group was going to take over the world.

On top of that, our church community hadn't been supportive of her. They'd implied that Amy could be helped and healed if she only had enough faith—which ultimately was a hurtful and shaming message for her. Although she'd been helped significantly with counseling, her PTSD was still part of our daily reality.

The only time she seemed like her old self was when we were hiking. It was the natural beauty that drew her initially, but as she and Kristina began taking backpacking trips, she found that the excursions helped her anxiety. "I *like* being in a vulnerable position when I'm out in the wilderness," she explained to me one night. I was complaining about the fact that she had chosen a hike that would traverse a high snowpack where the trail would be covered for much of the time. "If I do something that scares me on purpose, it forces me to confront my fears and stretch myself. By the time we're hiking out, I feel more confident and more skilled. I don't feel as anxious and scared. And that makes returning to normal life just a tiny bit easier." Despite my misgivings with some of the risky hikes she and Kristina planned, I couldn't argue with how they seemed to help Amy.

Luckily, that May we had the chance to get ourselves back into the mountains. My younger brother, Luke, was going to be graduating from his undergrad in Colorado right after my MBA graduation ceremony. Amy and I flew to her parents' house in South Dakota for a visit, then left the kids with them and headed to Colorado to see Luke. After his graduation ceremonies, we planned to go backpacking in the Lost Creek Wilderness in the Colorado Rocky Mountains.

Amy planned the trip. After all the serious hikes she and Kristina had done together, Amy had turned into an impressive backpacker. They never took it easy, hiking higher and farther than I would ever have considered safe or sane.

I was less enthusiastic about roughing it. Ironically, one of the ways I had comforted myself about not being able to return to duty as an Infantry Officer was considering that I wouldn't have to sleep in the dirt ever again. If I ever slept "outside," I told myself, it would be in a forty-foot RV with access to a bed with a mattress, a kitchen, and a hot shower. There was no need to deprive myself of the comforts of life if a mission didn't require it, I thought.

But Amy had other ideas—and she'd convinced me to do my first backpacking trip "civilian style," post-Army. Because she had become so experienced, she planned the trip, assembled our gear, and led us to the Lost Creek trailhead. "Come on, Captain Brown!" she called over her shoulder.

"Yes, ma'am, Captain Brown!" I called back. I grinned. It was a relief to see Amy like this.

On the trail, Amy exuded confidence and vivacity. She teased me and laughed easily. It was such a stark contrast to the Amy that I'd become used to at home in Dallas.

We paused to drink water beside a creek, and Amy looked up at the clouds, breathing in with deep satisfaction. "Sam, if I could do nothing other than hike through mountains for the rest of my life, I think I could die happy."

I loved seeing her thrive. "Do you remember the hike near Lake Tahoe?" I asked.

She laughed. "The one where we got chased by a bear on the trail to Spooner Lake? *Yes.* Of course I do. But do you remember how *beautiful* Lake Tahoe was, Sam? How clear the water was? I loved Nevada."

"I loved it too," I reminded her. "I remember going back to San Antonio and looking at real estate in Reno, trying to figure out how we could move there. But you were still in the military. We had no idea where life was going to take us at that point."

"True." She twisted the top on her water bottle and pulled her pack back on. "Come on, Soldier. We've got three more miles before camp."

The trail took us through fields of wildflowers and past vistas of snowy peaks. I couldn't get over how happy Amy seemed in this environment. I considered what she'd said: *If I could do nothing other than hike through mountains for the rest of my life, I think I could die happy.* I thought about the wilderness in Nevada and how much we'd enjoyed that Reno trip.

"You know," I told her that night as we cuddled beside the pot of boiling water for our meals and hot cocoa. "With this job falling through…we could consider moving. There's no reason we need to stay in Dallas."

She furrowed her eyebrows. "Move? You don't think you need to stay and lean on your connections here?"

I shrugged. "I've been 'leaning on my connections' for the past five years in Dallas. It hasn't really gotten me anywhere. I've got a business idea that I think could take off. And it's one I could do from anywhere. I'd need to find some sort of steady work to sustain us while I got the business off the ground, but that doesn't need to be in Dallas."

I pulled back from her so I could look her in the eyes. "I want us to live in a place where you can thrive. Wouldn't you like to live in a place like this? Among the Rockies? Or somewhere in the Sierra Nevada Mountains, where we can do hikes all the time?"

Her eyes grew wide. "The Sierra Nevadas. Oh my gosh, yes please." She snuggled back into me. "You really think we could move?"

"I loved Nevada," I said. "I think that would be a great place to raise a family. We could find a new church. Get ourselves a little house. Go hiking on the weekends. What do you think?"

"I'll plan all the backpacking trips," Amy said.

I laughed. "Deal."

The next morning as we hiked out, I rallied myself behind the new plan. *I just need to find a job to help us move and get us a steady income while I get my own business off the ground,* I thought. Fresh out of business school, I felt confident in my ability to find something that could work for our family. I had more to offer and no shortage of motivation to see this version of Amy on a daily basis.

"What about Amazon?" I asked Amy as we made the drive back to South Dakota. "I like where that company seems to be heading.

And it seems like they're everywhere. Maybe I could get a job with them. Like—manage a warehouse, or something."

Amy pulled out her phone. "I'm Googling 'Amazon fulfillment centers...'" Amy looked up from the screen, bright-eyed. "Sam, there are *a couple of* fulfillment centers in northern Nevada."

"*Really.* Well, that seems promising. And doesn't Nevada have favorable tax laws for small business owners? I feel like someone told me that."

Amy was still studying the map on her phone. "SAM. Do you have any idea how many beautiful places to hike there are in Nevada? Great Basin, Ruby Mountains, Lake Tahoe, Red Rock Canyon—plus it's near Crater Lake, Volcanic National Park, *Yosemite...*"

"Wow."

"And we could easily get to Sequoia, Kings Canyon, Death Valley, Joshua Tree..." She looked up from her phone. "Oh my gosh. We have to make this move happen."

By that autumn, moving to Nevada was no longer a pipe dream, but our firm plan. I landed an interview with Amazon, and they made me an offer to be a baseline ops manager at one of the warehouses. It wasn't an impressive job—it was an entry-level position that any college graduate would have qualified for. But I saw it as a means to an end.

Provided it got us to Reno.

"We're going to place you at one of our US fulfillment centers," the HR lady told me over the phone. She rattled off several locations—one in California, one in Washington, and one in Florida. "Those are the places where we currently have positions available..."

"What about Reno?" I asked.

"Nothing's available in Reno. Take a day or two to think about it and get back to me."

I dragged my feet on making a decision, hunting for other jobs in Nevada while still hoping the Amazon opportunity might work out. Finally, another HR guy from the company called me.

"Has anything come available in Nevada?" I asked.

"It's very seldom that we see anything opening up in Nevada," he said. "The Reno center is a small worksite. Did you think about Florida? Or, there are now openings in Kentucky and Texas too. You said you live in the Dallas area, right? You wouldn't even have to move for one of the openings we have. You could start in as soon as three weeks."

"Well, what are the odds that something might come up soon?" I asked. "We're really hoping to end up in Nevada."

"Look," the man said impatiently. "Your options haven't changed. If you want to get started with Amazon, you need to pick one of the available sites."

"How often do openings pop up for the Reno fulfillment center? Maybe I can wait until one of those spots opens up."

"You think if I just refresh my screen, I'm going to see a job opening in Nevada when there wasn't one a second ago? Fine, if it will make you happy, I'll refresh."

There was a pause. "What the…?" The man's voice trailed off. "Hold on," he said. "I think this is probably a mistake. Let me refresh again."

I waited. "Anything?"

I heard him blow air out of his lips in disbelief. "Well, you are one lucky SOB. Or else someone up there is looking out for you. I thought this was a mistake because it wasn't here earlier, but they've just posted a job opportunity for your specific managerial role in Reno. You want it?"

"Yes! I want it!"

"The post won't be open until July, though," the man said. "Can you wait that long?"

"I can wait that long," I said. That would give me plenty of time to get my ducks in a row as I laid the groundwork to set up my own business in Nevada. A longer timeline would be better for the kids and Amy, anyway.

In May of 2018, Amy and I once again dropped the kids off with her parents in South Dakota and began driving west on Highway 50 to Nevada, planning to scout out a place to live. My experience of Nevada up to that point had really been confined to the tiny bubble around Reno we'd explored. I had stereotypical impressions of Las Vegas but had no idea what the rest of the state was like. I expected eastern Nevada to look like a flat, sandy desert.

Instead, we found ourselves driving through mountain range after mountain range. The views were vast and striking. "Sam, Nevada is the most mountainous state in the *country*," Amy informed me, reading an article on her phone. "There are three *hundred* mountain ranges!"

"Unbelievable." The scenery backed up her fact-finding. The highway wound up and through passes, taking us through a seemingly never-ending series of mountain ranges that dropped down into basins, then up into peaks again. Every time we crossed over a pass, we could see the next range stretching in front of us.

"Amy, I feel like something inside of me is actually *singing*. This is so incredibly beautiful."

"I know! Me too! It never gets boring."

We drank it in, mile after mile. After a long, contented silence, Amy spoke up. "I wonder how long it will take us to make friends in Nevada. Or find a new church."

I nodded. "Do you think many of our friends in Dallas will come visit?"

She shrugged. "Not sure. I don't know how many of those relationships will translate to long distance." She named a few of our closest friends. "They might come visit."

The conversation drifted into a lull again. I began thinking of all that we were leaving behind in Dallas: our friends, the campus where I'd gotten my MBA, the house we'd been raising our kids in. But also the unpleasant things: humidity, the concrete cities, the people who viewed me as a payday—like some of the nonprofit fundraisers and political consultants. Then I had a new thought which made me chuckle. "You know—all that heartache that we had with campaigns and politics back in Texas is behind us now. No need for us to worry about that again."

Amy laughed. "You mean you don't think the people who used you are going to pay us a visit?" She shook her head. "I won't miss them *at all*."

The move to Nevada felt like almost a magical reset for Amy and me. For the first time in our history of being together, we both felt excited about where we were at in life: physically, emotionally, professionally, and geographically.

We *laughed* again. The stress we'd experienced in Dallas had taken such a toll on us—I don't think we'd even realized how hard and dark things had been until we broke out of it, finding ourselves laughing while unpacking boxes in Reno. We hadn't laughed in so long—it felt like an abnormal experience. The first time it happened, we looked at each other, shocked.

"Well, *that* was fun!" Amy said.

Everything seemed lighter, and happier, and easier nestled among the Sierra Nevadas—including work, at long last.

At the Balloon Festival in Reno, September 2018.

I enjoyed the job at Amazon. I liked leading a team and working with people to accomplish a clear, tangible outcome every day. In that way, it wasn't unlike crew at West Point, or working with my platoon in Afghanistan—only, instead of winning a regatta or providing security for a convoy, our goal was to pack and load boxes onto pallets, then move the pallets onto the semi-truck trailers for shipment. It was simple and straightforward: we had a clear goal, distinct roles, and we knew exactly whether or not we'd succeeded.

I also liked being among such a range of employees. The warehouse crew seemed to represent all different facets of the state—there were college-age young people, working Amazon as a part-time job; there were retirees working there to supplement their social security; there were people in their twenties, trying to save up to buy a home, and so on. I liked getting to know them and hearing their stories. It gave me the opportunity to serve people again—like I'd tried to serve my soldiers, and the patients and medical providers in the burn unit. Being able to serve felt like finding my equilibrium: it's when my upbringing, my passions, my skills, and my experiences finally seemed to find congruence.

I tried to organize people according to their skill set and abilities. Amazon's quotas were relentless, so there was no truly "easy" job, but some tasks were more physically grueling than others. I usually assigned the young men and women to load pallets, which was more physically demanding. The boxes we handled might be two pounds, or they might be a hundred pounds—sometimes, two people were required to lift them onto the pallets. Another tough job was the "Tetris master." That person stood at the end of a long conveyor belt that stretched into the actual tractor trailer. As boxes fell off the conveyor belt, the person moved and stacked them to fill the trailer— another task that required a young, strong body.

The actual packing of the boxes was less physically demanding, especially the lighter-weight packages that were under a pound. That's where I tried to slate people who needed a task that would be easier on their bodies. It required speed because of the high-volume quotas, but it wasn't as physically taxing.

At any station though, the work was relentless. I didn't mind the fast pace—it made the hours go fast. But it concerned me when people struggled to keep up.

Rick, for instance. Rick was an older guy—late sixties, I'd guess—who lived in an RV park along the Truckee River. Rick probably would have preferred to hang out on a golf course somewhere but needed income beyond his social security check. He was always asking me for overtime hours because he needed the money—but then he'd struggle to meet his quotas. His body simply couldn't keep up with his work ethic. I could relate to that.

I kept an eye on Rick. Whenever he started getting behind, he got grumpy—sometimes, I'd learn he was struggling by way of a complaint that made its way to me about something he'd said to a co-worker. I'd go check on him and try to get him into an easier spot. I recognized Rick's stress—it was stress I'd felt in my own life, teetering on the brink of failure. He knew he didn't have any margin for error in his life. He needed the hours, he needed the job, and he needed the income and health benefits. But in trying to do such physical work as an older man, he worked himself so hard that his performance would start to decline.

Despite me trying to get Rick in spots where he could succeed, his pattern of missed quotas got him put on probation. I started taking his seat when he went on his lunch break to try to clear his backlog and bump up his quota a little bit. I did the same thing for other employees on the bubble—packing up stuff that added to their numbers, and trying to ease bottlenecks at their stations while they caught a breather. Even so, it didn't always help.

One day, during Rick's probation, I went by to check on him. I was alarmed at what I saw. He'd fallen asleep.

"Hey. Rick," I said, shaking his shoulder. He jolted awake. "Rick—I've looked it up and I know you've got some PTO available. I've got to insist that you consider taking a half day off so that you don't end up missing your goals again."

He scowled. "I know it." Then his expression became worried. "I'm not sure I'll be able to drive myself home safely. I just can't seem to stay awake."

I went and found my manager and got permission to drive Rick home. We got into my car, and he directed me to his little trailer at the RV park. "Thanks for the ride," he said. He looked glum.

"You bet. Get some rest. On Monday, you can come in refreshed and hit your numbers."

"That's all they care about," he said gruffly. "You're the only leader at Amazon who treats me like a human being." He stared bleakly ahead. We were facing the Truckee River, and I looked out the windshield, following his gaze. The water flowed by, looking steel gray under the cloud cover. Rick looked back at me. "*You* get it."

I furrowed my brows. "Get what?"

He nodded like he'd made up his mind. "You get it." He opened the car door and climbed out.

"Get some rest, bud," I repeated. "Take an extra day if you need it." He waved and slowly climbed the steps of his trailer, hunched over.

The following week, Rick was back, but missed his quotas again, two days in a row. That Wednesday, Rick walked past me with a bleak expression on his face. He held up a paper in his hands—a summons to the front office. We both knew what it meant.

"I'm sorry, Rick," I said.

He shook his head. "Can't say I didn't try."

I didn't see him again after that day.

The initial enjoyment I'd felt in the teamwork and goals-driven environment of the Amazon job started to be tempered with frustration over people like Rick. I was getting to know my team—I was learning about their lives and hopes and dreams. But the giant arm of the company seemed to treat everyone there as expendable—not unlike the military. The employees were doing labor-intensive jobs for a low hourly wage, but Amazon didn't care. All the company cared about was if they were meeting their quotas.

In many cases, the workers seemed to be trapped. I heard some of the younger employees talk about their dreams of getting married or buying a home, but they were so exhausted at the end of every day, they didn't have time to learn a new skill that would get them higher on the pay scale, or send out applications to a better-paying job. They got stuck.

I talked about it with Amy in the evenings, sometimes. "It makes me wonder how many people across the state and even the country are in this same spot," I said, scrubbing the dishes after dinner. "They've done all the right things—they got through high school, pursued college, found a job. But now they've got no upward mobility. And the corporation just sees them as expendable. If they can't keep up, they get fired and replaced with someone else."

"That's disappointing," Amy said. "It's sad that people like Rick can't skate by, not even with government help."

"The government seems like part of the problem. These people could use help, but it seems like the government only offers temporary or insufficient help, which gets people stuck waiting on the government's aid—even though it's not enough. And politicians either don't know about what these people are going through, or don't care. The solutions they come up with are temporary, rather than doing anything that would change the overarching environment or system."

"You thinking about politics again, Sam?" Amy looked over at me teasingly from where she was loading the dishwasher.

"*No,*" I said. "Absolutely not. I'm just saying…the people on my team need freedom to pursue a meaningful life. And their environment isn't providing them that freedom."

As my disenchantment with Amazon grew, I put more energy into starting up my business. I'd decided to name it Palisade Strategies, and its function was to help veterans get their medications from local community pharmacies when they were in urgent need of prescriptions and the Veterans Affairs hospitals and clinics couldn't meet the need that same day. Amy and I had both received medical care through the VA, and there were basically only two ways to get medication from them: either at the hospital's onsite pharmacy, or via the mail. For any non-urgent medications, the mail order worked fine. But in the case of an emergency, you couldn't get medication without driving to a VA hospital, and that wasn't great for people who lived far away. My company started managing the relationships between the VA pharmacy and other local pharmacies so that veterans had better local emergency options.

I loved being an entrepreneur. My business helped veterans, which felt incredibly gratifying; and as the business started to grow, it was providing my family with a good standard of living. I also felt proud of the fact that it was a legitimate *business*. As opposed to all my work in the nonprofit sector, which had been donor driven, this business was creating its own revenue. For someone with a complex about being a charity case, this was hugely validating.

Hiking in the Ruby Mountains, in Elko Nevada. September 2022

One weekend, shortly after I'd left Amazon and gone full time with my business, Amy remarked on my change in attitude. We were out on a hike, and the kids scampered ahead of us on the trail.

"You seem *happy*," Amy said.

I grinned. "I am happy. I have a beautiful family, and we live in a place we love. I finally have a launchpad that enables us to dream and plan. And I feel like I've discovered a version of Sam Brown that isn't obsessed with the military or pigeonholed as a wounded warrior."

"You seem more confident too."

I nodded. "Back in Dallas, I always felt like a wannabe, trying to find a professional career. But now I feel competent and prepared. When I call up another business and set up relationships, it feels more peer-to-peer. Like—I am of equal standing with these other leaders. And it's exciting. Stressful too, obviously. But it's exciting to see the business succeed and grow."

I looked over at Amy. As usual, she seemed particularly full of life out here, in her happy place. "What about *you?*" I asked. "*You seem happy.*"

She grinned. "It's a pretty good life right now. Hiking mountains. School for Roman and Esther. Bonding with Ezra and working out most days. Doing our thing." She glanced over at me and seemed to hesitate over her next thought. "Would you be happy if this is what the next twenty years look like?"

"What do you mean?"

She shrugged. "I guess I just wondered…if this feels *satisfying* to you. If you feel like you're living into the purpose God saved you for."

I thought about that. Her question took me back to the horrible, blinding moment in the desert—screaming out, "Jesus, save me!" while engulfed in flames. That night had made me certain that my life had been saved for some sort of higher calling—*the life I live is not my own.* Was I living into the mission that God had for me?

"I remember a guy I met who encouraged me right after Mother and I moved into the hotel across the street from the hospital," I said. "Cliff Dugosh. Do you remember him?"

"Of course I do," she said. "You guys were still getting together a lot when we were dating."

I nodded. "He was such…an anomaly. He's one of the greatest people I've ever met, but he wasn't doing impressive work. He was a full-time substitute teacher. But he just *radiated* God's love. And I remember him telling me that I had a mission right where I was at. That was part of the reason I approached other people in the burn unit with so much intention, trying to encourage them."

"Which got *my* attention." She grinned.

"You know, for so much of my life, I've tried to find something *big* or *impressive* to do. It's like, if it wasn't something huge, it would be a waste of the skills and preparation God gave me. But I'm not sure I feel that anymore. I think I can be used by God in a burn unit, or in an Amazon warehouse, or running my business, or in the context of our family. Mostly, I just want to use the gifts and talents and opportunities in front of me to serve my God. And ideally, be humble and faithful in how I do that."

Amy looked at me thoughtfully, as though she was tempted to say something—then seemed to change her mind.

"Well, I love that," she said. "And I'm so glad."

* * *

Despite my intention to never get involved in politics again, Amy and I picked up volunteer work with the Republican Party in our local community—but *only* as volunteers, and *only* to remain civically engaged. Political engagement had been a big part of our life in Dallas, and—while I didn't want to abandon that form of civic engagement altogether, I also didn't want to be involved the same way I had before. Rather than trying to provide counsel to candidates, I decided to just do grunt work for them.

During campaign seasons, I helped out by knocking on doors, making calls, and delivering campaign literature. I'd made the decision that I didn't have any right to complain about political dysfunction unless I was actually seeking to help create positive change. That meant doing more than just showing up and voting on election day.

During the 2020 election, I started getting to know some of the young people working on the Nevada Republican campaigns. They weren't paid well, but they were passionate—the exact opposite of Aaron and Marty. I enjoyed being around them, and several of them sought me out as a mentor. They were fascinated when they realized I had some prior experience running in a political campaign.

"Why don't you run again?" one of them asked.

I shook my head. "*Here's* why," I said, then launched into my familiar cautionary tale.

But that didn't dissuade them, and they didn't let go of the idea that I should be a candidate. In the spring of 2021, after the 2020 election drama had started to die down, the guys called me up and asked me to grab breakfast with them.

"Sam. We seriously think you should run for office," Tanner said.

"We know you don't like the idea," Andy continued. "But you're the type of person our country needs. You get what the average person is experiencing. You're smart. You have integrity. You're a veteran, you're a small business owner, you're a man of faith—you *are* the kind of candidate we need!"

I didn't have the heart to tell them that I had zero interest in being a political candidate again—nor did I have the bandwidth for a campaign. "Tell you what," I told them. "Why don't I have you guys over for dinner and we can talk with Amy about it."

THERE, I thought. *Amy will deliver a firm "NO," and save me from being the bad guy.*

I didn't tell Amy about what the guys were planning to talk with us about. I figured her negative reaction would be more dramatic if they sprung their idea on her. I knew she'd have no tolerance for another political campaign and she'd squash the whole thing.

A week later, the guys came over. Amy made us chicken enchiladas and set the kids up with a movie. Right after we prayed over the food, I began serving up the enchiladas. *Now,* I thought. *I'm going to get ahead of this.*

"Hey, Amy," I said. "The guys here have been asking me for a couple of months if I would consider running for office. I've told them that you and I always do everything together. So, I just want to give you the floor right now to provide your thoughts and feedback on that." I sat down, feeling confident that Amy would issue an unequivocal "NO."

She looked at me, startled, then looked at the guys with the same surprised expression. *Here it comes*, I thought. *This is the last time I have to hear this idea and then we can all move on.*

But that's not what she did.

"I've been waiting for you to come to that conclusion, Sam."

My jaw dropped open. The two guys stared at her, then turned to look at me.

"I'm sorry—what?" I asked.

"I've been waiting for you to come to that conclusion," she repeated. "The Lord told me in prayer that we've been wasting our time." She looked at me, her eyes soft and full. "We're called to do more than just hike through mountains, Sam."

I stared at her in disbelief. "I can't believe you're saying this."

"The Lord has given you *gifts*, Sam," she said. "You're exceptionally intelligent. You're a gifted orator and leader. And you have an amazing story. We've been out gallivanting around in the mountains, having fun—and obviously, I love that. But I feel like God has been telling me that He didn't give us these gifts to waste."

"This is so epic," one of the guys whispered to the other.

I shook my head, trying to come to terms with Amy's declaration. "How long have you felt like this?"

"A couple months."

"Why didn't you say anything?"

"I was waiting for God to make it clear to you."

I wasn't sure God *had* made it clear to me—if anything, Amy's statement seemed to confuse things. *Was* I wasting my gifts?

The rest of the meal passed easily enough. The guys were both elated to have Amy's vote of support, and Amy seemed lighthearted after unburdening herself of her confession. I was the only one who felt awkward and preoccupied.

That night, as the two of us were getting ready for bed, I brought it up again. "You know, I was really banking on you breaking those guys' hearts," I said, my mouth full of toothpaste.

She smiled sympathetically. "Sorry to disappoint you."

"You said you've been feeling this way for a couple months?"

She cocked her head, thinking. "I remember having that prayer with God...back in the fall."

"That was like five months ago!" I spat out my toothpaste.

"I just felt like the Lord was telling me that it wasn't my job to tell you to do this. That was His job. He told me, 'I've prepared your heart. Now I've got to prepare his heart.' I knew it couldn't be me or anyone else making you want to do this. You had to see the need on your own. And you needed to get to a point where you saw what you could contribute." She paused and studied me. "*Do* you see the need?"

I grimaced and shrugged. "Of course I see the need for good leaders. That's the easy part."

"And do you see that you have incredible talents you could contribute?"

I sighed. "Those two made a pretty good case for it." She shot me a look, wordlessly rebuking my cop-out answer. "Okay, yes—I know that I would be a good leader. And my experiences have given me a lot of exposure to some of the struggles people are dealing with in this state."

Amy rubbed cold cream on her face. "And you're incredibly capable at leading people in teams. You can endure tough circumstances. You're able to make objectively good decisions on behalf of others. Sam, I feel like those talents are *needed* in the political arena, and..." She looked at me apologetically. "I think those gifts are being underutilized by you right now."

I didn't want to admit that I agreed with her. "But I'm not sure I *want* this."

"Don't you? If you're being really honest with yourself? Haven't you felt frustrated by the people making laws and policies, and considered the fact that you might do a better job?"

I shifted my weight uncomfortably. "No. Well. Maybe."

She sighed. "I *know* you, Sam Brown. You've always wanted to live a life of service. And I totally agree with what you said on our hike last fall, about God being able to use us in whatever context we're in. But I can't help thinking He's calling you to a broader level of service than what you're doing right now."

I sat down on the bed and stared at my hands. "What about what happened last time?"

"You're not the same person you were last time," she said, sitting down next to me. "You're so much more sure of yourself and your beliefs. We wouldn't be entering this as naive, clueless little lambs. We know *exactly* how awful the political machine can be. But that doesn't mean you're not still called to enter into the fray."

I thought about that. "I *do* have pretty thick skin," I acknowledged. I glanced at Amy with a grin, hoping she'd pick up on the joke.

She smiled and rolled her eyes. "Yes, you literally have very thick skin." She laughed. "Honestly, that's part of the draw. Your scars inspire people. Think about the people you worked with at Amazon. They're not in a position to represent themselves. They would never have the resources or the capacity to run for political office. They have a lot of suffering in their lives, and when they look at *you,* they think, 'This guy knows what it is to suffer.' And they see that your suffering hasn't *broken* you. It hasn't deterred you from trying to help other people, like them. What if you could help them, Sam? What if you were in a position of leadership that could lead to a noticeable improvement in their lives?"

"Amy. I'm not going to lie and say that doesn't appeal on some level. But haven't you thought about what this would mean for our family? For our kids? This would be brutal for all of us."

She nodded. "I know. I don't look forward to it. But...this guy I know is always quoting this motto—'No mission too difficult, no sacrifice too great. Duty first.'"

"Oof! You hit below the belt!"

Amy smiled. "Sorry, not sorry."

I stood up and began pacing at the foot of the bed. "Amy. I have learned over the years that you have so much wisdom."

"Aw." She smiled.

"I think you probably understand me better than I understand myself. So, when you speak on an issue like this…even if I don't agree with it, I know I have to consider it."

She took my hand as I walked past and paused my pacing. "Can we pray about it?"

I nodded. I sank back down on the bed next to her.

We held each other and prayed.

I struggled to fall asleep that night. For some reason, I kept thinking of Rick staring out at the Truckee River, remembering what he'd said to me just before he got out of the car. "You get it."

What did he mean by that? I wondered. *What did he think I "got"?*

Was it true what Amy had said about my scars? *People see that you know what it means to suffer.* I thought about what Rick had tried to endure every day at Amazon. *He* suffered. And maybe he related to me, because he saw evidence of my own suffering.

My road had looked vastly different than his, but in the end—suffering was suffering. By now, I'd heard plenty of stories of desperation, and broken dreams, and missed opportunities. I'd seen the deflation of hope and optimism in people's faces. Maybe my scars' visibility caused people to recognize their own pain in me. Maybe it even caused them to feel hope when they saw me fighting to keep going and striving and working to make things better, because that was a sign they could achieve the same thing.

Spreading hope, I thought. *Now THAT would be a mission worth sacrificing for.*

God. Do you want me to do this? I prayed. *I'd really be okay living a quiet life at home with Amy and the kids, running my business and keeping things chill. But I want to live my life for You. Is this something You're calling me into?*

While waiting for His answer, I fell asleep.

The next morning, I got up early, let the dogs out, poured myself some coffee, and went into the living room. I flipped my Bible open to the story of "the talents." It was a familiar story to me. Jesus tells a parable of a master leaving on a trip, and giving the care of his money—gold talents—to three different servants. When the master returns, two of the servants have invested the money and stewarded it well, so they're rewarded. But the third servant buried his gold talent in the ground. The master gets angry with him for wasting the talent and he's disciplined.

I shut my Bible and took my coffee out onto the back porch. The dogs ran up to me, eager for a walk. I patted their heads and threw a ball as a compromise. I'd take them on a walk later.

Lord, I prayed, *am I burying my talent in the ground?*

The sky was pink as the sun started to rise. I could see thick dew on the grass, and registered that the season had already moved beyond the spring frosts.

Lord, I could work toward solving problems that help people, but that could only ever be part of the answer. The thing that actually brings peace in the midst of it all is You.

I thought about the journey He'd taken me on. How strange and bizarre that the terrible explosion that had upended my life and left me permanently scarred might now be a reason for people to feel hope.

What if I get too caught up in it all? I wondered. *What if a political campaign becomes one more version of me wanting to feel important? What if my ego gets in the way and causes me to lose sight of what matters?*

I remembered Mother's remark during our long stretch together about how I'd been so prideful in high school. She'd said, "If getting burned is what it took for the Lord to draw you to Himself, so be it." That was the gift she could see in the accident: a humbling in the desert.

But I didn't just need a humbling in the desert, I thought. *I needed a thorn in my side.*

That was the gift of the scars: they were my grounding rod. Every time I looked in the mirror, I saw both the miracle and the reminder of who I was. I was not invincible. I was a fallible man, and I'd been hurt, and I *had* suffered. But I had also survived. And in that moment after surviving, even as I stood there on the battlefield before getting to the helicopter, I knew that *all of it* was for a reason.

The scars were a literal physical reminder that God saved my life for a purpose. Was a political campaign supposed to be part of that purpose?

The sun pushed its bright light over the horizon, spilling into our backyard. I could hear stirrings in the house—cupboards opening. Amy's voice calling for the kids to get up.

Lord, I'll explore this political thing, I prayed. *And if You don't want me to move forward, just send me a "No." Shut doors, so it can't happen. Either way, God, I want to hold up my end of the bargain: the life I live is not my own. It's Yours. Whether or not I do a political campaign, whether I win or lose—I just want to serve You. I want to show people the hope that You've given me.*

"Sam?" I heard Amy call.

I turned toward the deck and lifted my mug so she would spot me. She gave me an impatient smile and motioned me inside. I grinned.

Another day was beginning. It was another day I'd never been entitled to. Another day that may never have been. And there was my bride, and my three children who lit up when they saw my face, and there was hope and dreams and purpose that joined hands with eternity.

I headed inside.

It was time to keep living.

EPILOGUE

ABUNDANT LIFE

Amy and Sam in Reno, Nevada, in 2024.

It's a strange thing to try to write an epilogue for a life I'm still living.

As I write these words, I'm in the midst of a US Senate campaign. Most people who read this book will have the benefit of knowing information I don't currently have: was the campaign successful or unsuccessful? Did I win or lose?

But if there's one thing I've learned over the last sixteen-plus years since my Alive Day, it's that those sorts of questions are not the ones which truly matter.

Is there hope?

Will some purpose emerge out of this current trial?

Can I root my identity in something other than my current circumstances, or position, or profession, or physical form?

These are the questions that matter. These are the thoughts with eternal ramifications.

If you've been willing to read up to this point, I hope you'll allow my best attempt at answering those questions.

Yes, there is hope. If you get anything out of my story, let it be that goodness and beauty can come out of suffering. That doesn't mean hope is easy, and it may not mean you get what you want. There were times in my healing journey when I experienced crushing disappointment, like when I learned I could never return to Afghanistan to lead my platoon. Hope can't anchor itself in any person, place, or thing, because all of that is temporary and fallible.

But there's a different kind of hope that can sustain you. It's what sustained me. In my own darkest times—the horribly long minute of burning alive; the hellscape of the ketamine nightmare; the agony of a painful healing process; the shattering realization that my life's plans were no longer possible; the certainty that marriage and family were out of my reach—I struggled. It was only the hope in something *bigger* than myself that I was able to endure.

I call that hope Faith.

For me, faith served as a bridge that enabled me to climb out of despair. It stretched between the pain of where I was, to the purpose of where I was going. I remember lying on the stretcher at the HLZ in the Kandahar desert, waiting to be MEDEVACed out, my eyes blinded by gauze and my body in torment. But in that moment, I felt certain that my life had been spared for a purpose. Only by having faith that a greater purpose *existed* was I able to endure the days, weeks, and years that followed. Even though I had no idea what might be on the other side of the bridge and what the destination was, the path forward was there. I had faith in a good God. I had faith that I would find something meaningful on the other side of the journey. In that hope, I wasn't disappointed.

Which brings us to question number two: will some purpose emerge out of this trial?

Yes—but I believe it will only come if you're open to it. We've all heard that phrase, "Everything happens for a reason." It's a cliche, but on my own journey, I knew I needed to *choose* to believe it. I couldn't imagine what potential gifts might come out of the trauma. But I knew none of those gifts could ever come unless I chose to expect that there *could* be something more.

I wanted those gifts to come fast. If someone had told me that it would be three years before I was done going in and out of the hospital, I'm not sure I would have had the motivation to keep going. I had only ever planned a life that involved military leadership and valor, under fire if necessary. My life plan required a healthy body and a successful string of medals that represented leadership triumphs and missions accomplished. I had no life plan for medical retirement or a disfigured and broken frame. How could any silver lining make up for the loss of everything I'd wanted? "Everything happens for a reason"—so, what was the reason?

I had no idea. But I had hope that my pain *wouldn't be wasted.* I lived with anticipation that a good story would unfold with time, and I kept looking to the Divine Author for His direction.

Now, I see gifts all around me—and their existence is rooted in the ashes of that fiery day. Because of the faith I found in the midst of dying, I experienced freedom. Because of that freedom, I experienced joy in the midst of my painful disfigurement, which caused Amy to fall in love with me and experience freedom of her own through Christ. Because of my scars and my story, I've been able to encourage countless people who carry their own internal and external scars.

That doesn't negate the pain and suffering that defined so much of my journey. But it means the pain of trauma is no longer the defining aspect of my story.

What *does* define me? That's the essence of question number three: is there an identity to be found in something other than circumstances, or position, or profession, or physical form?

Yes! It's an identity that can never be taken away. My Alive Day put to death everything I used to value about myself. On the other side of those flames, I was no longer a leader of men; I no longer fought for the US Army; I was no longer fit, strong, or healthy. I was humbled to the point of death.

But with those temporary identities burned away, I was left with a true awakening of who I am: I only exist by God's grace and for His purpose. The "control" I wield in this human form falls infinitely short of His reign over my life.

I think that's why I feel so thankful for my scars. They remind me daily of the fragile state of my physical life—of *all* of our physical lives. And because of that reminder, I don't feel scared or limited anymore by what is temporary. I've had people tell me they feel amazed that I so freely engage with the world around me, despite my obvious disfigurement. They assume it would be a natural response to avoid the public eye, when my physical identity has been so distorted.

But I've gotten to a place where that doesn't bother me at all. My physical strength and appearance doesn't define my identity anymore. My identity is in Jesus Christ, and it's something no one can see, touch, or harm, because it's inside of me. I find the truth of who I am in my relationship to God. When I ground myself in that, it becomes possible to take risks without fear, regardless of what other people think of me, and even regardless of the outcome.

I don't ever want to find myself in a position like I was before my

Alive Day, where I believed I could do all things through my own strength, and that I could define my own purpose and mission. That was an empty existence. When it was incinerated on the battlefield, my old self died.

That death was when I began to live. It started when I cried out to God: "Jesus save me!"

"The life I live is not my own." In this frail form, I live to serve others through serving the Lord. It's my hope that, in being faithful to God, I will be a faithful servant to the people around me. And by sharing my story, I hope you recognize that purpose may emerge out of your own struggles. I hope *you* see that bridge of faith: rising out of despair, guiding you toward hope.

Even as my brother, Daniel, approached his final days in this life, he looked forward with hope and expectancy to the eternal life that follows. If you're in search of the peace Daniel and I both found through our faith and relationship with God but you don't know where to start, his final journal entry is the answer that will lead you to hope: "Said prayer to Jesus Christ to manifest to me and asked for forgiveness of my sins."

The pain in our lives is the preface of an eternal story. That's the gift I've found in faith: living life is like reading a good book, where I can expectantly turn the page and look forward to getting to the next chapter, because I trust that my Divine Author has written a happy ending—eternal peace.

There is *peace* that comes through surrendering to God.

In my story—in your story—we can have hope.

This is only the beginning.

ACKNOWLEDGMENTS

I want to start by noting that there are so many people and experiences that played a role in shaping me into the man I was prior to my Alive Day, as well as the years that followed. To those who do not get listed below, thank you for your role in shaping me. Some of you provided me with competition that pushed me to be the best version of myself. Others provided me with an example of leadership worth emulating—at home, in business, or life in general. Many of you prayed for me along my journey. You rightfully believed that there was a purpose for my life. And still others of you saw something within me—from my childhood to this present day—that led you to encourage me to set high goals, live with high standards, and be a person who could provide hope to others.

Amy Brown: My wife and closest friend, thank you for loving me and choosing this tough life journey with me. I fully know no one else would pursue such hardship as the starting point for their marriage. You are one of my heroes. You have profound endurance, and you pursue the right things; you seek excellence from yourself as well as those you love, which has produced many blessings for the people who know you and countless others who will never know that you were the genesis of a blessing in their life. Your love, trust, and support through our marriage has been the most consequential blessing in my life. I thank God for you and love you with all of my heart. These words are a worthy and accurate description of you as a wife and a mother: "*She is clothed with strength and dignity, and she laughs without fear of the future. When she speaks, her words are wise, and she gives instructions with kindness. She watches everything in her household and suffers nothing from laziness. Her children stand and bless her. Her husband praises her: 'There are many virtuous and capable women in the world, but you surpass them all!'*" *Proverbs 31:25–29*

Roman, Esther, and Ezra: My sons and daughter, you too have been brought into this world for a reason and a purpose. I pray that you will learn and apply the lessons from the experiences that your mom and I have shared with you so that you can live with the proper perspective that the "life you live is not your own." Your mom and I love you and know that you are capable of doing even greater things than we have done. Live your life with humility and never forget that the foundation of wisdom is fear of the Lord (Proverbs 9:10). Love the Lord your God with all your heart, soul, mind, and strength (Mark 12:30).

Scott and Tanya Brown: My parents, thank you for raising me to be a man who loves and serves my Lord and others. You have both lived a life that set the example to follow. I know that the journey for our family has had very challenging seasons. You both have forged through the challenges with unwavering faith and determination that even in hardship, we can serve others and your pain can be the tool that God uses to help others find true peace and hope. I love you. I'm proud of you. I'm grateful for the blessing to be your son.

Daniel and Kristina Brown: My brother and "sister" forever, you showed us what it meant to be vulnerable and truly live in your marriage and endeavors. You introduced us to the joy of being absolutely lost in the beauty of nature and admiration for His creation. You found purpose and joy in the midst of suffering that so few even knew existed. You lived and loved with such passion for each other and those around you that the impact of your time together will be felt for generations. I love you both with all my heart and look forward to the adventures we will have together in eternity. Kristina, I am so grateful for your love and support of Daniel throughout your marriage. You were to Daniel what Amy is to me. No one got to live and celebrate the best things in life with Daniel as intimately as you did. But, you also had the unimaginable burden of being the one who had to suffer alongside him as his brain injuries tortured him and led to us losing Daniel completely. And, until we have that rendezvous with Daniel in eternity, I look forward to the adventures we will share together in the years to come.

Anthony Roszko and Steven Smith: You both set the standard for accomplishing the mission while leading and taking care of your soldiers with profound love and respect. You have both also become husbands and fathers and continue to live your life in service to your family and others even since you retired from the Army. I'm honored to consider you both brothers. And, I have repeatedly said that you both gave me the most significant recognition a leader could ever hope to receive from his time in combat or service: love, respect, and friendship.

Kevin Jensen: You are so much more than "my gunner." On my Alive Day, in the moments of lost hope and desire to escape the pain through death, you delivered the words that changed my life: "I've got you!" Those words have become my anthem as I must share that message with others who have found themselves in a position of hopelessness or surrounded by chaos and fear. Your selfless service and valor will never be forgotten by those you aided on that fateful day. I'm proud of you for becoming a husband and father to a family that will continue your legacy of impacting the world.

Stephen Ruth and Cliff Dugosh: Of course two of the greatest servant leaders I've known would be from Texas A&M. Stephen, you demonstrated leadership both at West Point and in our time with the 1st Infantry Division. You prioritize mentorship and coaching, thus creating a generation of leaders who will forever have the mark of your impact on their lives. And, without your thoughtful care for me and asking Cliff to visit me in the hospital, I would have missed the blessing of knowing him. Cliff, you prioritize mentorship and coaching as well. But, your singular focus on challenging men to be leaders in the likeness of Jesus will have an eternal impact that no one can fathom. The legacy of your love for God and those desperate for hope or purpose will rightfully rival the most famous of evangelists. You live and serve with a rare humility that is an example to all of us and a hallmark of your character and impact.

Greta Myers: You were an answer to prayer. This book would not exist in this form without your talents and passion to help me put the stories of my life, hard lessons learned, and the love I have for others into written form. I put off this project for years because I knew I didn't have the skill to write and edit in such a professional form, and I was too afraid to explore working with someone else because I was concerned that a writer wouldn't share my beliefs and the greater mission. You have done an amazing job transferring my passion and purpose to paper. Thank you for believing in this project and guiding me through it despite the challenges and obstacles.

Carson: Your friendship has been a blessing these past few years. Thank you for spending the time to get to know Amy and me so well—to know our story and understand our mission with this book. Your help reading through the manuscript and offering thoughts and perspectives helped us add depth to the narrative to the great benefit of the readers who do not know us as well as you do. Thank you for your friendship, professionalism, and manuscript suggestions to help us connect with the audience in a more personal and meaningful way.

Scribe Team: You know the struggle and opportunity of dealing with unexpected hardship. Thank you for working with me to present this message of hope to those who need it most. This team has overcome adversity, risen to the challenge, and delivered a superior book. Thank you for being part of my journey and a member of the team in this process.

ABOUT THE AUTHOR

CAPTAIN SAM BROWN is an American politician, businessman, and veteran. After graduating from the United States Military Academy at West Point and completing training at the United States Army Infantry School, Ranger School, and Airborne School, Sam was proud to serve in the 3rd Brigade Combat Team of the 1st Infantry Division. During his military deployment in Afghanistan, Sam's vehicle detonated an improvised explosive device and he burned alive for nearly a minute before a fellow soldier was able to extinguish the blaze. He is the recipient of a Purple Heart, a Bronze Star, and an Army Commendation Medal with a "V" device for Valor.

Sam later went on to earn his MBA from Southern Methodist University and holds an honorary doctorate from Northwood University. He founded the company Palisade Strategies, a firm that enabled emergency pharmaceutical support to veterans. Sam sold his company in 2022, in part to devote his full attention to a political run for United States Senate. He has also had the privilege of sharing his inspirational story to groups all over the country.

An avid outdoorsman, Sam enjoys skiing and hiking in Nevada with his wife, Amy, also a veteran and former Army Captain. Tagging along on any adventure are their three beloved children—Roman, Esther, and Ezra—along with their Belgian Malinois dogs, which have been a Brown family fixture since Sam and Amy got married. The Browns live in Reno, Nevada, where Sam is a candidate for the US Senate and active in community service.

WRITER'S NOTE

A ghostwriter's comfort zone is backstage, hidden deep in the darkness of the wings. We are rarely asked to step into the light and comment on the nature of our contribution. But, as Sam and I finish our collaboration on his memoir, that's what he's asked me to do. If you know Sam, you shouldn't find that surprising. He is as eager to share credit as he has been eager to point to God as the source of his healing and transformation. So—per his request—I'll take a brief step onstage and share some of the choices we made in telling his story, listed roughly in the order we made them.

First: it was clear that Sam's faith needed to be a central element of his book. After being profiled by *GQ* in their Jan. 2012 article "Burning Man," Sam was impressed and happy with Jay Kirk's brilliant narration of his story. However, when Sam asked Jay if he might be willing to write his story in book form, Jay pushed back. "Your faith is such a huge part of who you are," he told Sam. "You should work with someone who can understand it and honor that side of you." I thank God for Jay's humble redirection of Sam, because it paved the way for us to connect. When I was first given Sam's name as a possible project assignment by my former company, I looked up his website. His story was instantly compelling, but it was our shared faith that made me determine I had to find the space in my schedule to take on his book. During our first phone call, Sam and I quickly bonded over the centrality of Jesus in our lives, and our desire to honor Him in our work. With that shared mission, we set about crafting *how* we might tell his story.

"I do NOT want this to be a political book," Sam told me during our first in-person meeting. His friend had joined us, but—as Sam pointed out—"You can see there's no one from my political team here. There's a reason for that. I don't want their influence on what we share." Sam and Amy have maintained that fencing throughout our work together. Although we have sought to be mindful of the implications of certain sections that touch on hot political issues, the foremost priority has always been a truthful and authentic narration of Sam's and Amy's stories.

I had the pleasure of spending several days with the Brown family at their home in Reno when we began the book's work in earnest. It was during those sessions that we made the decision to make the book a memoir, rather than a "knowledge share" book which would be driven by advice. That was a hard decision for Sam; he worried a memoir would come across as a vanity project, particularly as we knew the book was likely to launch in the midst of his political campaign. But with Daniel's amazing life and tragic death as the motivation behind writing the book, Sam's foremost objective was to give people hope. As he explains in the book's prologue, we ultimately felt that his story could do that even more effectively than didactics. We have written this to remind readers that they are not alone.

Once we settled on memoir as our genre, my task was to guide Sam and Amy in identifying the foremost transformation they experienced through Sam's accident, their love story, his healing journey, and their life together. What we uncovered was the theme of surrender. Sam's story is fascinating because the most dramatic part—the explosion and his experience being burned alive—is really just the beginning. If we were to place it in Joseph Campbell's "hero's journey," the explosion was Sam's threshold, when he crossed from the familiar, known world into the unknown world—the place where a hero's transformation begins.

Ironically though, Sam's "hero's journey" takes him in the opposite direction of a Marvel movie. His "before" is when he's Superman: tall, fit, strong, handsome, upwardly mobile, and a leader of men. The explosion in the desert rips that all away, leaving him utterly exposed, face-to-face with a searing truth: his life is not his own. His accomplishments and impressive external strengths are chaff, quickly consumed in the fire. What's left out of that crucible is eternal: certainty in a sovereign and loving God, unshakeable hope, and a purpose beyond his own ambitions. The rest of his story is the working out of those truths in each new context: physically, relationally, professionally, and missionally.

Some people may balk at a story that implies Superman's transformation into a scarred and disfigured Clark Kent is somehow heroic. In my opinion, it's profoundly inspiring. Sam's story gets at the crux of who we are as humans and who we are not; it reorients us to divine hope and the meaning of life. It reveals our inability to save ourselves, yet points us toward One who can. I have felt deeply privileged to bear witness to Sam's and Amy's testimonies, and to be trusted with conveying these profound truths to a wider audience.

Deconstructing a worldview is a painful, slow process and it felt important to honor the weight of Sam's former self in balance with the discoveries he was making on the other side of the explosion. For that reason, we made the decision to include flashbacks to open every chapter, with the intentional exceptions of Chapter 4, "Alive Day," and Chapter 10, "Amy's Chapter." The flashbacks are meant to remind the reader of the paradigms that shaped Sam's upbringing and identity formation, even while he was faced with deconstructing those beliefs on the other side of his accident. The deconstructive process is one many of us face in our adulthood as we seek greater meaning out of the incomplete truths we may have been raised with. Sam's disentangling process felt like an important piece to share in chronicling the full arc of his story.

A final few editorial choices to comment on: we elected to include profanity for the sake of realism, despite the risk of offense. (Sam and Amy could only laugh at my first draft of Chapter 4, which depicted Sam asking his soldier politely, "Please take off my glove." As they both patiently explained to me, there's no way in hell soldiers would get out of that battle without dropping a few f-bombs.) Also, it became clear to me as soon as I heard Amy's version of their love story that she had to have her own chapter, even though it was an unconventional choice. The themes of her story beautifully complement Sam's, and she was able to shed light on his character in a way his own narration couldn't. Plus, Sam has such a deep respect for Amy's wisdom in his life, his own story would have felt incomplete without her voice shared firsthand. For that reason, I sought to maintain Amy's first person voice as much as possible during the remaining chapters by conveying most of her thoughts and feelings via dialogue. In that way, she continued to speak for herself.

Sam's life was changed by fire. As a literary symbol, fire is catastrophic and destructive, yet also purifying and necessary for survival. Sam's experience reveals it to be all of the above. As you, the reader, navigate your own life-altering trials, may you discover hope through the flames, eternity out of the ashes, and purpose from the wreckage. And may this book offer you some warmth, some light, some ray of truth in its flickering flame.

With deep gratitude,
Greta Myers
Ghostwriter & Editor

Made in the USA
Middletown, DE
13 September 2024

60912877R00190